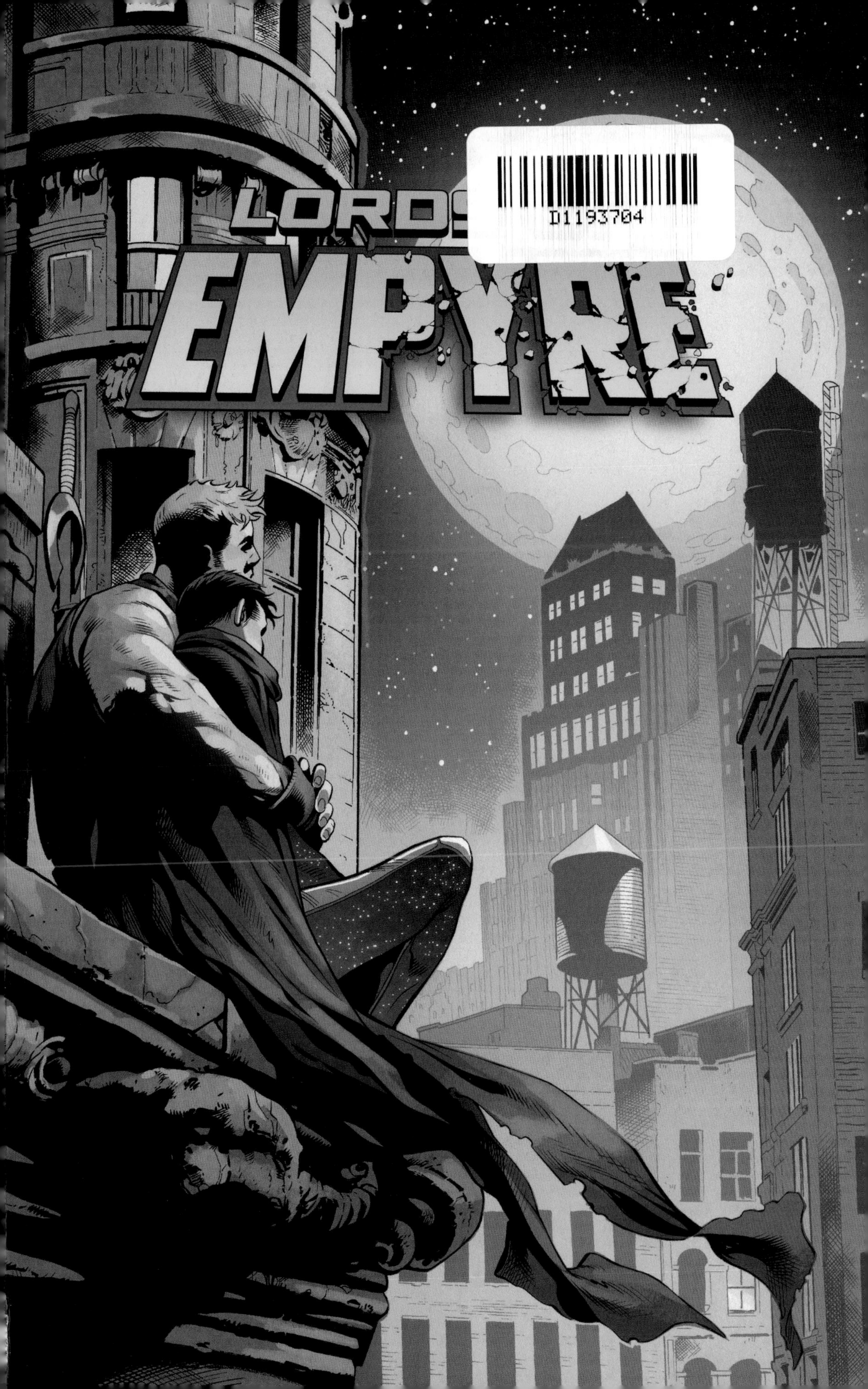
LORDS
EMPYRE

LORD EMP

The Kree and Skrull Empires have united under Emperor Hulkling to fight a common enemy: the Celestial Messiah Quoi and his plantlike Cotati, who have claimed Earth's Moon as their own!

But the Cotati want more than justice for the crimes the Kree and Skrulls committed against them — they want to exterminate all animal life, starting with Earth! Can Earth's heroes stop their deadly campaign before the Kree/Skrull Empire decides to sacrifice one world to save the universe?

LORDS OF EMPYRE: EMPEROR HULKLING

WRITERS	Chip Zdarsky & Anthony Oliveira
PENCILER	Manuel Garcia
INKER	Cam Smith
COLORIST	Tríona Farrell
LETTERER	VC's Travis Lanham
COVER ART	Patrick Gleason & Marte Gracia
ASSOCIATE EDITOR	Sarah Brunstad
EDITOR	Wil Moss

LORDS OF EMPYRE: CELESTIAL MESSIAH

WRITER	Alex Paknadel
ARTIST	Alex Lins
COLORIST	Matt Yackey
LETTERER	VC's Ariana Maher
COVER ART	Rod Reis
ASSOCIATE EDITOR	Lauren Amaro
EDITOR	Darren Shan

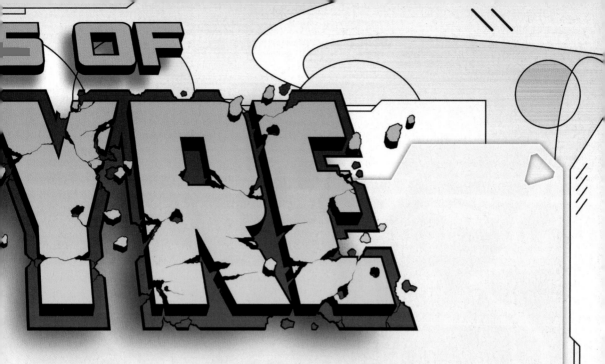

LORDS OF EMPYRE: SWORDSMAN

WRITER	**Alex Paknadel**
ARTIST	**Thomas Nachlik**
COLORIST	**Marcio Menyz**

LETTERER	**VC's Ariana Maher**
COVER ART	**Rod Reis**
EDITORS	**Darren Shan** & **Lauren Amaro**

EMPYRE: SAVAGE AVENGERS

WRITER	**Gerry Duggan**
ARTIST/COLORIST	**Greg Smallwood**

LETTERER	**VC's Travis Lanham**
COVER ART	**Greg Smallwood**
ASSISTANT EDITOR	**Martin Biro**
ASSOCIATE EDITOR	**Alanna Smith**
EDITOR	**Tom Brevoort**

FOR CONAN PROPERTIES INTERNATIONAL

COORDINATOR	**Mike Jacobsen**	EXECUTIVE VICE PRESIDENT	**Jay Zetterberg**
PRESIDENT	**Fredrik Malmberg**	CHIEF OPERATING OFFICER	**Steve Booth**

Conan and related characters copyright ©2020 Conan Properties International LLC

COLLECTION EDITOR **Jennifer Grünwald**	VP PRODUCTION & SPECIAL PROJECTS **Jeff Youngquist**
ASSISTANT MANAGING EDITOR **Maia Loy**	LAYOUT **Jeph York**
ASSISTANT MANAGING EDITOR **Lisa Montalbano**	BOOK DESIGNER **Jay Bowen**
ASSOCIATE MANAGER, DIGITAL ASSETS **Joe Hochstein**	SVP PRINT, SALES & MARKETING **David Gabriel**
EDITOR, SPECIAL PROJECTS **Mark D. Beazley**	EDITOR IN CHIEF **C.B. Cebulski**

EMPYRE: LORDS OF EMPYRE. Contains material originally published in magazine form as LORDS OF EMPYRE: EMPEROR HULKLING (2020) #1, LORDS OF EMPYRE: CELESTIAL MESSIAH (2020) #1, LORDS OF EMPYRE: SWORDSMAN (2020) #1 and EMPYRE: SAVAGE AVENGERS (2020) #1. First printing 2020. ISBN 978-1-302-92591-8. Published by MARVEL WORLDWIDE, INC., a subsidiary of MARVEL ENTERTAINMENT, LLC. OFFICE OF PUBLICATION: 1290 Avenue of the Americas, New York, NY 10104. © 2020 MARVEL No similarity between any of the names, characters, persons, and/or institutions in this magazine with those of any living or dead person or institution is intended, and any such similarity which may exist is purely coincidental. **Printed in the U.S.A.** KEVIN FEIGE, Chief Creative Officer; DAN BUCKLEY, President, Marvel Entertainment; JOHN NEE, Publisher; JOE QUESADA, EVP & Creative Director; TOM BREVOORT, SVP of Publishing; DAVID BOGART, Associate Publisher & SVP of Talent Affairs; Publishing & Partnership; DAVID GABRIEL, VP of Print & Digital Publishing; JEFF YOUNGQUIST, VP of Production & Special Projects; DAN CARR, Executive Director of Publishing Technology; ALEX MORALES, Director of Publishing Operations; DAN EDINGTON, Managing Editor; RICKEY PURDIN, Director of Talent Relations; SUSAN CRESPI, Production Manager; STAN LEE, Chairman Emeritus. For information regarding advertising in Marvel Comics or on Marvel.com, please contact Vit DeBellis, Custom Solutions & Integrated Advertising Manager, at vdebellis@marvel.com. For Marvel subscription inquiries, please call 888-511-5480. **Manufactured between 9/25/2020 and 10/26/2020 by FRY COMMUNICATIONS, MECHANICSBURG, PA, USA.**

10 9 8 7 6 5 4 3 2 1

LORDS OF EMPYRE: EMPEROR HULKLING

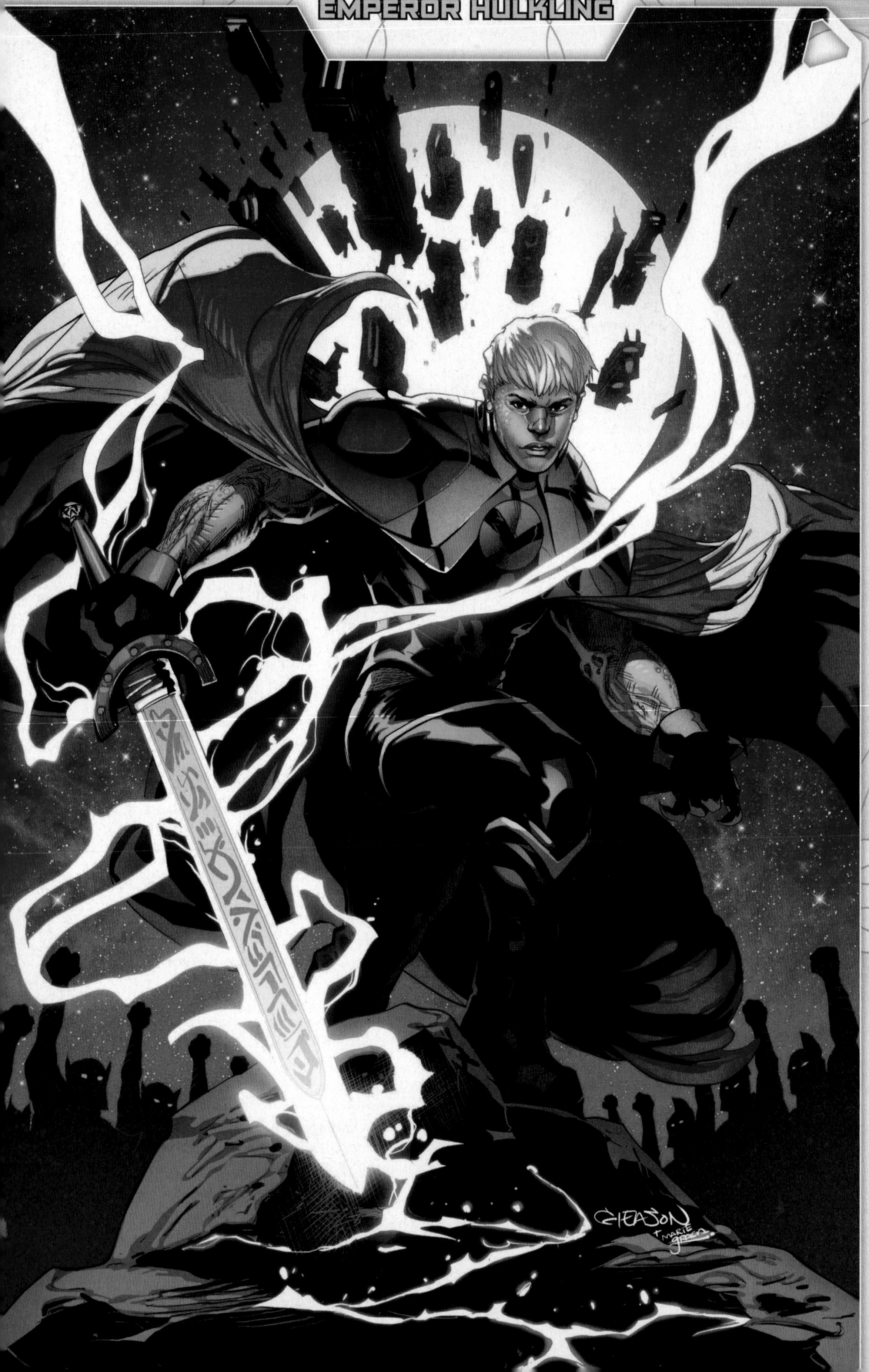

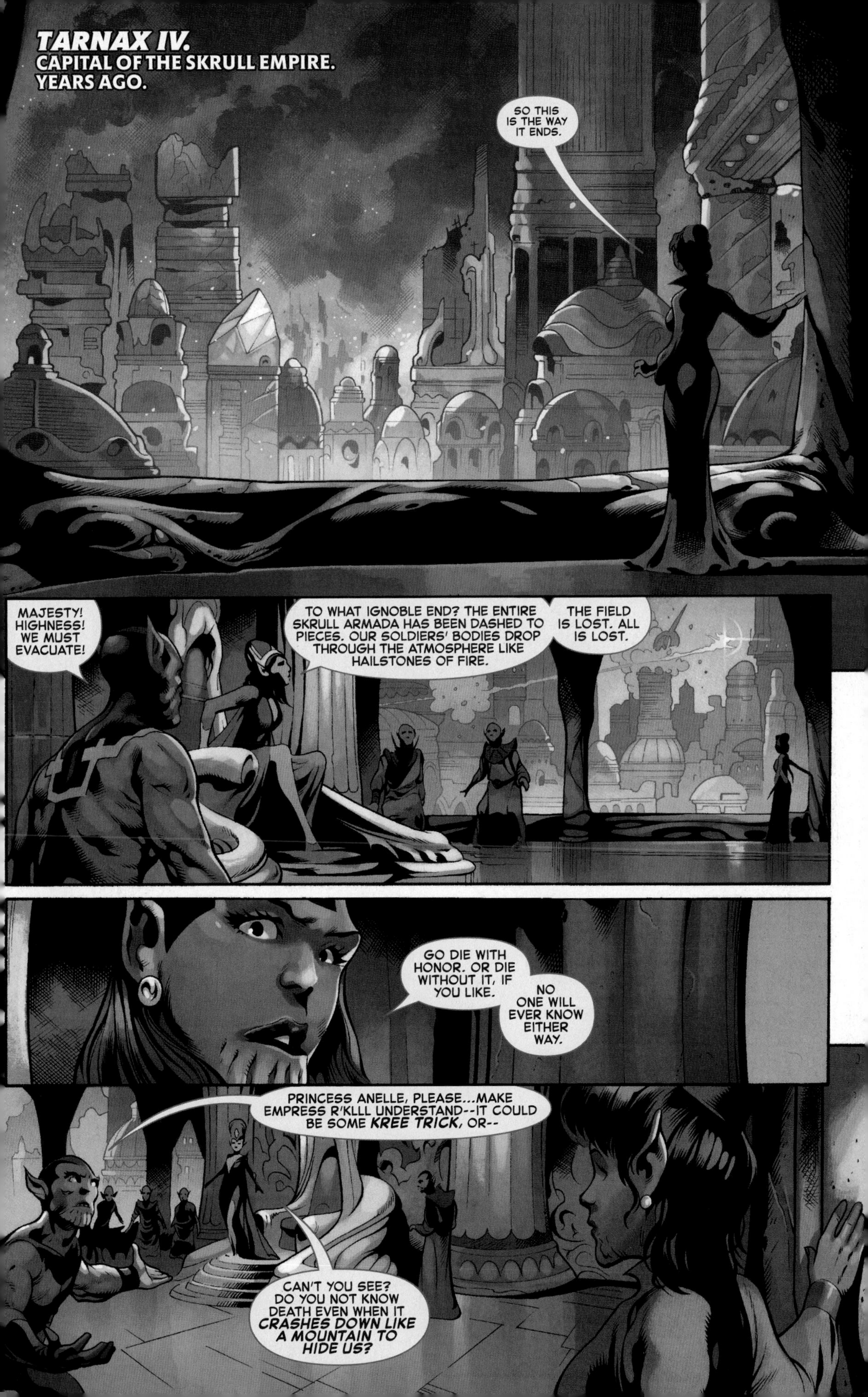
TARNAX IV.
CAPITAL OF THE SKRULL EMPIRE.
YEARS AGO.
SO THIS IS THE WAY IT ENDS.
MAJESTY! HIGHNESS! WE MUST EVACUATE!
TO WHAT IGNOBLE END? THE ENTIRE SKRULL ARMADA HAS BEEN DASHED TO PIECES. OUR SOLDIERS' BODIES DROP THROUGH THE ATMOSPHERE LIKE HAILSTONES OF FIRE.
THE FIELD IS LOST. ALL IS LOST.
GO DIE WITH HONOR. OR DIE WITHOUT IT, IF YOU LIKE.
NO ONE WILL EVER KNOW EITHER WAY.
PRINCESS ANELLE, PLEASE...MAKE EMPRESS R'KLLL UNDERSTAND--IT COULD BE SOME KREE TRICK, OR--
CAN'T YOU SEE? DO YOU NOT KNOW DEATH EVEN WHEN IT CRASHES DOWN LIKE A MOUNTAIN TO HIDE US?

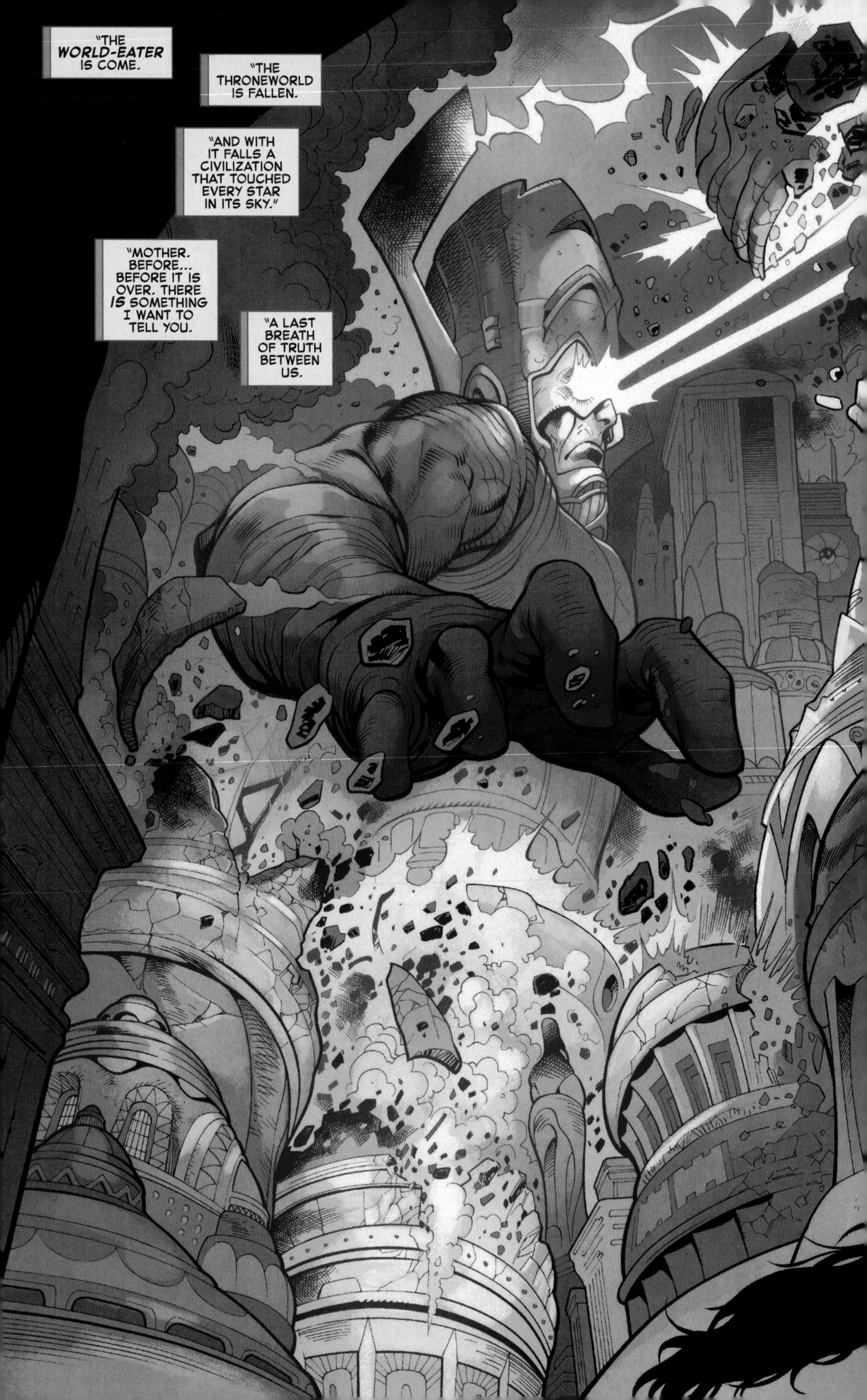
"THE WORLD-EATER IS COME.
"THE THRONEWORLD IS FALLEN.
"AND WITH IT FALLS A CIVILIZATION THAT TOUCHED EVERY STAR IN ITS SKY."
"MOTHER. BEFORE... BEFORE IT IS OVER. THERE IS SOMETHING I WANT TO TELL YOU.
"A LAST BREATH OF TRUTH BETWEEN US.

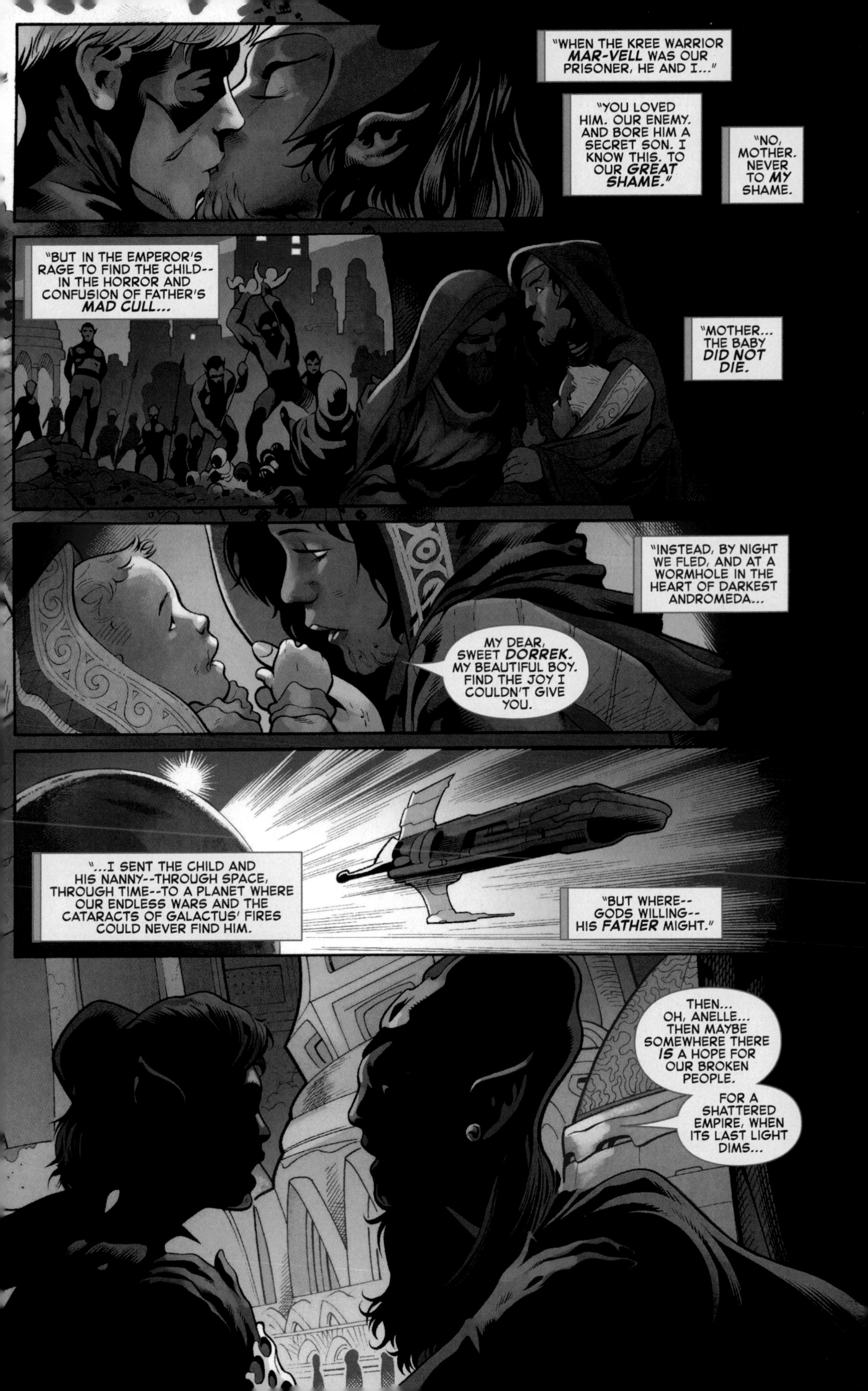
"WHEN THE KREE WARRIOR MAR-VELL WAS OUR PRISONER, HE AND I..."
"YOU LOVED HIM. OUR ENEMY. AND BORE HIM A SECRET SON. I KNOW THIS. TO OUR GREAT SHAME."
"NO, MOTHER. NEVER TO MY SHAME.
"BUT IN THE EMPEROR'S RAGE TO FIND THE CHILD-- IN THE HORROR AND CONFUSION OF FATHER'S MAD CULL...
"MOTHER... THE BABY DID NOT DIE.
"INSTEAD, BY NIGHT WE FLED, AND AT A WORMHOLE IN THE HEART OF DARKEST ANDROMEDA...
MY DEAR, SWEET DORREK. MY BEAUTIFUL BOY. FIND THE JOY I COULDN'T GIVE YOU.
"...I SENT THE CHILD AND HIS NANNY--THROUGH SPACE, THROUGH TIME--TO A PLANET WHERE OUR ENDLESS WARS AND THE CATARACTS OF GALACTUS' FIRES COULD NEVER FIND HIM.
"BUT WHERE-- GODS WILLING-- HIS FATHER MIGHT."
THEN... OH, ANELLE... THEN MAYBE SOMEWHERE THERE IS A HOPE FOR OUR BROKEN PEOPLE.
FOR A SHATTERED EMPIRE, WHEN ITS LAST LIGHT DIMS...

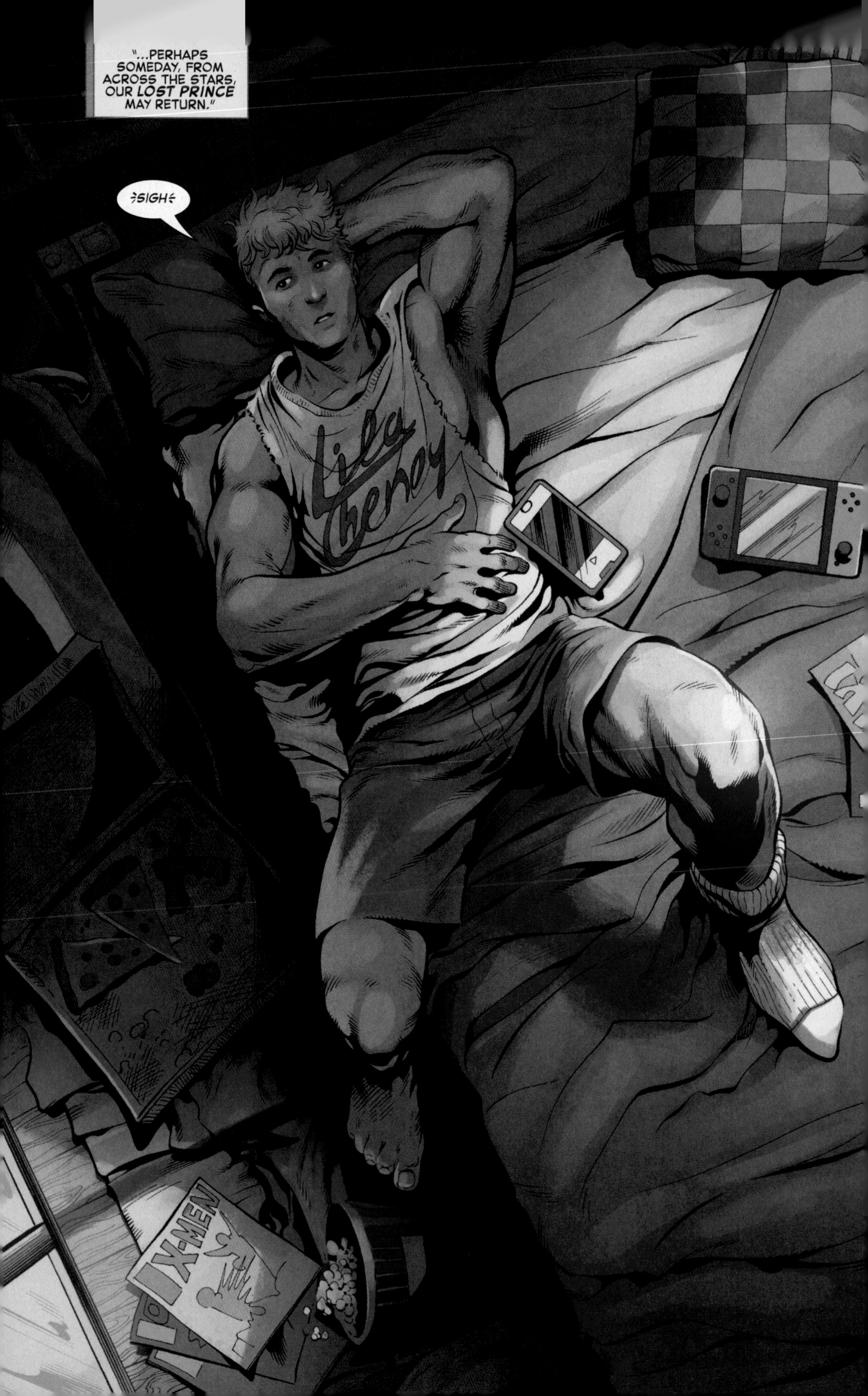
"...PERHAPS SOMEDAY, FROM ACROSS THE STARS, OUR *LOST PRINCE* MAY RETURN."
SIGH
Lila Cheney
X-MEN

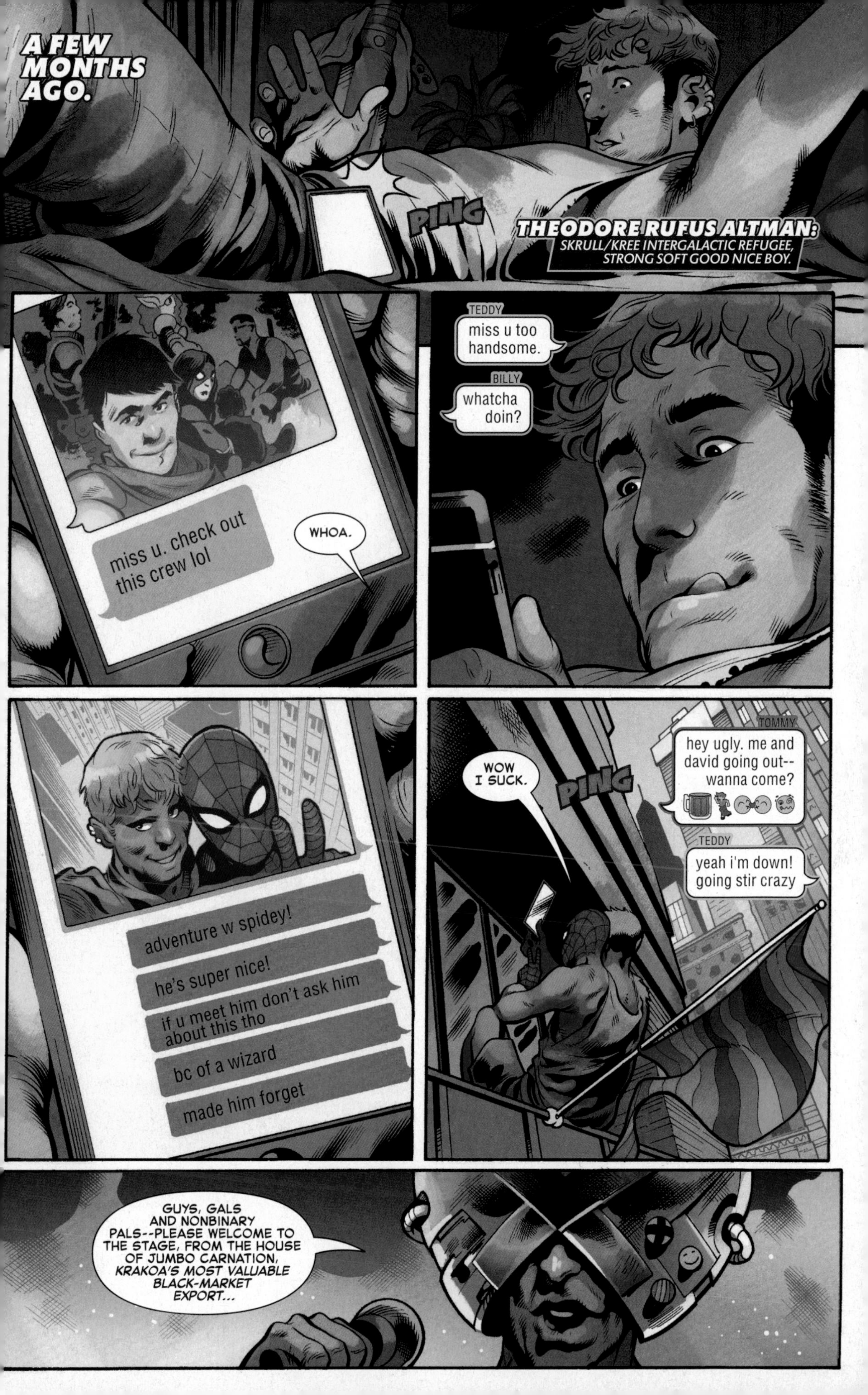
A FEW MONTHS AGO.
PING
THEODORE RUFUS ALTMAN:
SKRULL/KREE INTERGALACTIC REFUGEE, STRONG SOFT GOOD NICE BOY.
miss u. check out this crew lol
WHOA.
TEDDY
miss u too handsome.
BILLY
whatcha doin?
adventure w spidey!
he's super nice!
if u meet him don't ask him about this tho
bc of a wizard
made him forget
WOW I SUCK.
PING
TOMMY
hey ugly. me and david going out--wanna come?
TEDDY
yeah i'm down! going stir crazy
GUYS, GALS AND NONBINARY PALS--PLEASE WELCOME TO THE STAGE, FROM THE HOUSE OF JUMBO CARNATION, KRAKOA'S MOST VALUABLE BLACK-MARKET EXPORT...

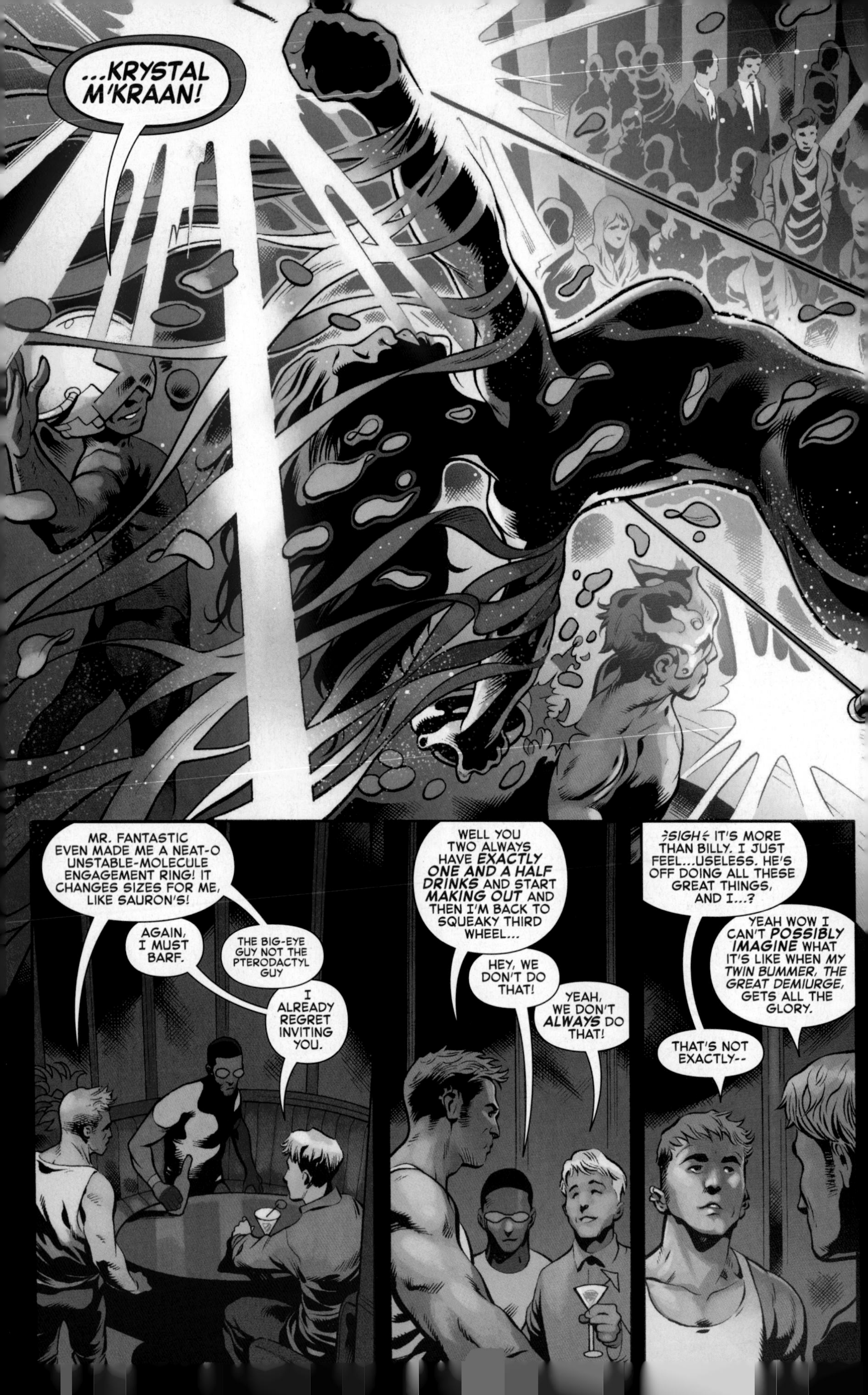

...KRYSTAL M'KRAAN!
MR. FANTASTIC EVEN MADE ME A NEAT-O UNSTABLE-MOLECULE ENGAGEMENT RING! IT CHANGES SIZES FOR ME, LIKE SAURON'S!
AGAIN, I MUST BARF.
THE BIG-EYE GUY NOT THE PTERODACTYL GUY
I ALREADY REGRET INVITING YOU.
WELL YOU TWO ALWAYS HAVE EXACTLY ONE AND A HALF DRINKS AND START MAKING OUT AND THEN I'M BACK TO SQUEAKY THIRD WHEEL...
HEY, WE DON'T DO THAT!
YEAH, WE DON'T ALWAYS DO THAT!
SIGH IT'S MORE THAN BILLY. I JUST FEEL...USELESS. HE'S OFF DOING ALL THESE GREAT THINGS, AND I...?
YEAH WOW I CAN'T POSSIBLY IMAGINE WHAT IT'S LIKE WHEN MY TWIN BUMMER, THE GREAT DEMIURGE, GETS ALL THE GLORY.
THAT'S NOT EXACTLY--

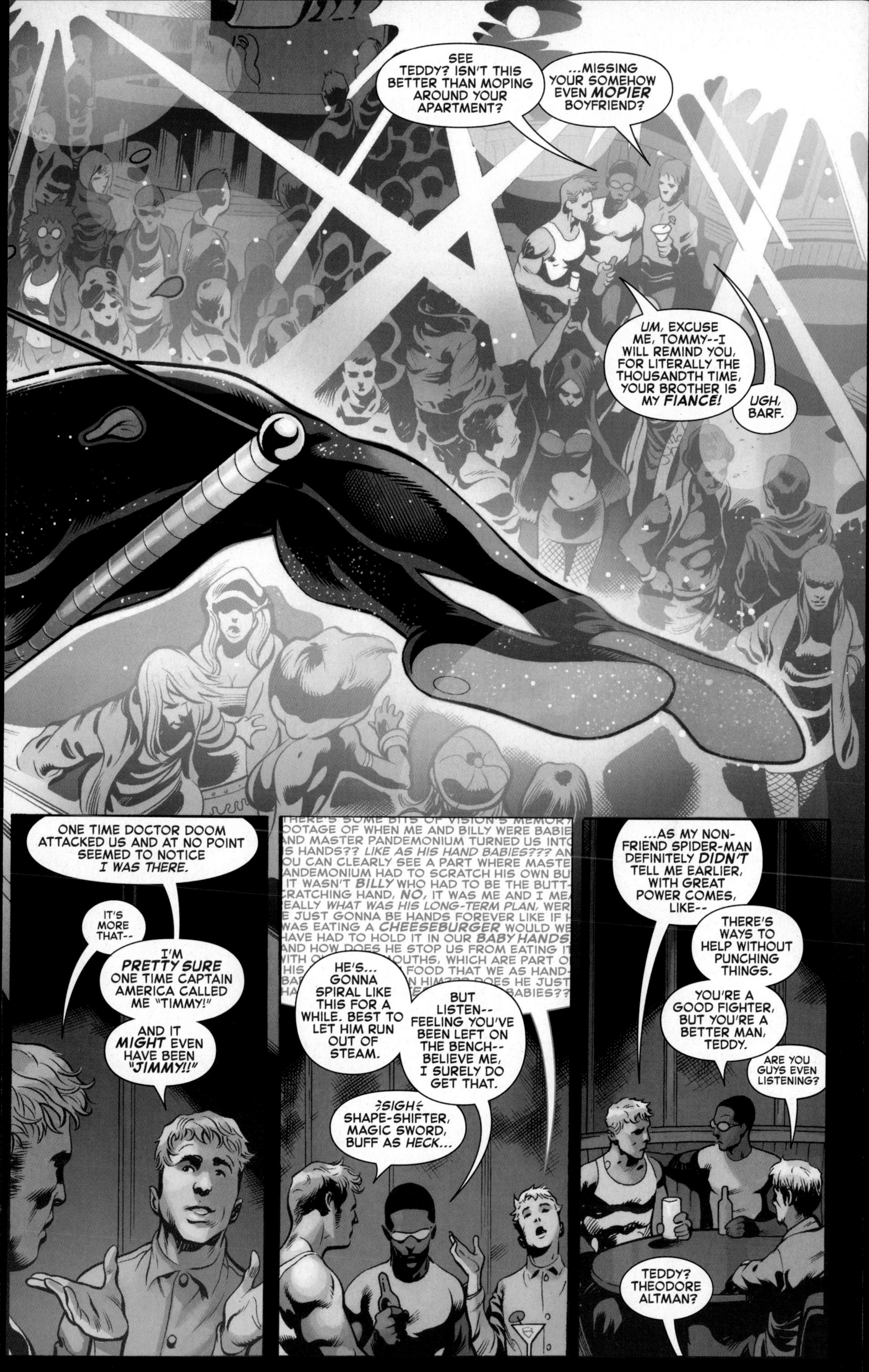
SEE TEDDY? ISN'T THIS BETTER THAN MOPING AROUND YOUR APARTMENT?
...MISSING YOUR SOMEHOW EVEN MOPIER BOYFRIEND?
UM, EXCUSE ME, TOMMY--I WILL REMIND YOU, FOR LITERALLY THE THOUSANDTH TIME, YOUR BROTHER IS MY FIANCE!
UGH, BARF.
ONE TIME DOCTOR DOOM ATTACKED US AND AT NO POINT SEEMED TO NOTICE I WAS THERE.
IT'S MORE THAT--
I'M PRETTY SURE ONE TIME CAPTAIN AMERICA CALLED ME "TIMMY!"
AND IT MIGHT EVEN HAVE BEEN "JIMMY!!"
OOTAGE OF WHEN ME AND BILLY WERE BABIE
AND MASTER PANDEMONIUM TURNED US INTO
S HANDS?? LIKE AS HIS HAND BABIES??? AN
OU CAN CLEARLY SEE A PART WHERE MASTE
ANDEMONIUM HAD TO SCRATCH HIS OWN BU
IT WASN'T BILLY WHO HAD TO BE THE BUTT-
CRATCHING HAND, NO, IT WAS ME AND I MEA
EALLY WHAT WAS HIS LONG-TERM PLAN, WER
E JUST GONNA BE HANDS FOREVER LIKE IF H
WAS EATING A CHEESEBURGER WOULD WE
HAVE HAD TO HOLD IT IN OUR BABY HANDS
AND HOW DOES HE STOP US FROM EATING IT
HE'S... GONNA SPIRAL LIKE THIS FOR A WHILE. BEST TO LET HIM RUN OUT OF STEAM.
BUT LISTEN-- FEELING YOU'VE BEEN LEFT ON THE BENCH-- BELIEVE ME, I SURELY DO GET THAT.
SIGH
SHAPE-SHIFTER, MAGIC SWORD, BUFF AS HECK...
...AS MY NON-FRIEND SPIDER-MAN DEFINITELY DIDN'T TELL ME EARLIER, WITH GREAT POWER COMES, LIKE--
THERE'S WAYS TO HELP WITHOUT PUNCHING THINGS.
YOU'RE A GOOD FIGHTER, BUT YOU'RE A BETTER MAN, TEDDY.
ARE YOU GUYS EVEN LISTENING?
TEDDY? THEODORE ALTMAN?

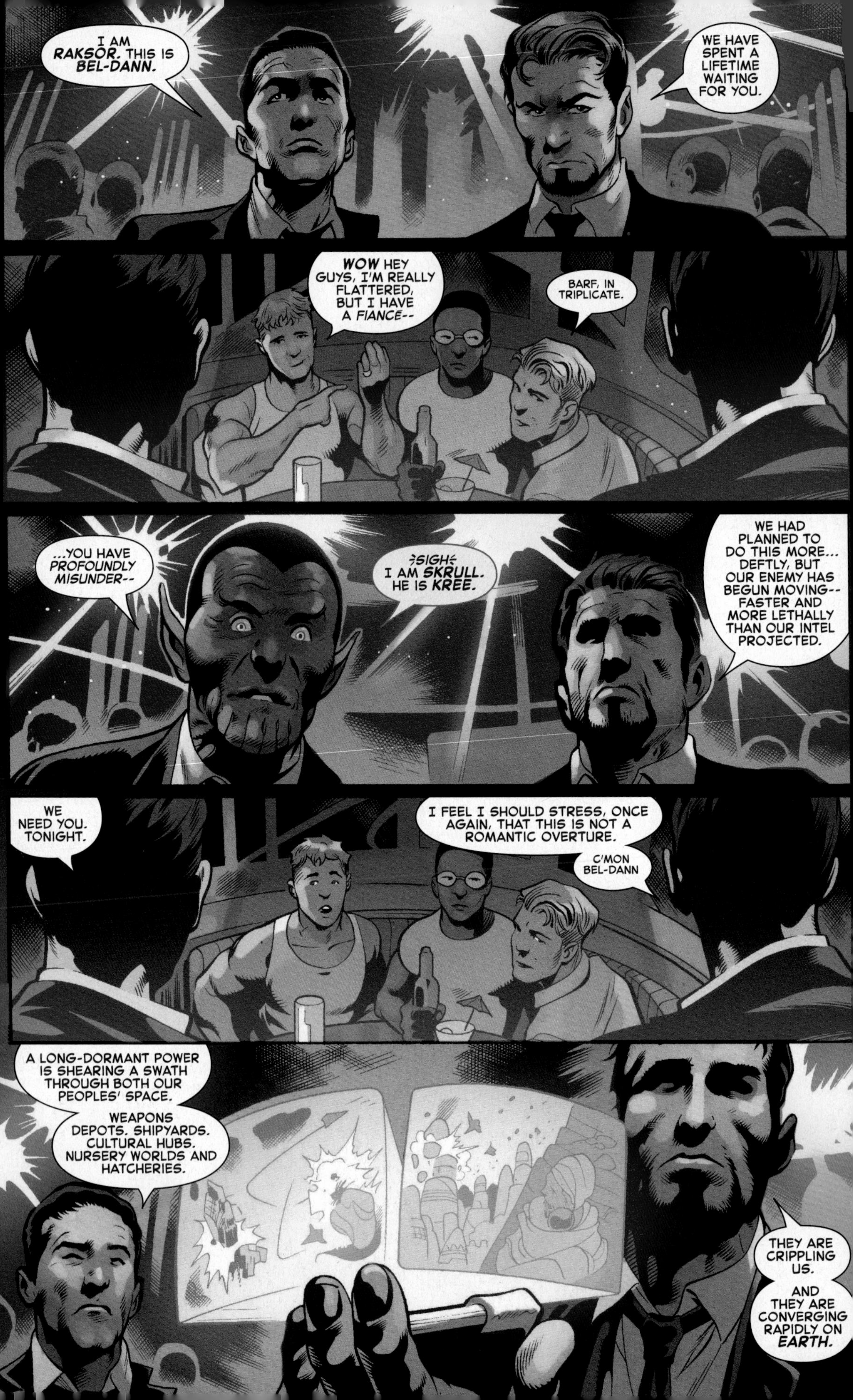
I AM RAKSOR. THIS IS BEL-DANN.
WE HAVE SPENT A LIFETIME WAITING FOR YOU.
WOW HEY GUYS, I'M REALLY FLATTERED, BUT I HAVE A FIANCE--
BARF, IN TRIPLICATE.
...YOU HAVE PROFOUNDLY MISUNDER--
SIGH I AM SKRULL. HE IS KREE.
WE HAD PLANNED TO DO THIS MORE... DEFTLY, BUT OUR ENEMY HAS BEGUN MOVING-- FASTER AND MORE LETHALLY THAN OUR INTEL PROJECTED.
WE NEED YOU. TONIGHT.
I FEEL I SHOULD STRESS, ONCE AGAIN, THAT THIS IS NOT A ROMANTIC OVERTURE.
C'MON BEL-DANN
A LONG-DORMANT POWER IS SHEARING A SWATH THROUGH BOTH OUR PEOPLES' SPACE.
WEAPONS DEPOTS. SHIPYARDS. CULTURAL HUBS. NURSERY WORLDS AND HATCHERIES.
THEY ARE CRIPPLING US.
AND THEY ARE CONVERGING RAPIDLY ON EARTH.

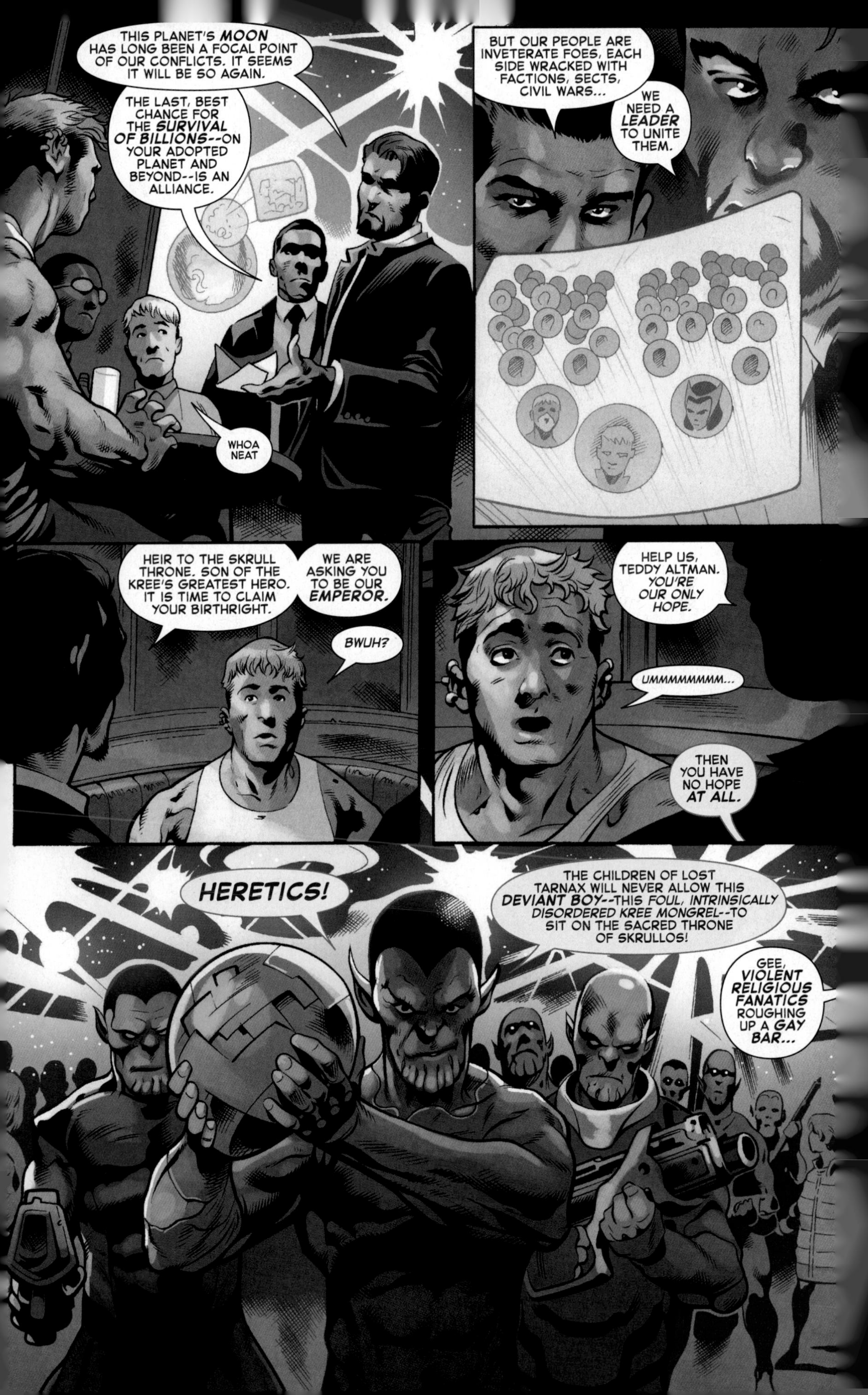

THIS PLANET'S MOON HAS LONG BEEN A FOCAL POINT OF OUR CONFLICTS. IT SEEMS IT WILL BE SO AGAIN.
THE LAST, BEST CHANCE FOR THE SURVIVAL OF BILLIONS--ON YOUR ADOPTED PLANET AND BEYOND--IS AN ALLIANCE.
WHOA NEAT
BUT OUR PEOPLE ARE INVETERATE FOES, EACH SIDE WRACKED WITH FACTIONS, SECTS, CIVIL WARS...
WE NEED A LEADER TO UNITE THEM.
HEIR TO THE SKRULL THRONE. SON OF THE KREE'S GREATEST HERO. IT IS TIME TO CLAIM YOUR BIRTHRIGHT.
WE ARE ASKING YOU TO BE OUR EMPEROR.
BWUH?
HELP US, TEDDY ALTMAN. YOU'RE OUR ONLY HOPE.
UMMMMMMMM...
THEN YOU HAVE NO HOPE AT ALL.
HERETICS!
THE CHILDREN OF LOST TARNAX WILL NEVER ALLOW THIS DEVIANT BOY--THIS FOUL, INTRINSICALLY DISORDERED KREE MONGREL--TO SIT ON THE SACRED THRONE OF SKRULLOS!
GEE, VIOLENT RELIGIOUS FANATICS ROUGHING UP A GAY BAR...

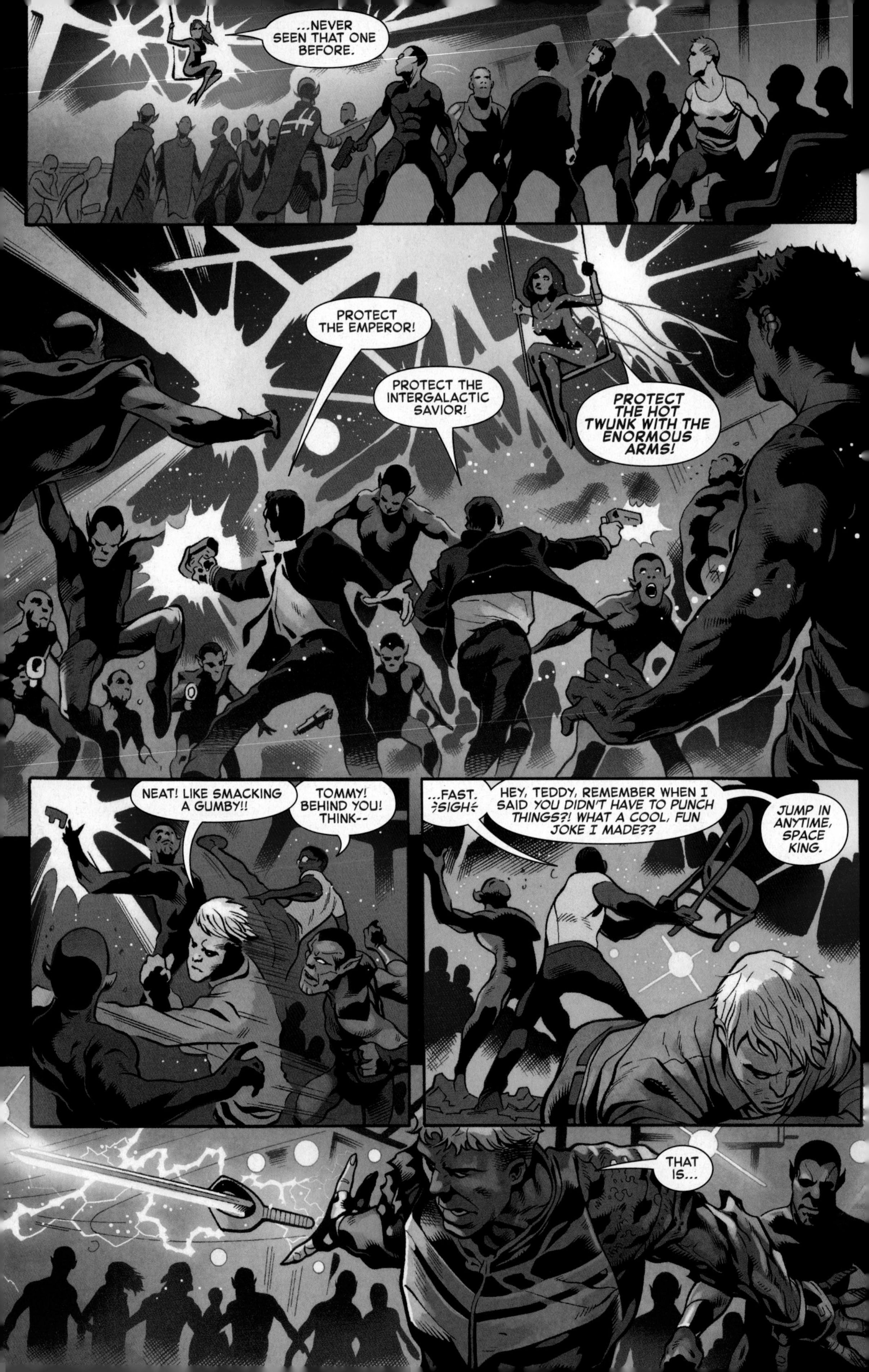
...NEVER SEEN THAT ONE BEFORE.
PROTECT THE EMPEROR!
PROTECT THE INTERGALACTIC SAVIOR!
PROTECT THE HOT TWUNK WITH THE ENORMOUS ARMS!
NEAT! LIKE SMACKING A GUMBY!!
TOMMY! BEHIND YOU! THINK--
...FAST. *SIGH*
HEY, TEDDY, REMEMBER WHEN I SAID YOU DIDN'T HAVE TO PUNCH THINGS?! WHAT A COOL, FUN JOKE I MADE??
JUMP IN ANYTIME, SPACE KING.
THAT IS...

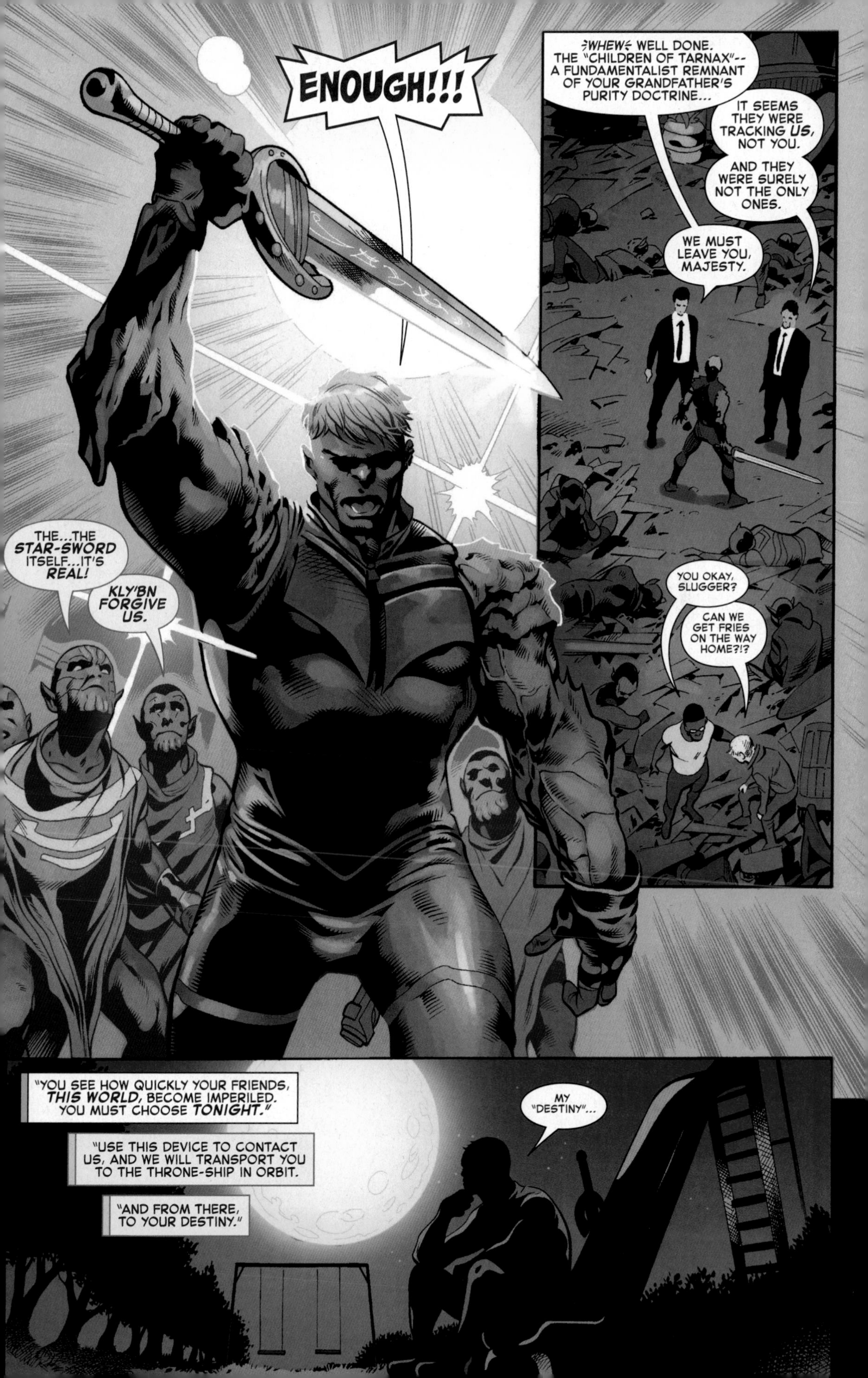
ENOUGH!!!
THE...THE STAR-SWORD ITSELF...IT'S REAL!
KLY'BN FORGIVE US.
WHEW WELL DONE. THE "CHILDREN OF TARNAX"-- A FUNDAMENTALIST REMNANT OF YOUR GRANDFATHER'S PURITY DOCTRINE...
IT SEEMS THEY WERE TRACKING US, NOT YOU.
AND THEY WERE SURELY NOT THE ONLY ONES.
WE MUST LEAVE YOU, MAJESTY.
YOU OKAY, SLUGGER?
CAN WE GET FRIES ON THE WAY HOME?!?
"YOU SEE HOW QUICKLY YOUR FRIENDS, THIS WORLD, BECOME IMPERILED. YOU MUST CHOOSE TONIGHT."
"USE THIS DEVICE TO CONTACT US, AND WE WILL TRANSPORT YOU TO THE THRONE-SHIP IN ORBIT.
"AND FROM THERE, TO YOUR DESTINY."
MY "DESTINY"...

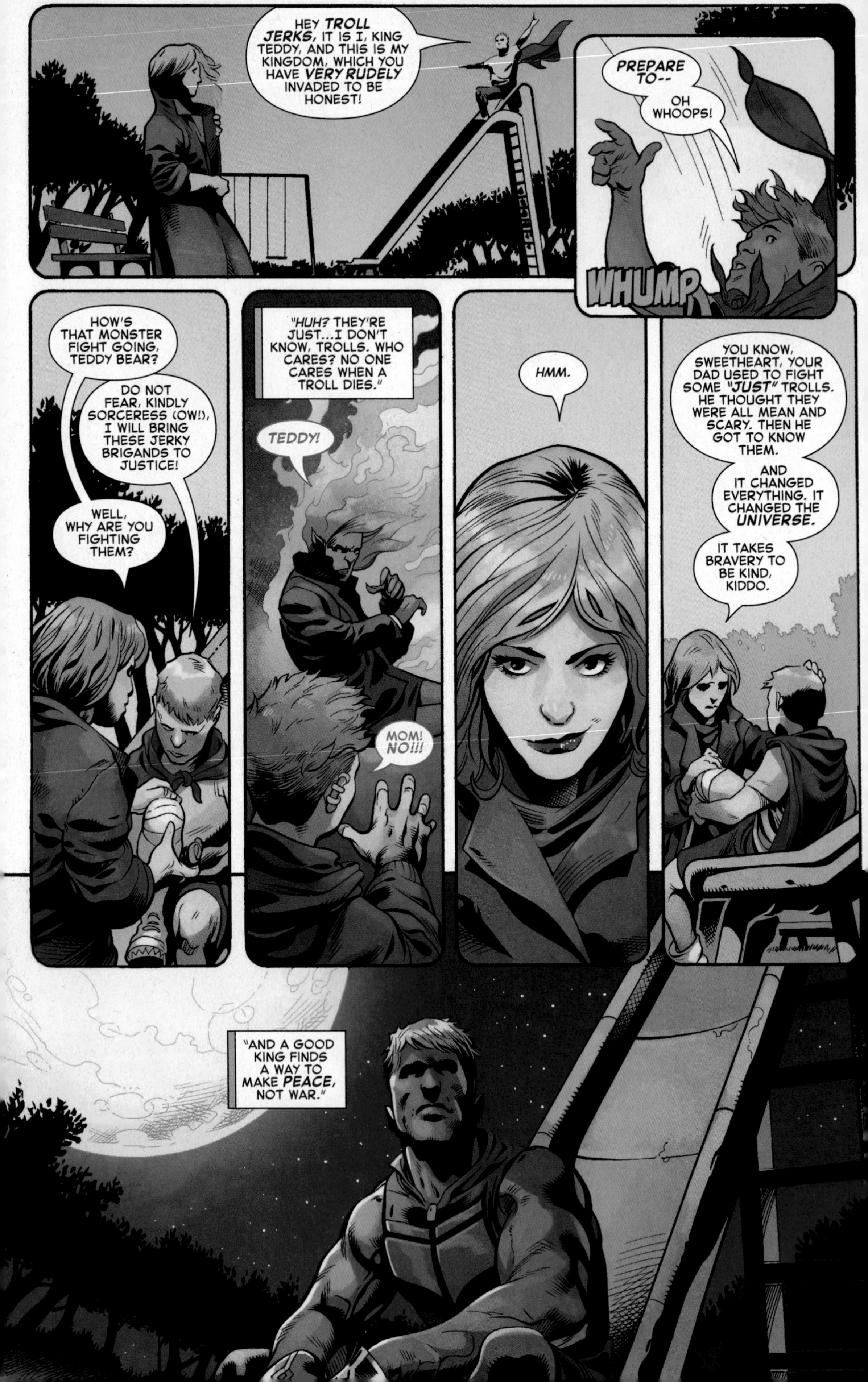

HEY TROLL JERKS, IT IS I, KING TEDDY, AND THIS IS MY KINGDOM, WHICH YOU HAVE VERY RUDELY INVADED TO BE HONEST!
PREPARE TO--
OH WHOOPS!
WHUMP
HOW'S THAT MONSTER FIGHT GOING, TEDDY BEAR?
DO NOT FEAR, KINDLY SORCERESS (OW!), I WILL BRING THESE JERKY BRIGANDS TO JUSTICE!
WELL, WHY ARE YOU FIGHTING THEM?
"HUH? THEY'RE JUST...I DON'T KNOW, TROLLS. WHO CARES? NO ONE CARES WHEN A TROLL DIES."
TEDDY!
MOM! NO!!!
HMM.
YOU KNOW, SWEETHEART, YOUR DAD USED TO FIGHT SOME "JUST" TROLLS. HE THOUGHT THEY WERE ALL MEAN AND SCARY. THEN HE GOT TO KNOW THEM.
AND IT CHANGED EVERYTHING. IT CHANGED THE UNIVERSE.
IT TAKES BRAVERY TO BE KIND, KIDDO.
"AND A GOOD KING FINDS A WAY TO MAKE PEACE, NOT WAR."

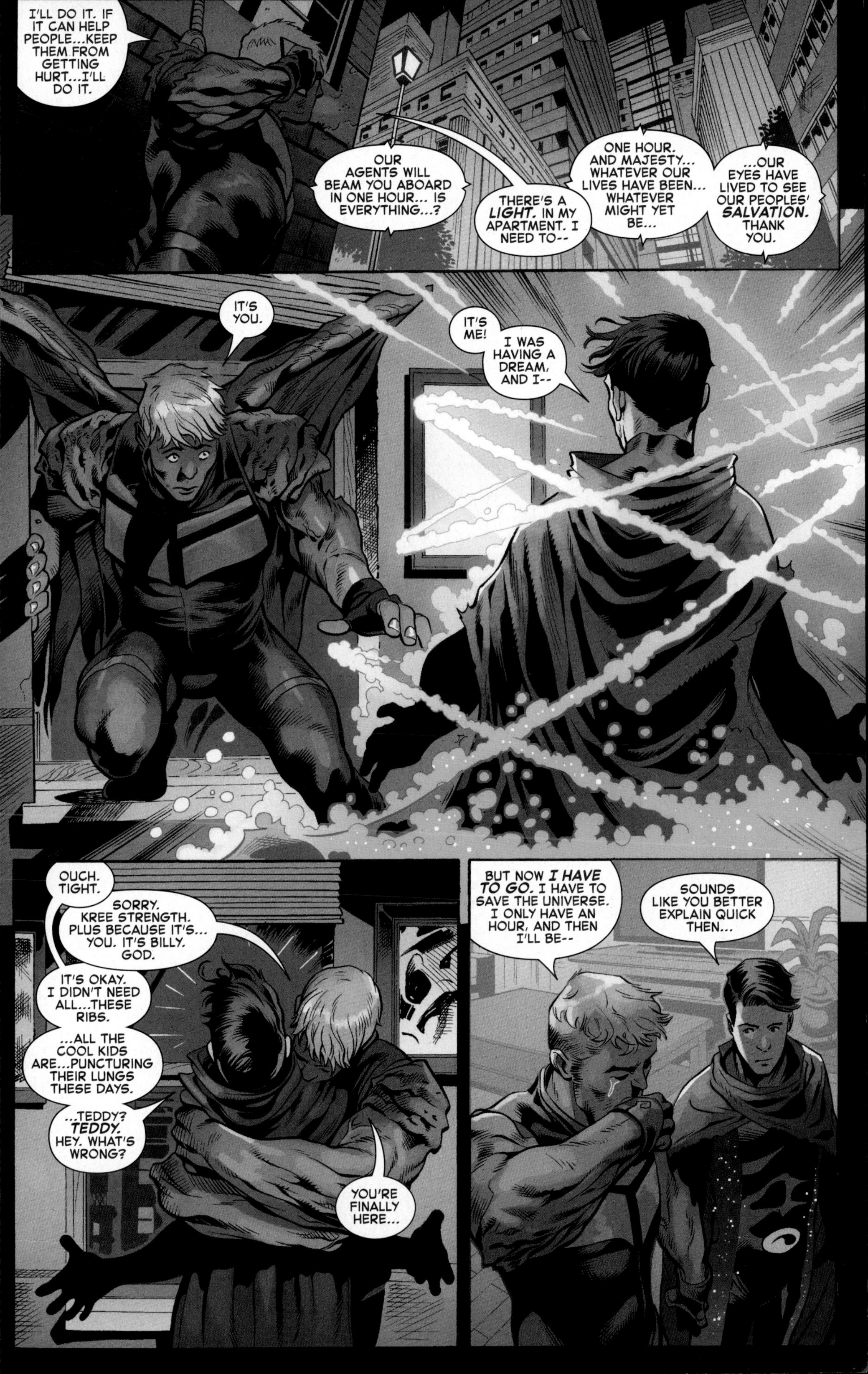
I'LL DO IT. IF IT CAN HELP PEOPLE...KEEP THEM FROM GETTING HURT...I'LL DO IT.
OUR AGENTS WILL BEAM YOU ABOARD IN ONE HOUR... IS EVERYTHING...?
THERE'S A LIGHT. IN MY APARTMENT. I NEED TO--
ONE HOUR. AND MAJESTY... WHATEVER OUR LIVES HAVE BEEN... WHATEVER MIGHT YET BE...
...OUR EYES HAVE LIVED TO SEE OUR PEOPLES' SALVATION. THANK YOU.
IT'S YOU.
IT'S ME!
I WAS HAVING A DREAM, AND I--
OUCH. TIGHT.
SORRY. KREE STRENGTH. PLUS BECAUSE IT'S... YOU. IT'S BILLY. GOD.
IT'S OKAY. I DIDN'T NEED ALL...THESE RIBS.
...ALL THE COOL KIDS ARE...PUNCTURING THEIR LUNGS THESE DAYS.
...TEDDY? TEDDY. HEY. WHAT'S WRONG?
YOU'RE FINALLY HERE...
BUT NOW I HAVE TO GO. I HAVE TO SAVE THE UNIVERSE. I ONLY HAVE AN HOUR, AND THEN I'LL BE--
SOUNDS LIKE YOU BETTER EXPLAIN QUICK THEN...

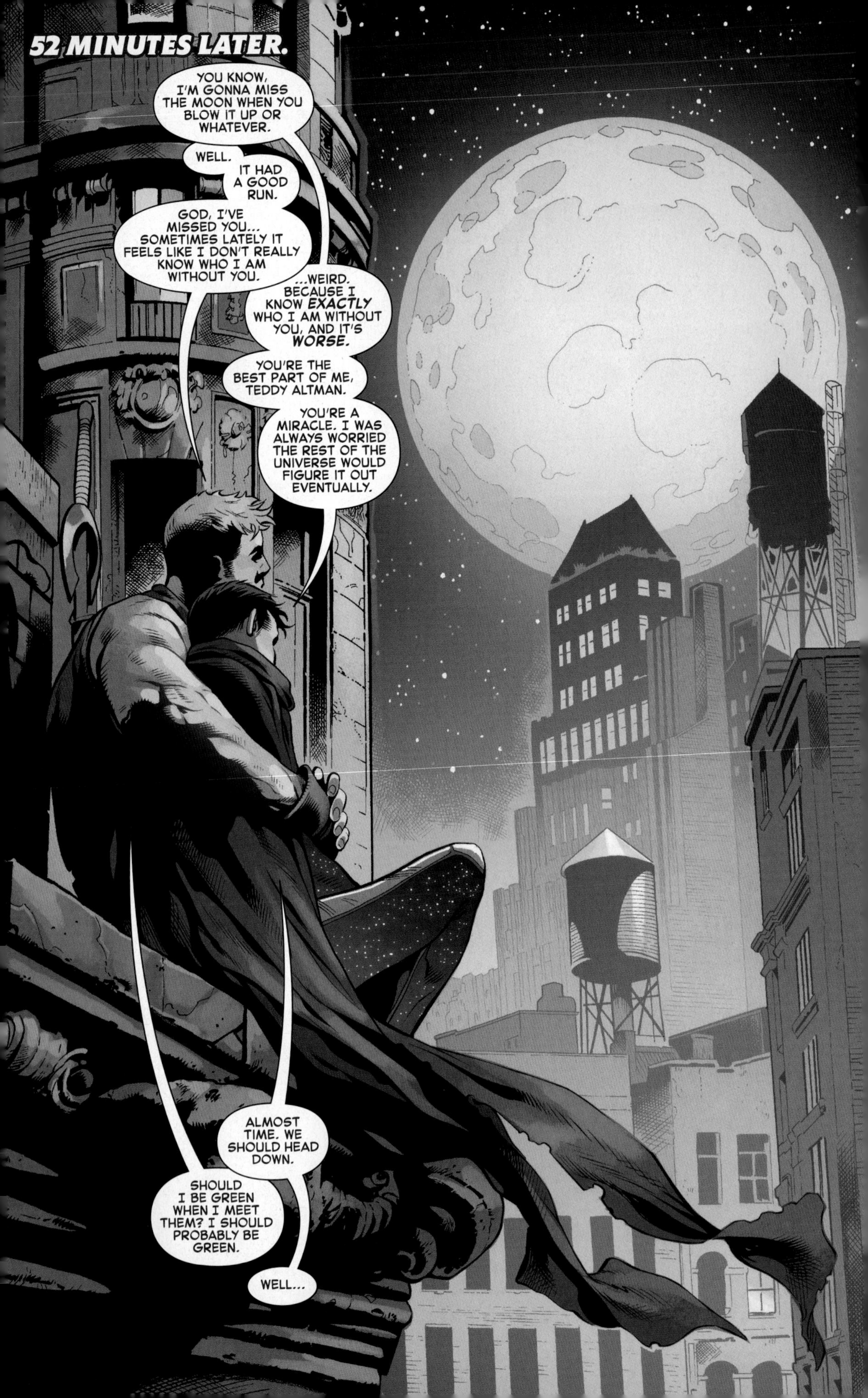
52 MINUTES LATER.
YOU KNOW, I'M GONNA MISS THE MOON WHEN YOU BLOW IT UP OR WHATEVER.
WELL.
IT HAD A GOOD RUN.
GOD, I'VE MISSED YOU... SOMETIMES LATELY IT FEELS LIKE I DON'T REALLY KNOW WHO I AM WITHOUT YOU.
...WEIRD. BECAUSE I KNOW EXACTLY WHO I AM WITHOUT YOU, AND IT'S WORSE.
YOU'RE THE BEST PART OF ME, TEDDY ALTMAN.
YOU'RE A MIRACLE. I WAS ALWAYS WORRIED THE REST OF THE UNIVERSE WOULD FIGURE IT OUT EVENTUALLY.
ALMOST TIME. WE SHOULD HEAD DOWN.
SHOULD I BE GREEN WHEN I MEET THEM? I SHOULD PROBABLY BE GREEN.
WELL...

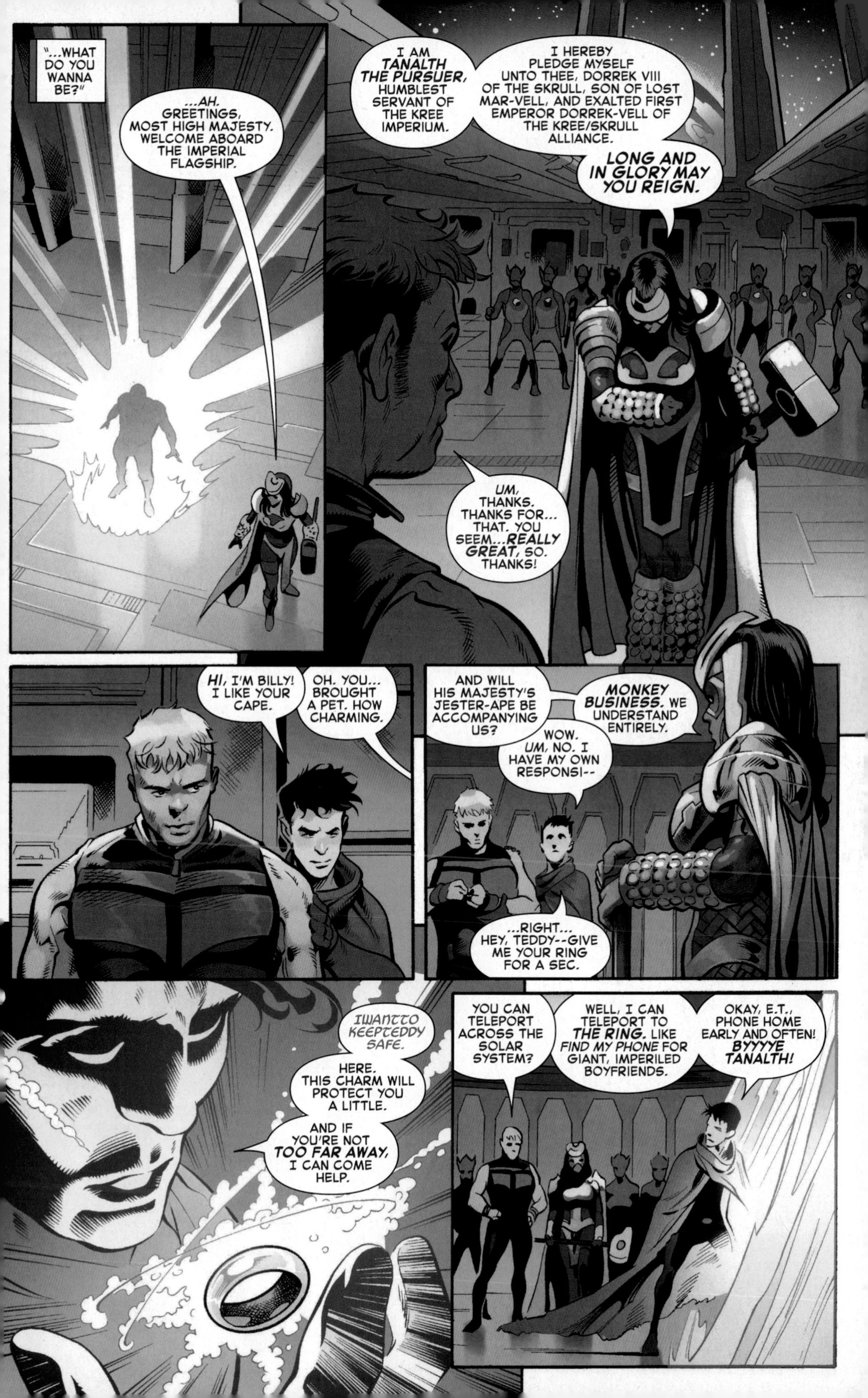
"...WHAT DO YOU WANNA BE?"
...AH. GREETINGS, MOST HIGH MAJESTY. WELCOME ABOARD THE IMPERIAL FLAGSHIP.
I AM TANALTH THE PURSUER, HUMBLEST SERVANT OF THE KREE IMPERIUM.
I HEREBY PLEDGE MYSELF UNTO THEE, DORREK VIII OF THE SKRULL, SON OF LOST MAR-VELL, AND EXALTED FIRST EMPEROR DORREK-VELL OF THE KREE/SKRULL ALLIANCE.
LONG AND IN GLORY MAY YOU REIGN.
UM, THANKS. THANKS FOR... THAT. YOU SEEM...REALLY GREAT, SO. THANKS!
HI, I'M BILLY! I LIKE YOUR CAPE.
OH. YOU... BROUGHT A PET. HOW CHARMING.
AND WILL HIS MAJESTY'S JESTER-APE BE ACCOMPANYING US?
MONKEY BUSINESS. WE UNDERSTAND ENTIRELY.
WOW. UM, NO. I HAVE MY OWN RESPONSI--
...RIGHT... HEY, TEDDY--GIVE ME YOUR RING FOR A SEC.
IWANTTO KEEPTEDDY SAFE.
HERE. THIS CHARM WILL PROTECT YOU A LITTLE.
AND IF YOU'RE NOT TOO FAR AWAY, I CAN COME HELP.
YOU CAN TELEPORT ACROSS THE SOLAR SYSTEM?
WELL, I CAN TELEPORT TO THE RING. LIKE FIND MY PHONE FOR GIANT, IMPERILED BOYFRIENDS.
OKAY, E.T., PHONE HOME EARLY AND OFTEN! BYYYYE TANALTH!

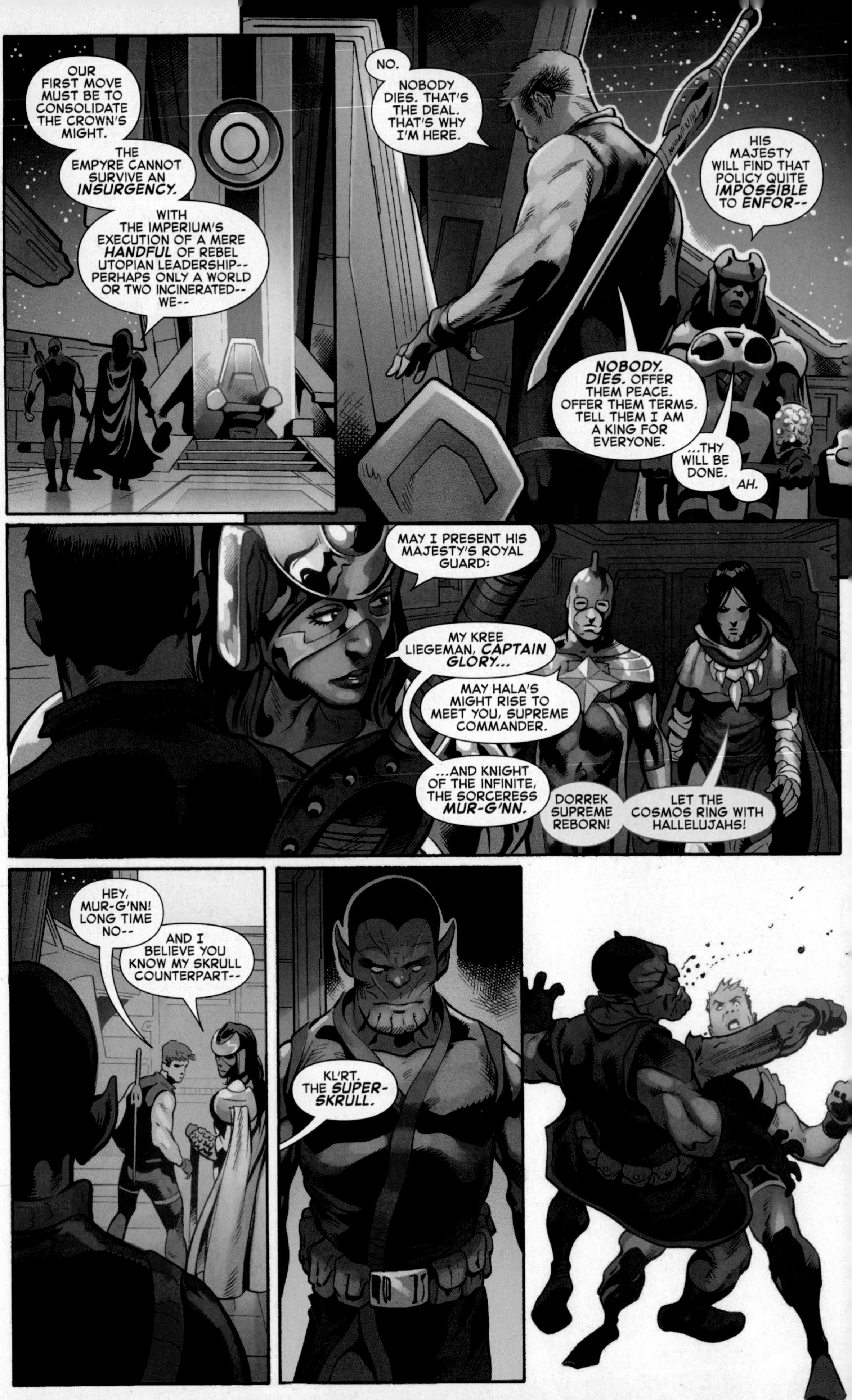
OUR FIRST MOVE MUST BE TO CONSOLIDATE THE CROWN'S MIGHT.
THE EMPYRE CANNOT SURVIVE AN INSURGENCY.
WITH THE IMPERIUM'S EXECUTION OF A MERE HANDFUL OF REBEL UTOPIAN LEADERSHIP-- PERHAPS ONLY A WORLD OR TWO INCINERATED-- WE--
NO.
NOBODY DIES. THAT'S THE DEAL. THAT'S WHY I'M HERE.
HIS MAJESTY WILL FIND THAT POLICY QUITE IMPOSSIBLE TO ENFOR--
NOBODY. DIES. OFFER THEM PEACE. OFFER THEM TERMS. TELL THEM I AM A KING FOR EVERYONE.
...THY WILL BE DONE.
AH.
MAY I PRESENT HIS MAJESTY'S ROYAL GUARD:
MY KREE LIEGEMAN, CAPTAIN GLORY...
MAY HALA'S MIGHT RISE TO MEET YOU, SUPREME COMMANDER.
...AND KNIGHT OF THE INFINITE, THE SORCERESS MUR-G'NN.
DORREK SUPREME REBORN!
LET THE COSMOS RING WITH HALLELUJAHS!
HEY, MUR-G'NN! LONG TIME NO--
AND I BELIEVE YOU KNOW MY SKRULL COUNTERPART--
KL'RT. THE SUPER-SKRULL.

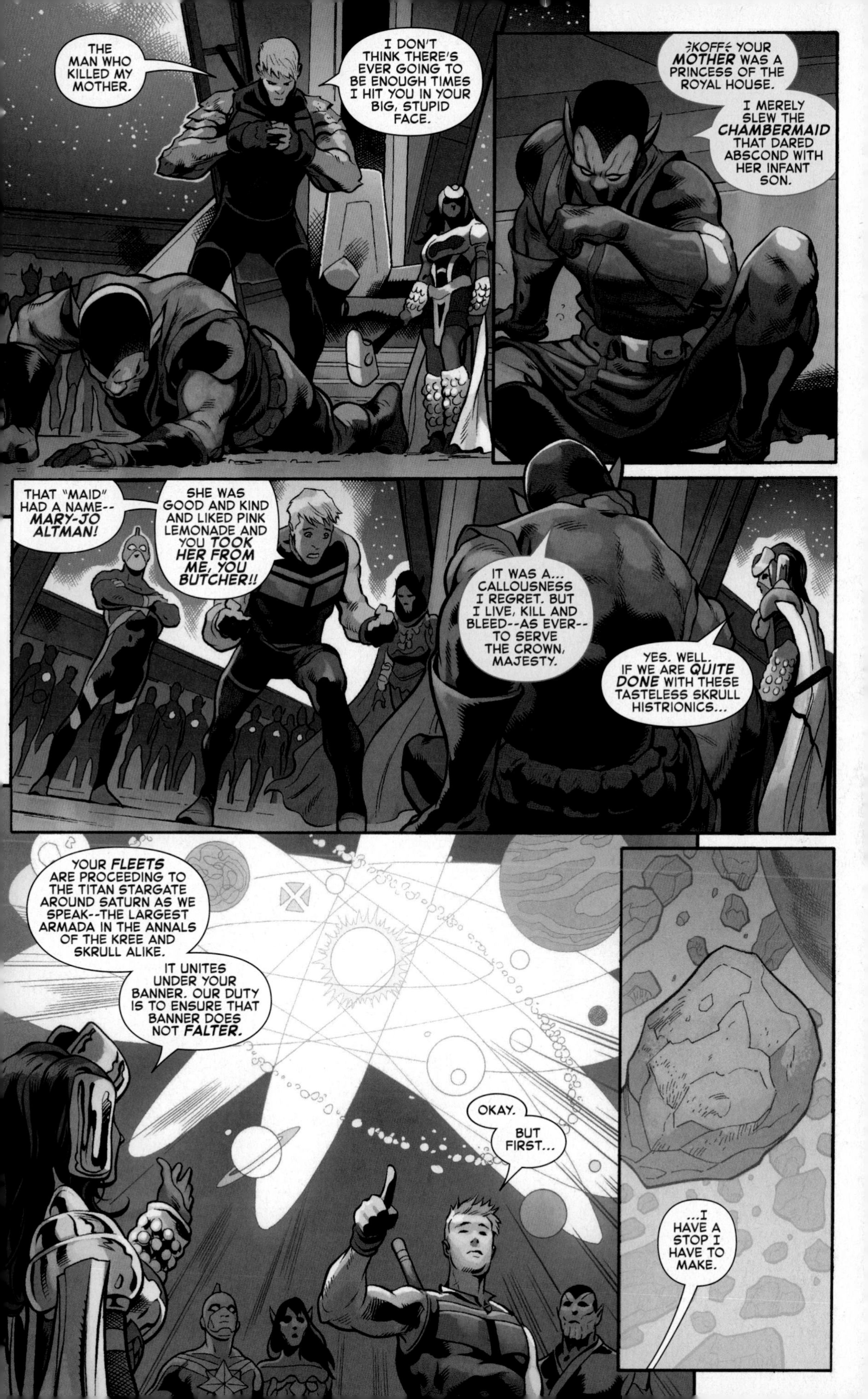
THE MAN WHO KILLED MY MOTHER.
I DON'T THINK THERE'S EVER GOING TO BE ENOUGH TIMES I HIT YOU IN YOUR BIG, STUPID FACE.
KOFF YOUR MOTHER WAS A PRINCESS OF THE ROYAL HOUSE.
I MERELY SLEW THE CHAMBERMAID THAT DARED ABSCOND WITH HER INFANT SON.
THAT "MAID" HAD A NAME-- MARY-JO ALTMAN!
SHE WAS GOOD AND KIND AND LIKED PINK LEMONADE AND YOU TOOK HER FROM ME, YOU BUTCHER!!
IT WAS A... CALLOUSNESS I REGRET. BUT I LIVE, KILL AND BLEED--AS EVER-- TO SERVE THE CROWN, MAJESTY.
YES. WELL. IF WE ARE QUITE DONE WITH THESE TASTELESS SKRULL HISTRIONICS...
YOUR FLEETS ARE PROCEEDING TO THE TITAN STARGATE AROUND SATURN AS WE SPEAK--THE LARGEST ARMADA IN THE ANNALS OF THE KREE AND SKRULL ALIKE.
IT UNITES UNDER YOUR BANNER. OUR DUTY IS TO ENSURE THAT BANNER DOES NOT FALTER.
OKAY.
BUT FIRST...
...I HAVE A STOP I HAVE TO MAKE.

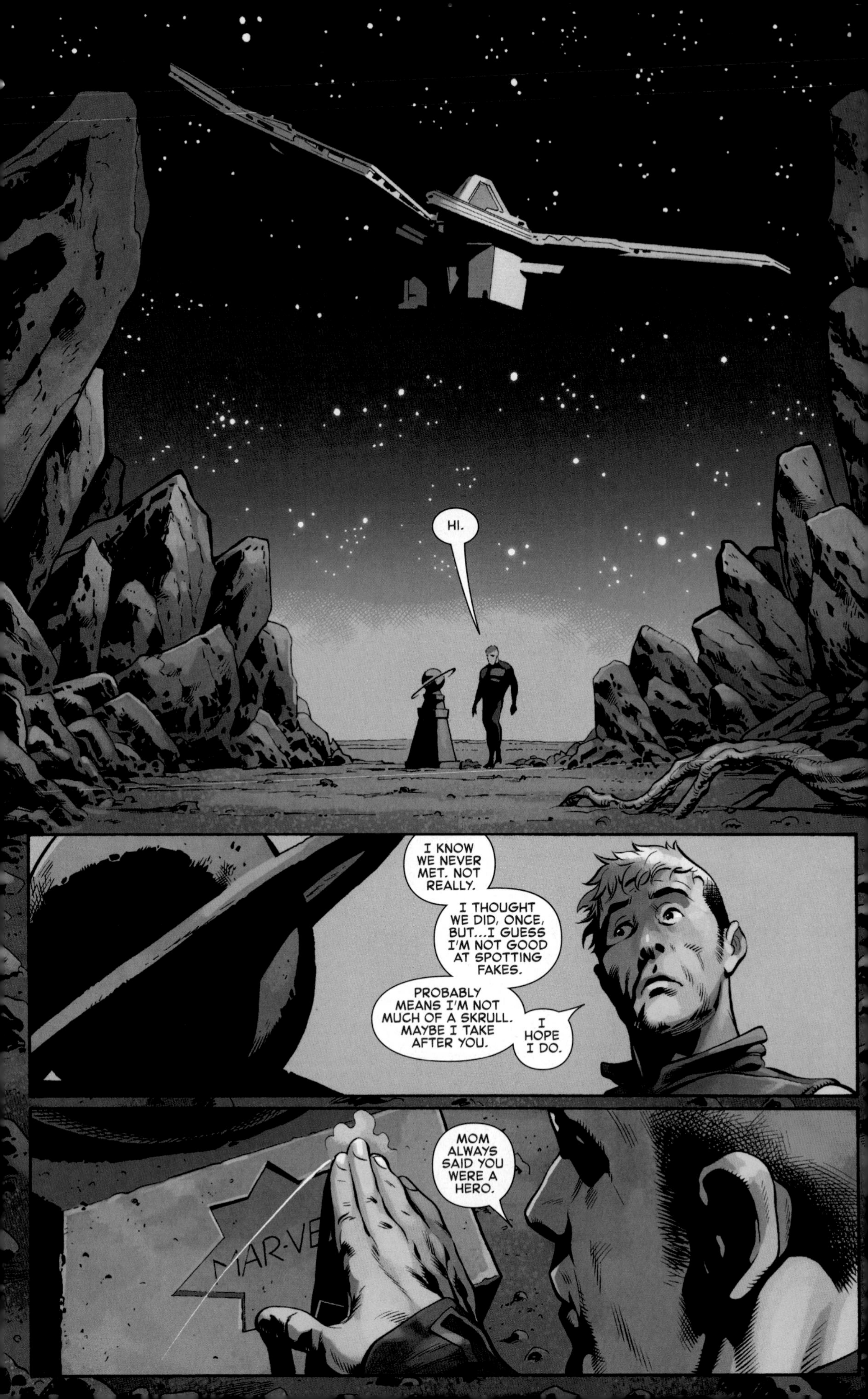
HI.
I KNOW WE NEVER MET. NOT REALLY.
I THOUGHT WE DID, ONCE, BUT...I GUESS I'M NOT GOOD AT SPOTTING FAKES.
PROBABLY MEANS I'M NOT MUCH OF A SKRULL. MAYBE I TAKE AFTER YOU.
I HOPE I DO.
MOM ALWAYS SAID YOU WERE A HERO.
MAR-VE

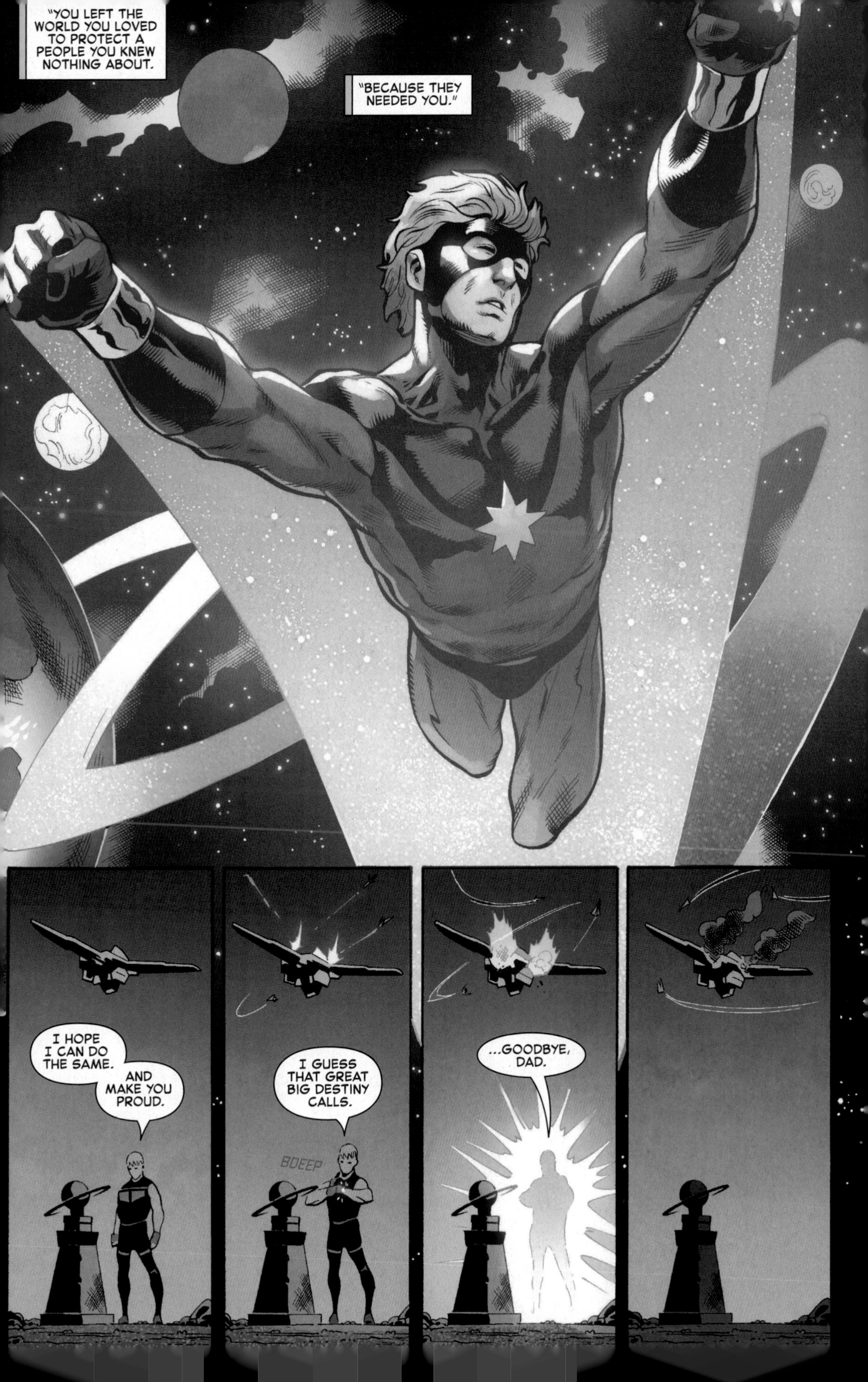
"YOU LEFT THE WORLD YOU LOVED TO PROTECT A PEOPLE YOU KNEW NOTHING ABOUT.
"BECAUSE THEY NEEDED YOU."
I HOPE I CAN DO THE SAME.
AND MAKE YOU PROUD.
I GUESS THAT GREAT BIG DESTINY CALLS.
BDEEP
...GOODBYE, DAD.

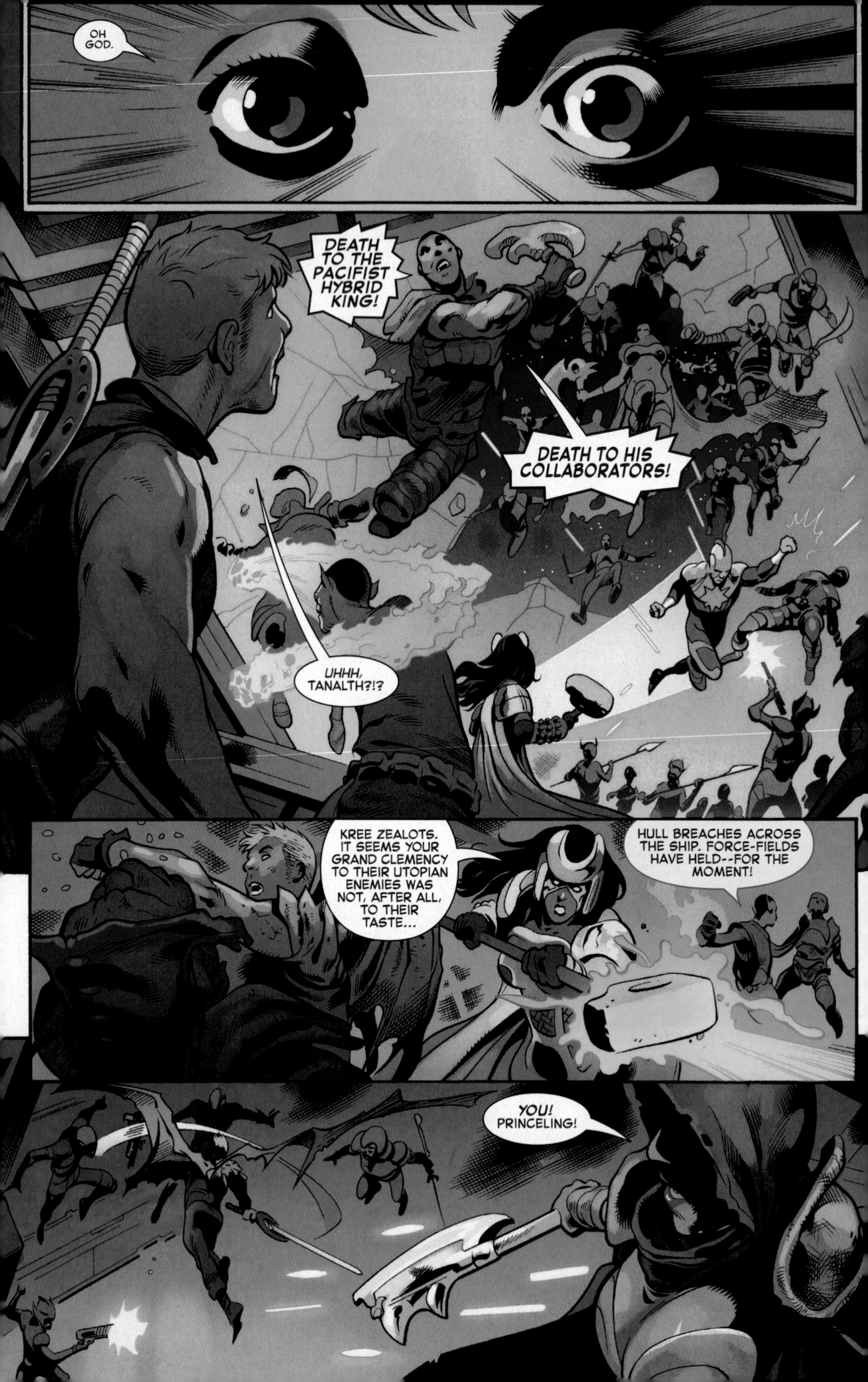
OH GOD.
DEATH TO THE PACIFIST HYBRID KING!
DEATH TO HIS COLLABORATORS!
UHHH, TANALTH?!?
KREE ZEALOTS. IT SEEMS YOUR GRAND CLEMENCY TO THEIR UTOPIAN ENEMIES WAS NOT, AFTER ALL, TO THEIR TASTE...
HULL BREACHES ACROSS THE SHIP. FORCE-FIELDS HAVE HELD--FOR THE MOMENT!
YOU! PRINCELING!

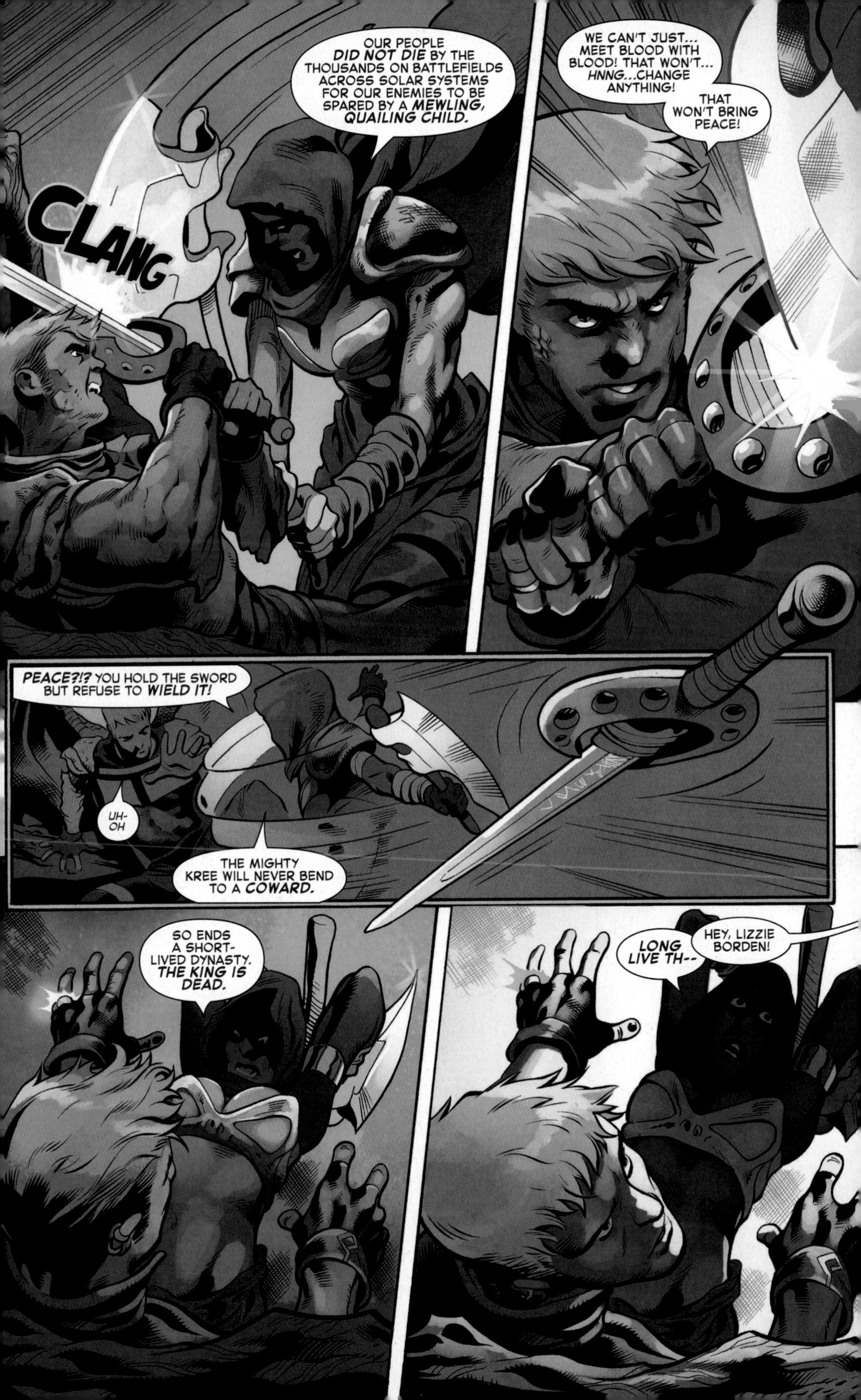

OUR PEOPLE DID NOT DIE BY THE THOUSANDS ON BATTLEFIELDS ACROSS SOLAR SYSTEMS FOR OUR ENEMIES TO BE SPARED BY A MEWLING, QUAILING CHILD.
CLANG
WE CAN'T JUST... MEET BLOOD WITH BLOOD! THAT WON'T... HNNG...CHANGE ANYTHING!
THAT WON'T BRING PEACE!
PEACE?!? YOU HOLD THE SWORD BUT REFUSE TO WIELD IT!
UH-OH
THE MIGHTY KREE WILL NEVER BEND TO A COWARD.
SO ENDS A SHORT-LIVED DYNASTY. THE KING IS DEAD.
LONG LIVE TH--
HEY, LIZZIE BORDEN!

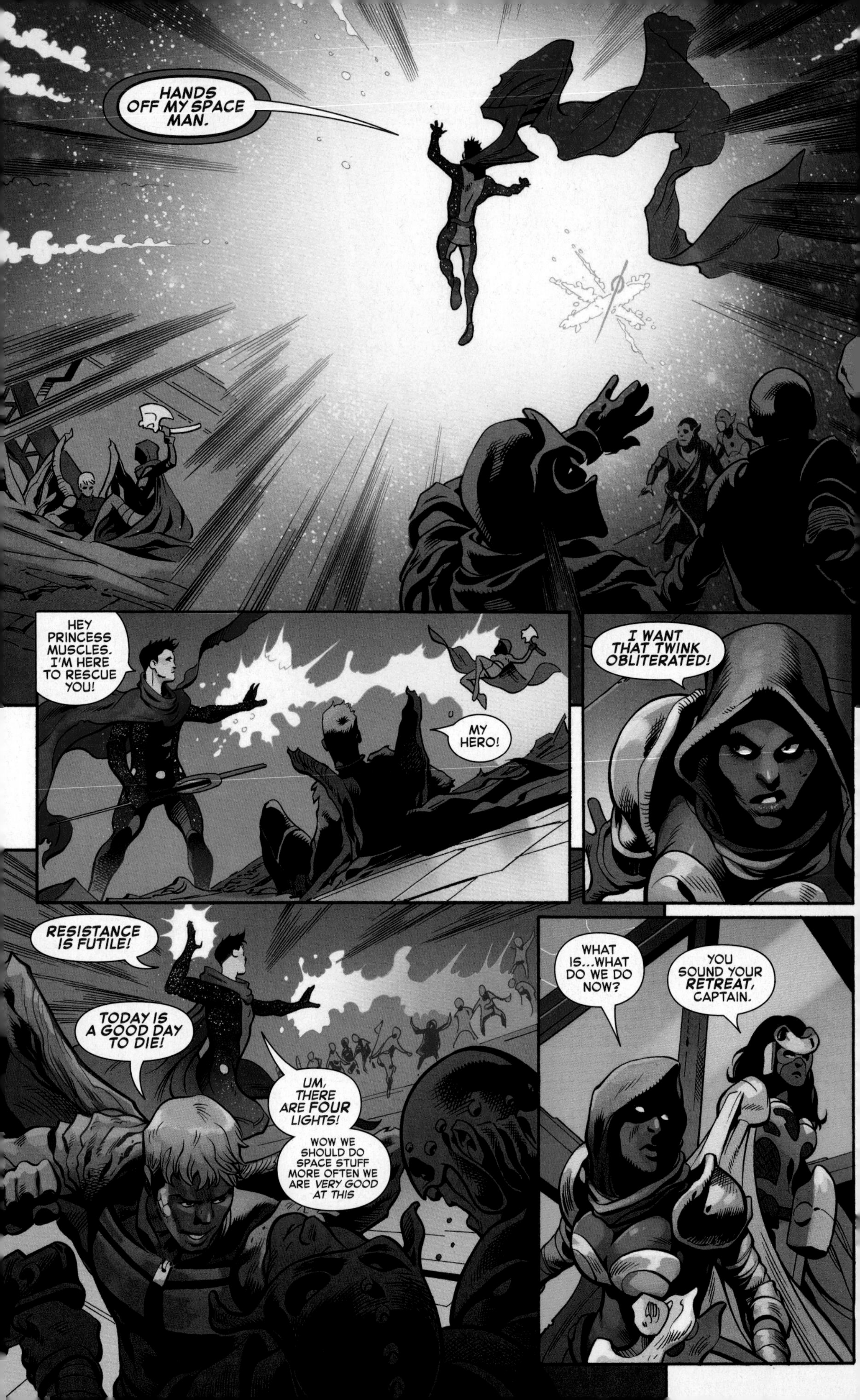
HANDS OFF MY SPACE MAN.
HEY PRINCESS MUSCLES. I'M HERE TO RESCUE YOU!
MY HERO!
I WANT THAT TWINK OBLITERATED!
RESISTANCE IS FUTILE!
TODAY IS A GOOD DAY TO DIE!
UM, THERE ARE FOUR LIGHTS!
WOW WE SHOULD DO SPACE STUFF MORE OFTEN WE ARE VERY GOOD AT THIS
WHAT IS...WHAT DO WE DO NOW?
YOU SOUND YOUR RETREAT, CAPTAIN.

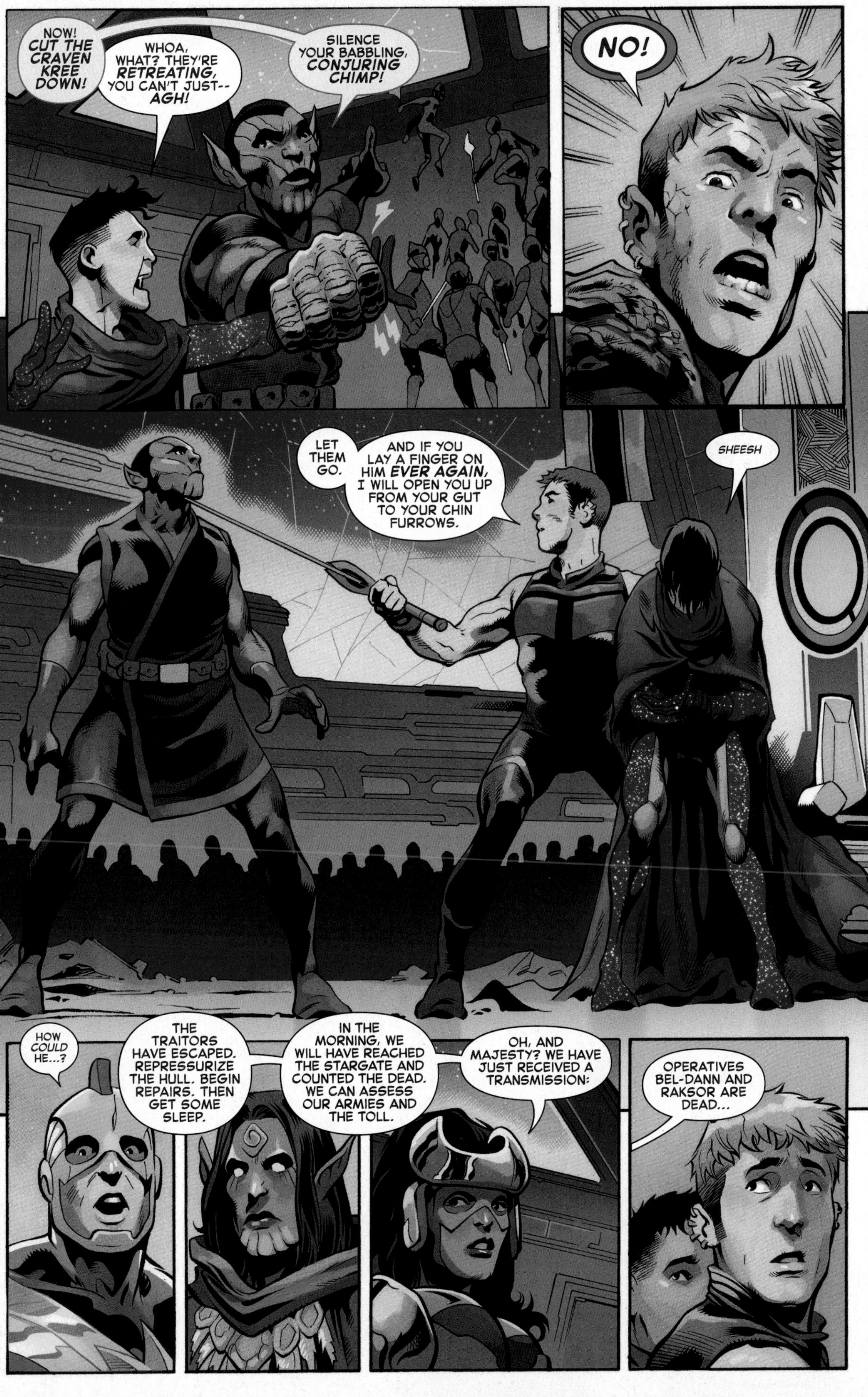
NOW! CUT THE CRAVEN KREE DOWN!
WHOA, WHAT? THEY'RE RETREATING, YOU CAN'T JUST-- AGH!
SILENCE YOUR BABBLING, CONJURING CHIMP!
NO!
LET THEM GO.
AND IF YOU LAY A FINGER ON HIM EVER AGAIN, I WILL OPEN YOU UP FROM YOUR GUT TO YOUR CHIN FURROWS.
SHEESH
HOW COULD HE...?
THE TRAITORS HAVE ESCAPED. REPRESSURIZE THE HULL. BEGIN REPAIRS. THEN GET SOME SLEEP.
IN THE MORNING, WE WILL HAVE REACHED THE STARGATE AND COUNTED THE DEAD. WE CAN ASSESS OUR ARMIES AND THE TOLL.
OH, AND MAJESTY? WE HAVE JUST RECEIVED A TRANSMISSION:
OPERATIVES BEL-DANN AND RAKSOR ARE DEAD...

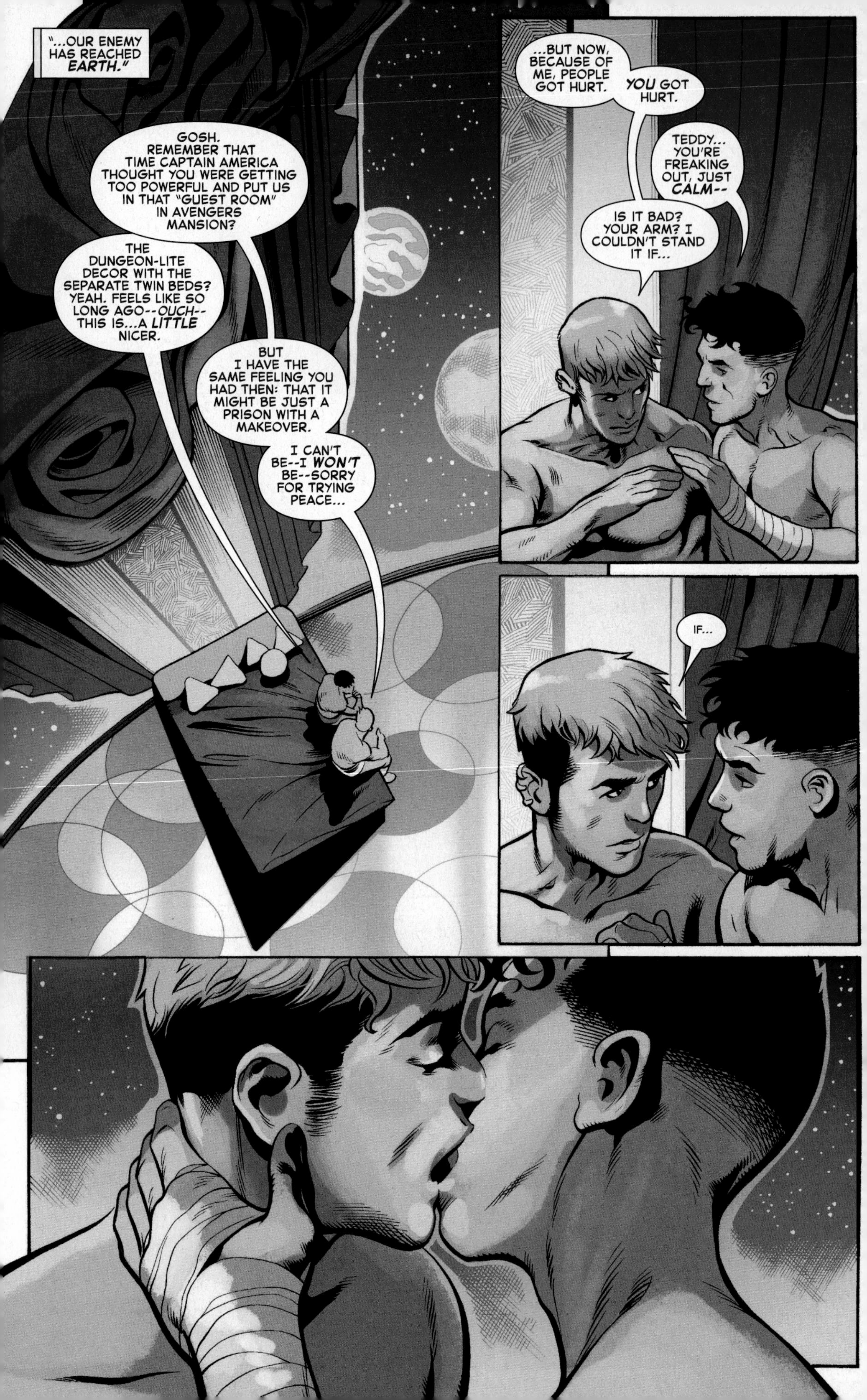
"...OUR ENEMY HAS REACHED EARTH."
GOSH. REMEMBER THAT TIME CAPTAIN AMERICA THOUGHT YOU WERE GETTING TOO POWERFUL AND PUT US IN THAT "GUEST ROOM" IN AVENGERS MANSION?
THE DUNGEON-LITE DECOR WITH THE SEPARATE TWIN BEDS? YEAH. FEELS LIKE SO LONG AGO--OUCH--THIS IS...A LITTLE NICER.
BUT I HAVE THE SAME FEELING YOU HAD THEN: THAT IT MIGHT BE JUST A PRISON WITH A MAKEOVER.
I CAN'T BE--I WON'T BE--SORRY FOR TRYING PEACE...
...BUT NOW, BECAUSE OF ME, PEOPLE GOT HURT.
YOU GOT HURT.
TEDDY... YOU'RE FREAKING OUT, JUST CALM--
IS IT BAD? YOUR ARM? I COULDN'T STAND IT IF...
IF...

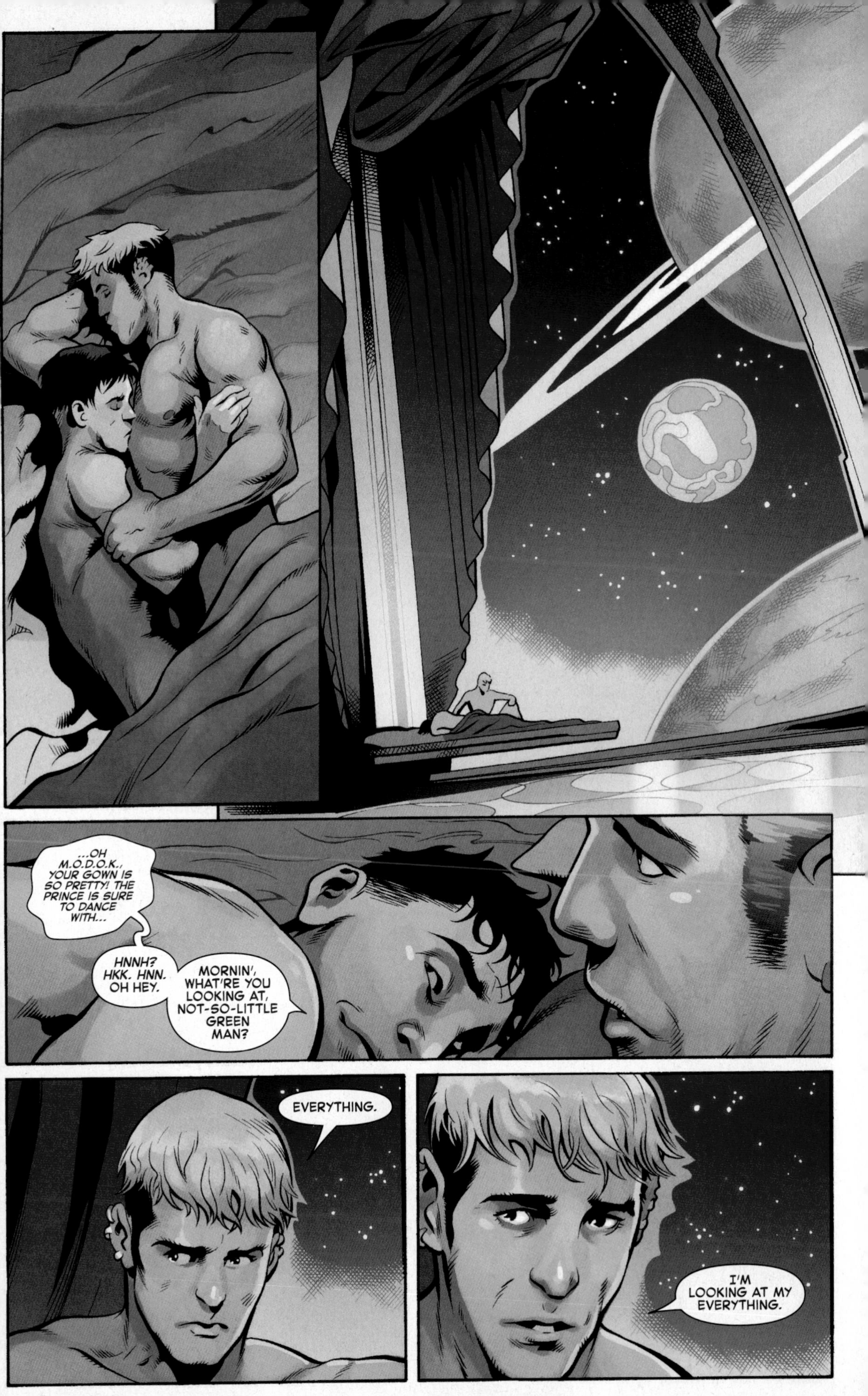
...OH M.O.D.O.K., YOUR GOWN IS SO PRETTY! THE PRINCE IS SURE TO DANCE WITH...
HNNH? HKK. HNN. OH HEY.
MORNIN', WHAT'RE YOU LOOKING AT, NOT-SO-LITTLE GREEN MAN?
EVERYTHING.
I'M LOOKING AT MY EVERYTHING.

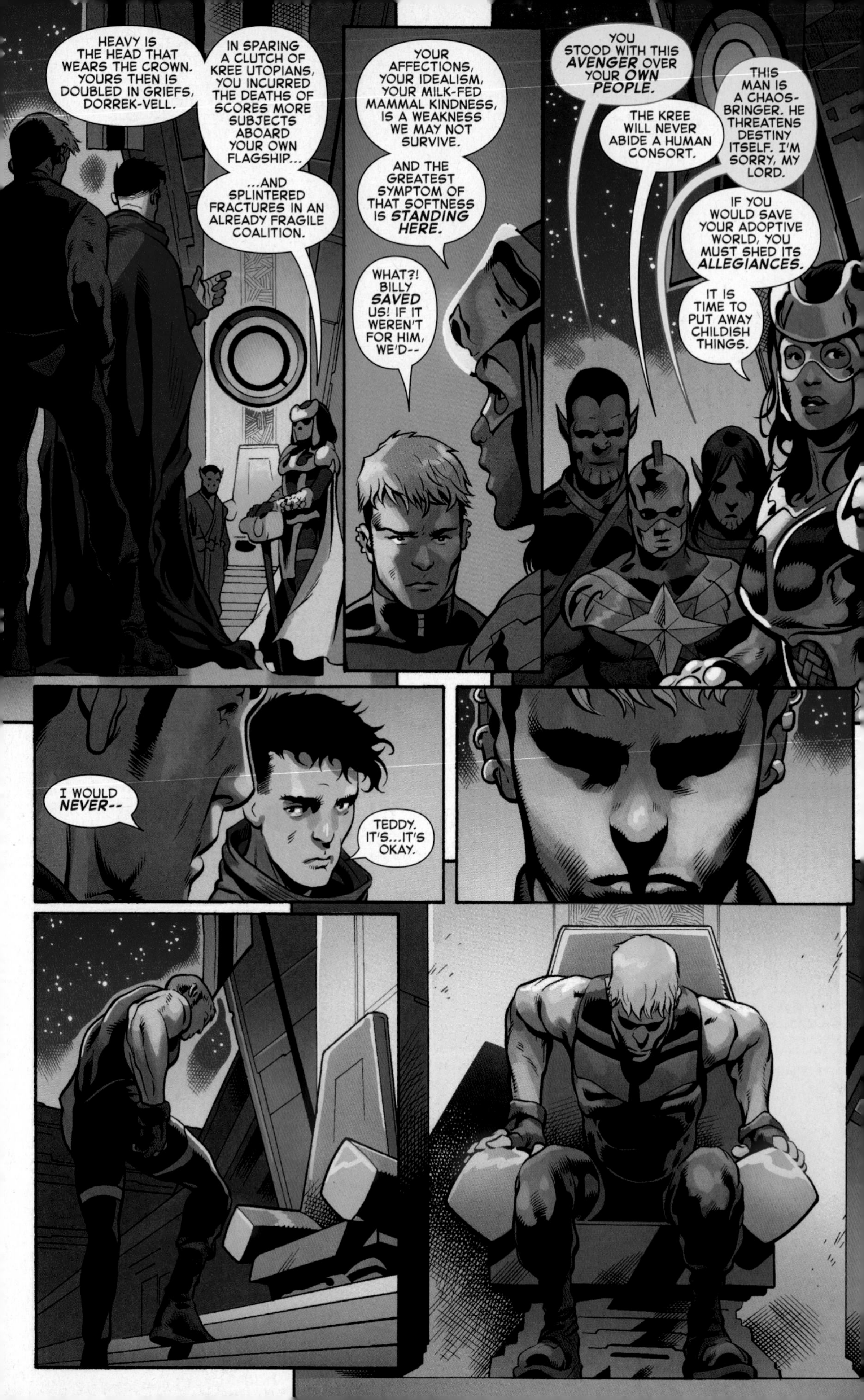

HEAVY IS THE HEAD THAT WEARS THE CROWN. YOURS THEN IS DOUBLED IN GRIEFS, DORREK-VELL.
IN SPARING A CLUTCH OF KREE UTOPIANS, YOU INCURRED THE DEATHS OF SCORES MORE SUBJECTS ABOARD YOUR OWN FLAGSHIP...
...AND SPLINTERED FRACTURES IN AN ALREADY FRAGILE COALITION.
YOUR AFFECTIONS, YOUR IDEALISM, YOUR MILK-FED MAMMAL KINDNESS, IS A WEAKNESS WE MAY NOT SURVIVE.
AND THE GREATEST SYMPTOM OF THAT SOFTNESS IS ***STANDING HERE.***
WHAT?! BILLY ***SAVED*** US! IF IT WEREN'T FOR HIM, WE'D--
YOU STOOD WITH THIS ***AVENGER*** OVER YOUR ***OWN PEOPLE.***
THE KREE WILL NEVER ABIDE A HUMAN CONSORT.
THIS MAN IS A CHAOS-BRINGER. HE THREATENS DESTINY ITSELF. I'M SORRY, MY LORD.
IF YOU WOULD SAVE YOUR ADOPTIVE WORLD, YOU MUST SHED ITS ***ALLEGIANCES.***
IT IS TIME TO PUT AWAY CHILDISH THINGS.
I WOULD ***NEVER--***
TEDDY. IT'S...IT'S OKAY.

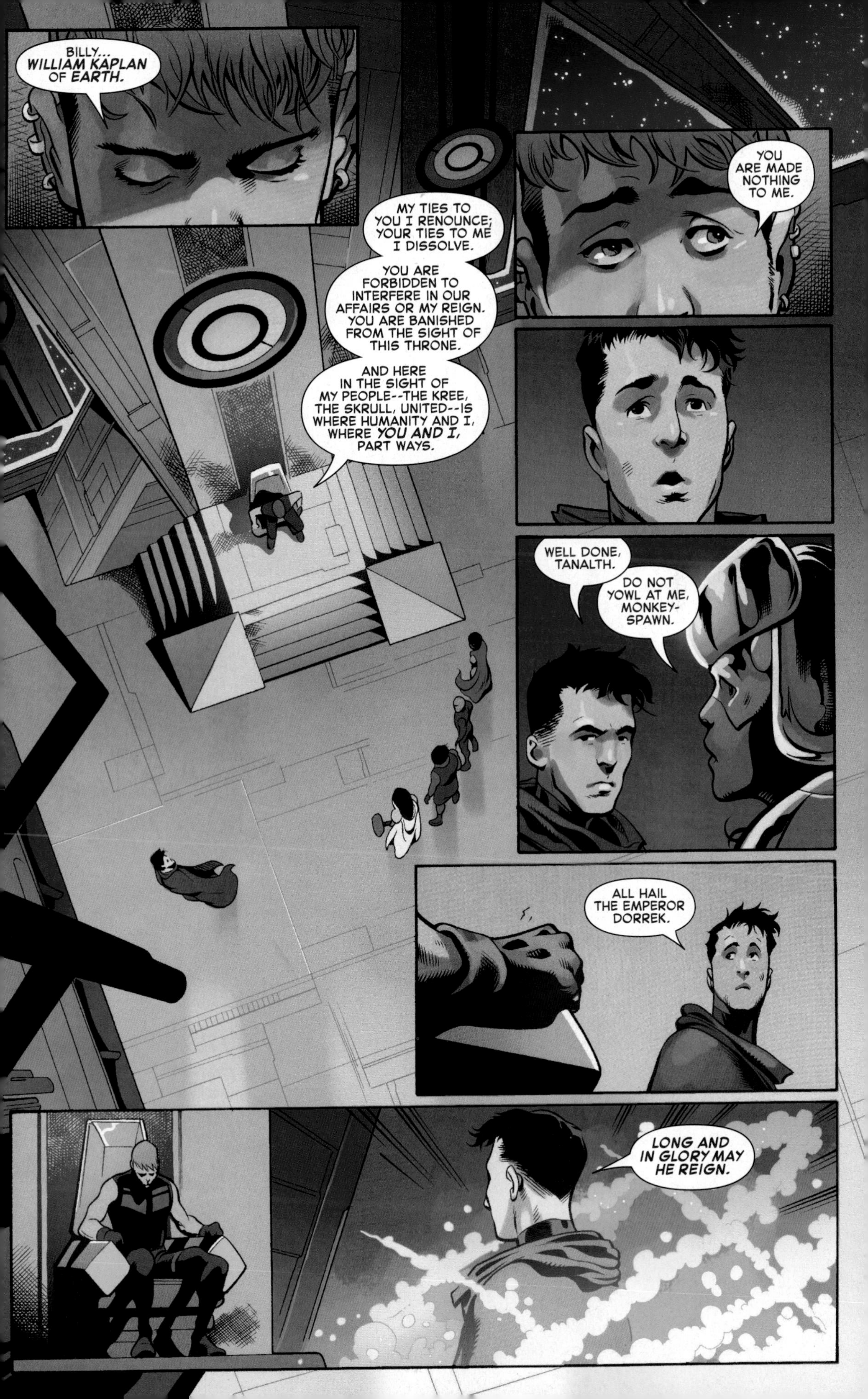
BILLY... WILLIAM KAPLAN OF EARTH.
YOU ARE MADE NOTHING TO ME.
MY TIES TO YOU I RENOUNCE; YOUR TIES TO ME I DISSOLVE.
YOU ARE FORBIDDEN TO INTERFERE IN OUR AFFAIRS OR MY REIGN. YOU ARE BANISHED FROM THE SIGHT OF THIS THRONE.
AND HERE IN THE SIGHT OF MY PEOPLE--THE KREE, THE SKRULL, UNITED--IS WHERE HUMANITY AND I, WHERE YOU AND I, PART WAYS.
WELL DONE, TANALTH.
DO NOT YOWL AT ME, MONKEY-SPAWN.
ALL HAIL THE EMPEROR DORREK.
LONG AND IN GLORY MAY HE REIGN.

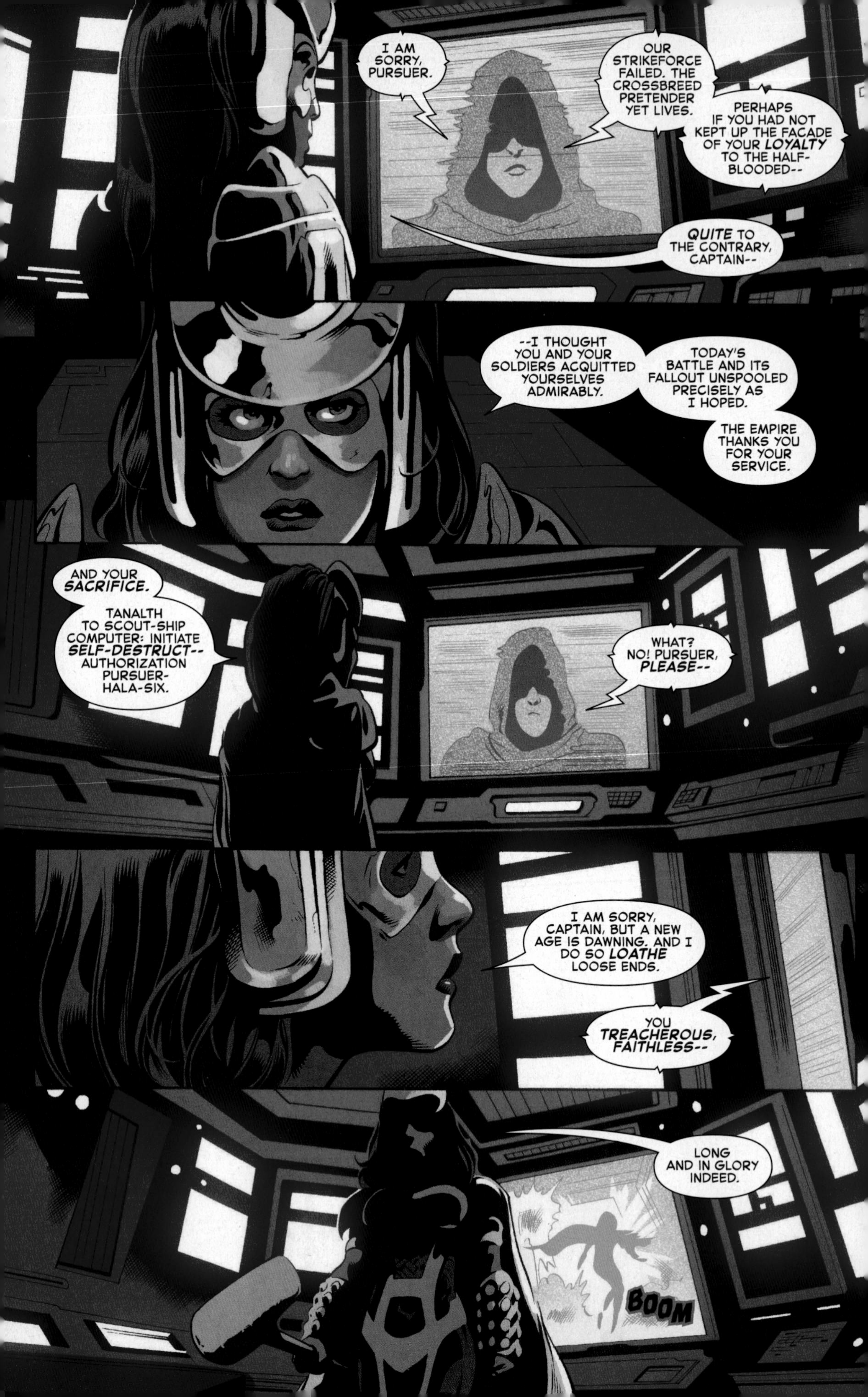
I AM SORRY, PURSUER.
OUR STRIKEFORCE FAILED. THE CROSSBREED PRETENDER YET LIVES.
PERHAPS IF YOU HAD NOT KEPT UP THE FACADE OF YOUR LOYALTY TO THE HALF-BLOODED--
QUITE TO THE CONTRARY, CAPTAIN--
--I THOUGHT YOU AND YOUR SOLDIERS ACQUITTED YOURSELVES ADMIRABLY.
TODAY'S BATTLE AND ITS FALLOUT UNSPOOLED PRECISELY AS I HOPED.
THE EMPIRE THANKS YOU FOR YOUR SERVICE.
AND YOUR SACRIFICE.
TANALTH TO SCOUT-SHIP COMPUTER: INITIATE SELF-DESTRUCT-- AUTHORIZATION PURSUER-HALA-SIX.
WHAT? NO! PURSUER, PLEASE--
I AM SORRY, CAPTAIN, BUT A NEW AGE IS DAWNING. AND I DO SO LOATHE LOOSE ENDS.
YOU TREACHEROUS, FAITHLESS--
LONG AND IN GLORY INDEED.
BOOM

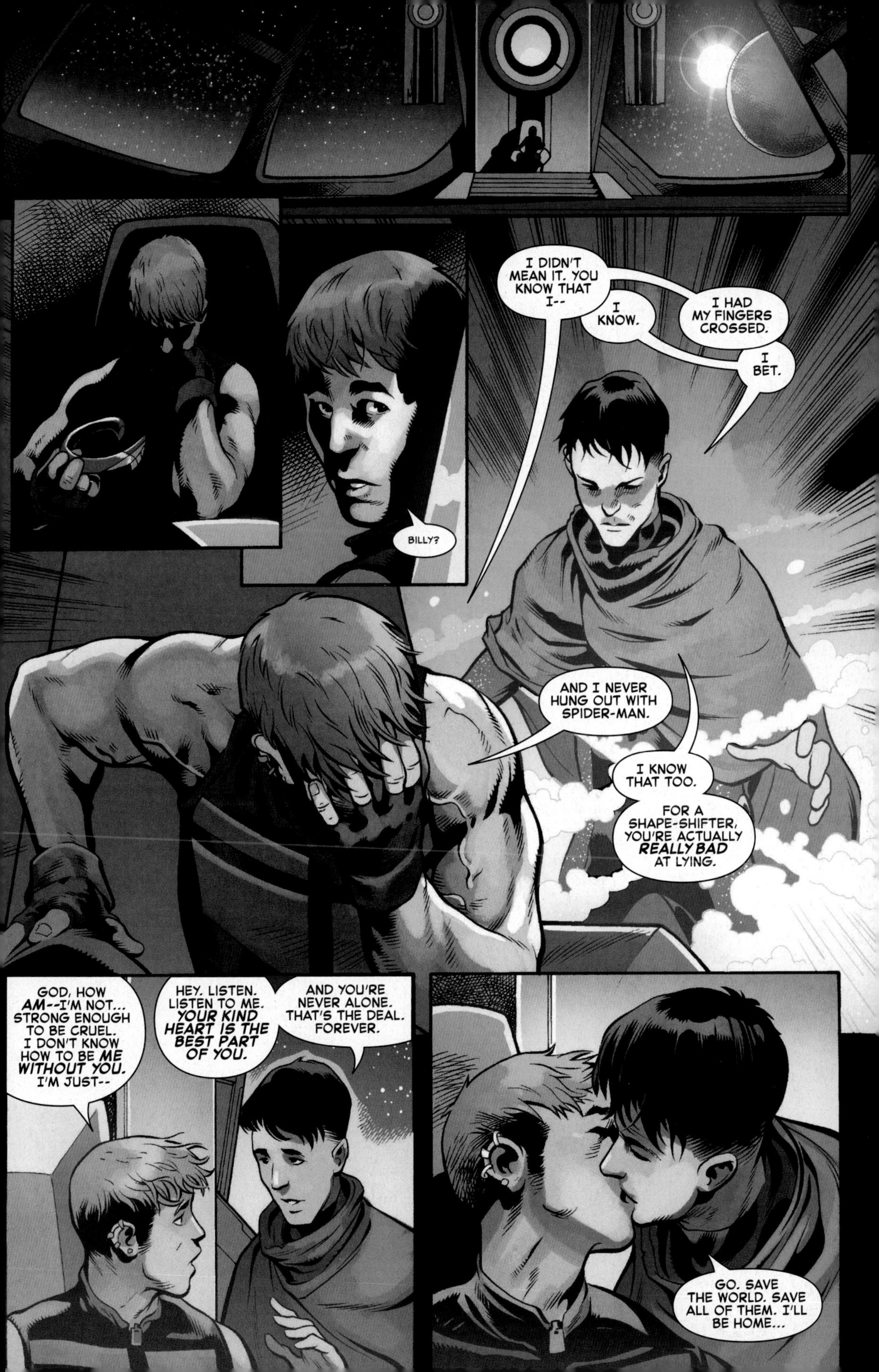
BILLY?
I DIDN'T MEAN IT. YOU KNOW THAT I--
I KNOW.
I HAD MY FINGERS CROSSED.
I BET.
AND I NEVER HUNG OUT WITH SPIDER-MAN.
I KNOW THAT TOO.
FOR A SHAPE-SHIFTER, YOU'RE ACTUALLY REALLY BAD AT LYING.
GOD, HOW AM--I'M NOT... STRONG ENOUGH TO BE CRUEL. I DON'T KNOW HOW TO BE ME WITHOUT YOU. I'M JUST--
HEY. LISTEN. LISTEN TO ME. YOUR KIND HEART IS THE BEST PART OF YOU.
AND YOU'RE NEVER ALONE. THAT'S THE DEAL. FOREVER.
GO. SAVE THE WORLD. SAVE ALL OF THEM. I'LL BE HOME...

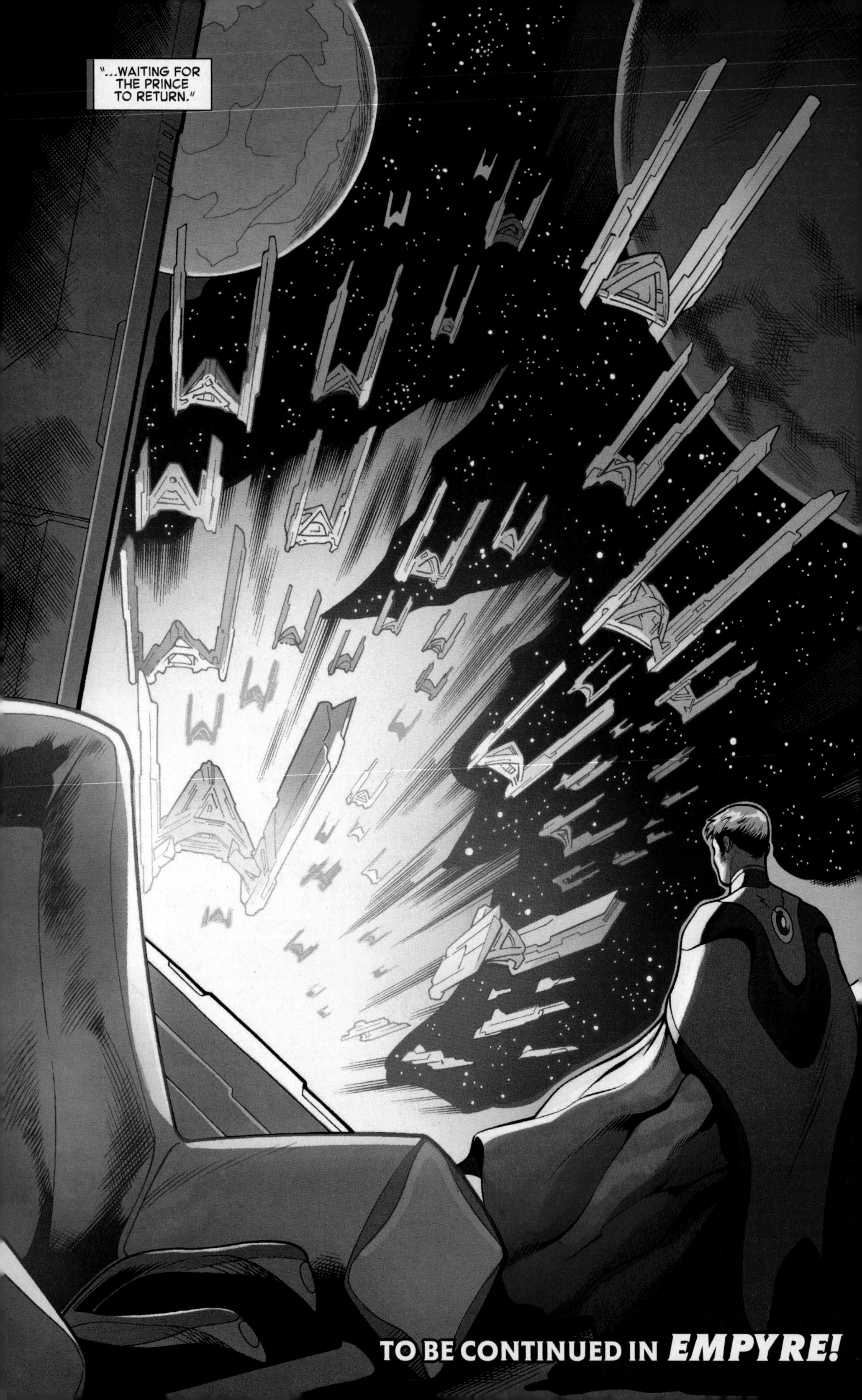
"...WAITING FOR THE PRINCE TO RETURN."
TO BE CONTINUED IN EMPYRE!

LORDS OF EMPYRE: CELESTIAL MESSIAH

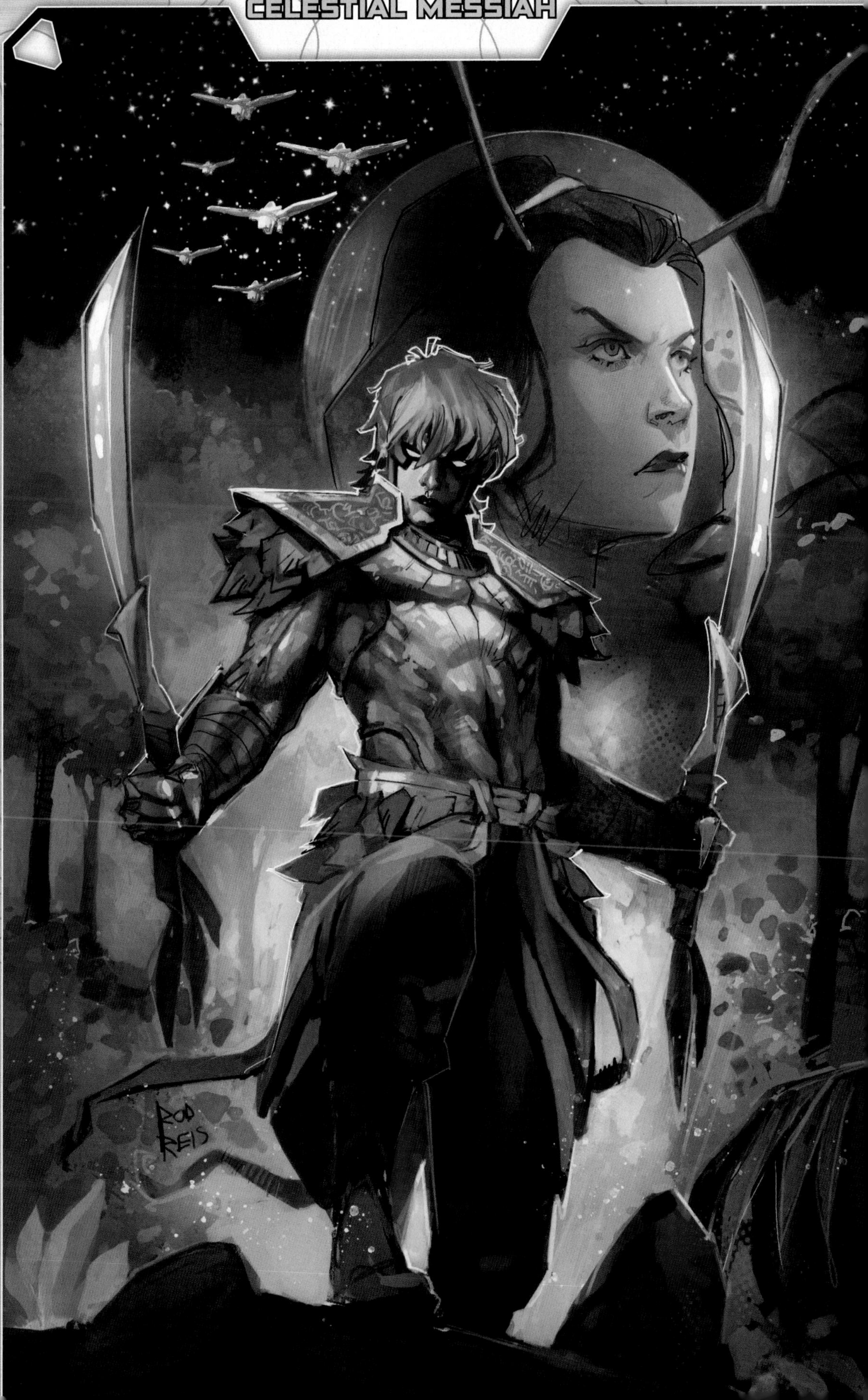
ROD REIS

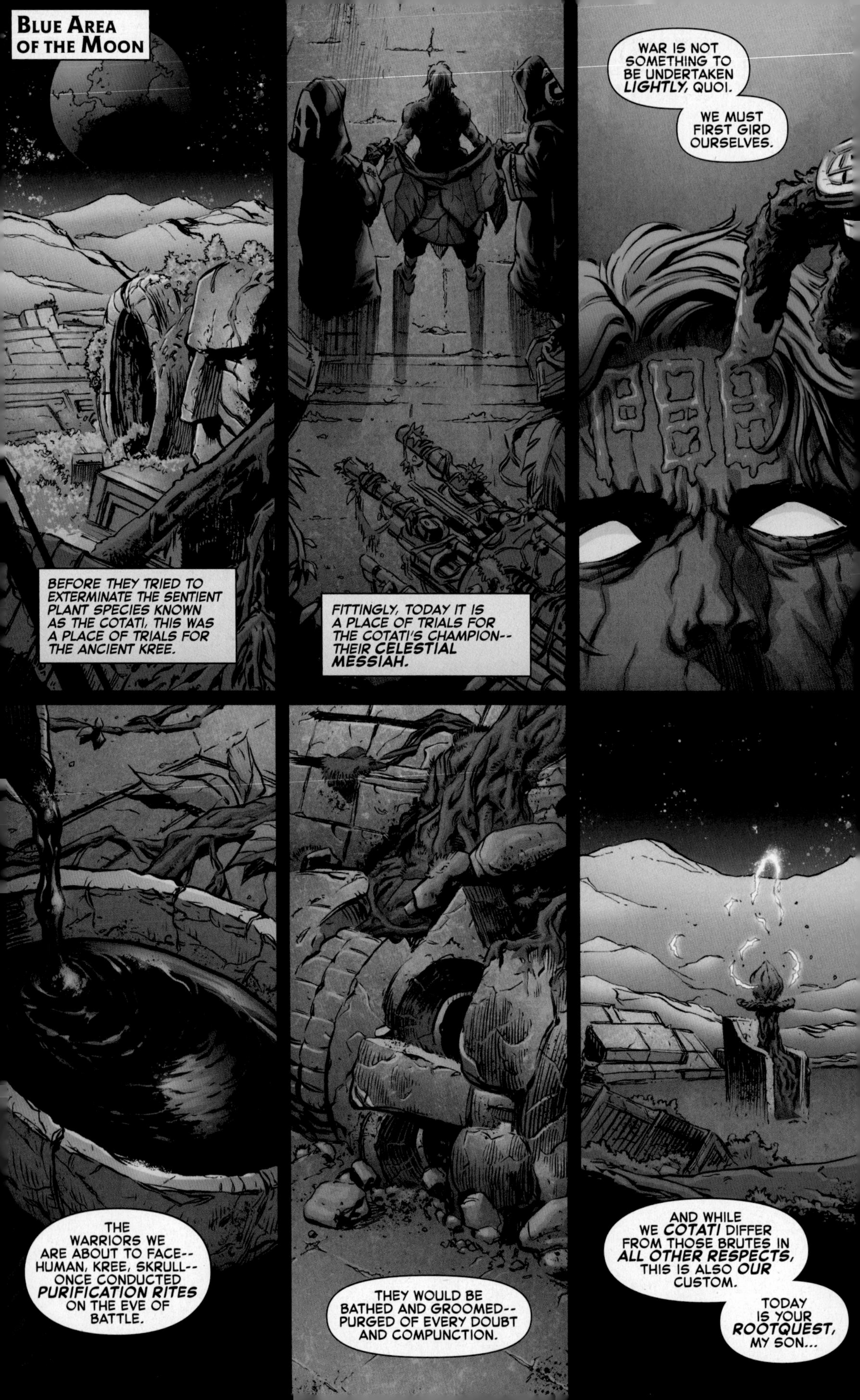
BLUE AREA OF THE MOON
BEFORE THEY TRIED TO EXTERMINATE THE SENTIENT PLANT SPECIES KNOWN AS THE COTATI, THIS WAS A PLACE OF TRIALS FOR THE ANCIENT KREE.
FITTINGLY, TODAY IT IS A PLACE OF TRIALS FOR THE COTATI'S CHAMPION-- THEIR CELESTIAL MESSIAH.
WAR IS NOT SOMETHING TO BE UNDERTAKEN LIGHTLY, QUOI.
WE MUST FIRST GIRD OURSELVES.
THE WARRIORS WE ARE ABOUT TO FACE-- HUMAN, KREE, SKRULL-- ONCE CONDUCTED PURIFICATION RITES ON THE EVE OF BATTLE.
THEY WOULD BE BATHED AND GROOMED-- PURGED OF EVERY DOUBT AND COMPUNCTION.
AND WHILE WE COTATI DIFFER FROM THOSE BRUTES IN ALL OTHER RESPECTS, THIS IS ALSO OUR CUSTOM.
TODAY IS YOUR ROOTQUEST, MY SON...

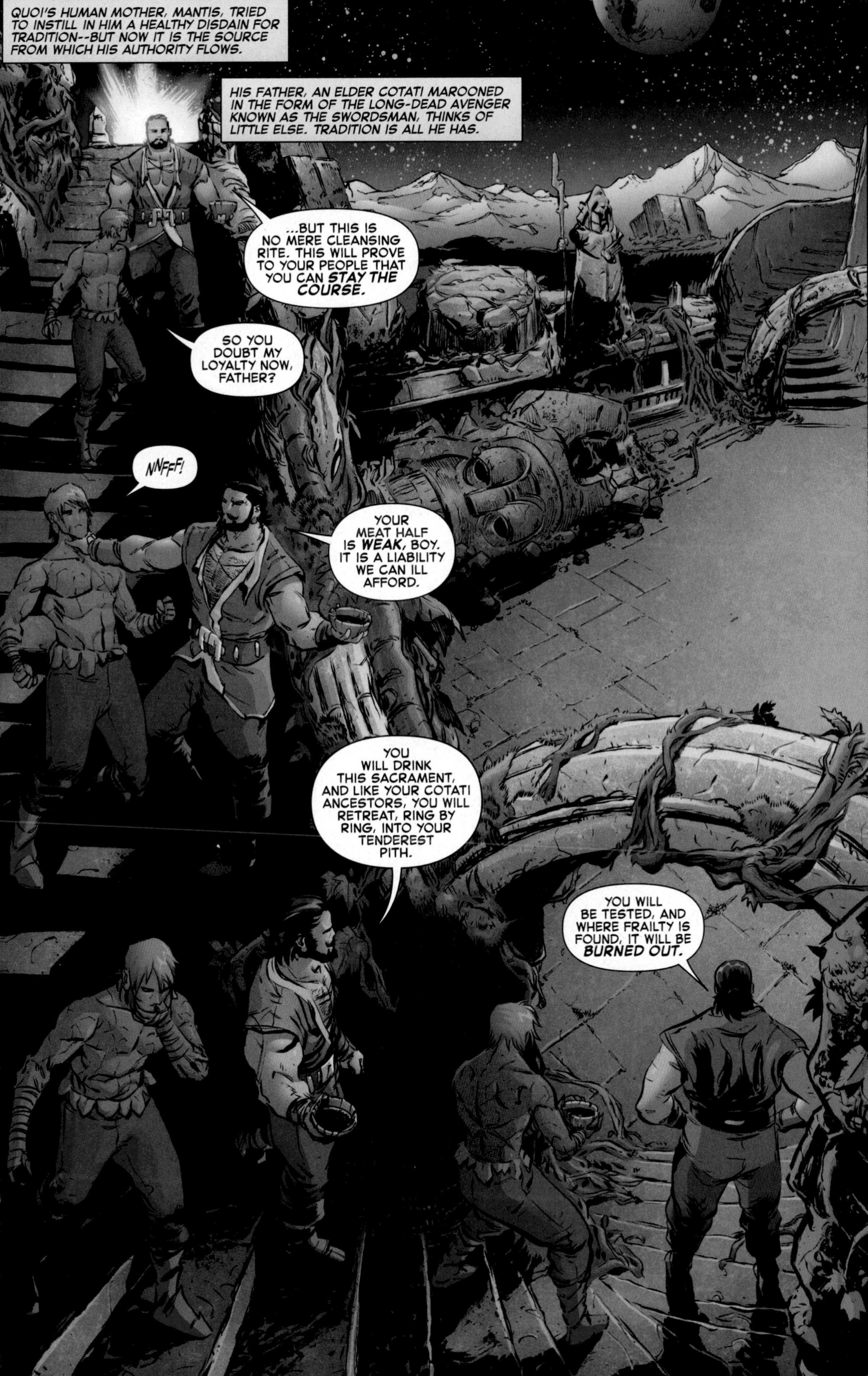
QUOI'S HUMAN MOTHER, MANTIS, TRIED TO INSTILL IN HIM A HEALTHY DISDAIN FOR TRADITION--BUT NOW IT IS THE SOURCE FROM WHICH HIS AUTHORITY FLOWS.
HIS FATHER, AN ELDER COTATI MAROONED IN THE FORM OF THE LONG-DEAD AVENGER KNOWN AS THE SWORDSMAN, THINKS OF LITTLE ELSE. TRADITION IS ALL HE HAS.
...BUT THIS IS NO MERE CLEANSING RITE. THIS WILL PROVE TO YOUR PEOPLE THAT YOU CAN STAY THE COURSE.
SO YOU DOUBT MY LOYALTY NOW, FATHER?
NNFFF!
YOUR MEAT HALF IS WEAK, BOY. IT IS A LIABILITY WE CAN ILL AFFORD.
YOU WILL DRINK THIS SACRAMENT, AND LIKE YOUR COTATI ANCESTORS, YOU WILL RETREAT, RING BY RING, INTO YOUR TENDEREST PITH.
YOU WILL BE TESTED, AND WHERE FRAILTY IS FOUND, IT WILL BE BURNED OUT.

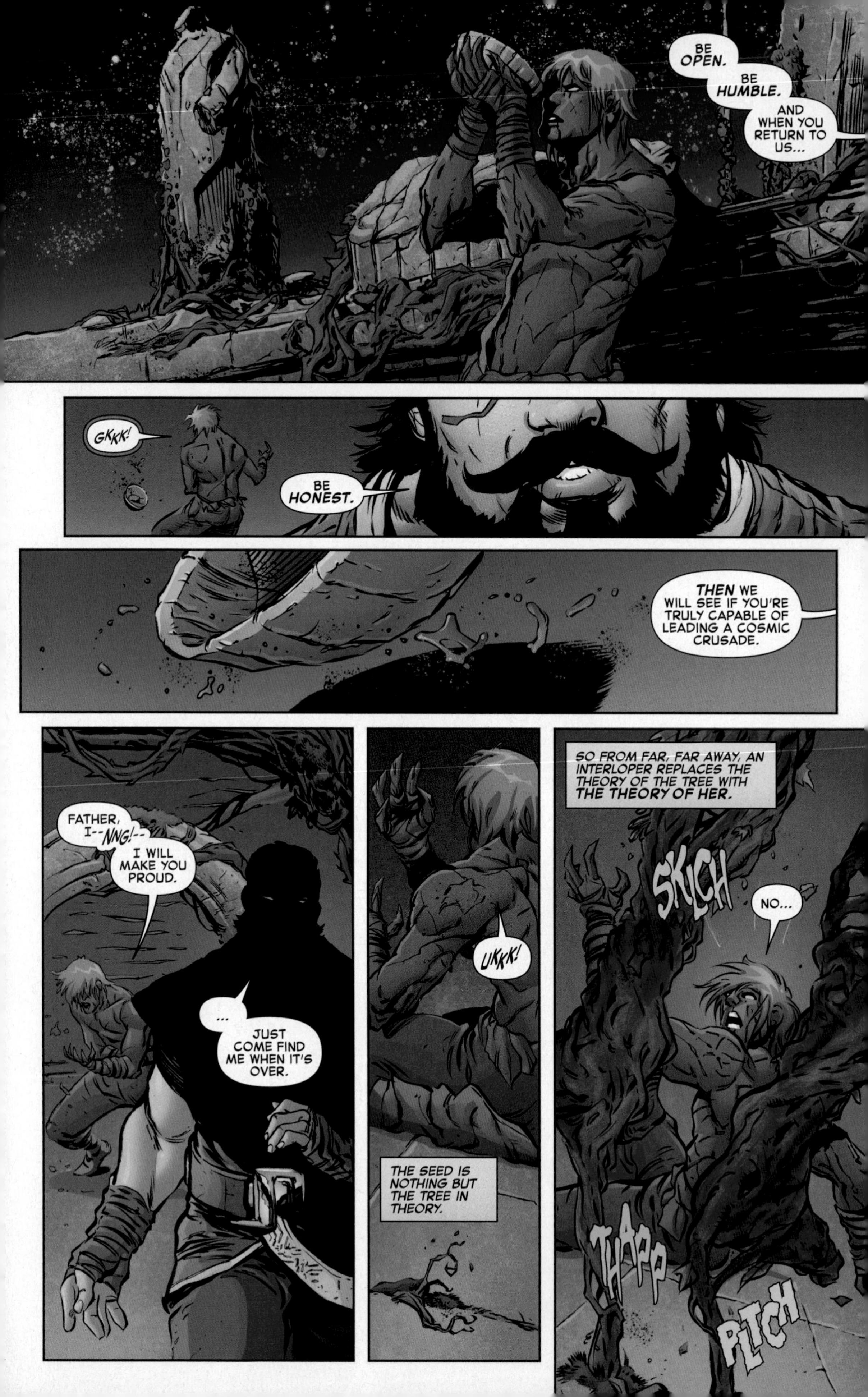
BE OPEN.
BE HUMBLE.
AND WHEN YOU RETURN TO US...
GKKK!
BE HONEST.
THEN WE WILL SEE IF YOU'RE TRULY CAPABLE OF LEADING A COSMIC CRUSADE.
FATHER, I--NNG!-- I WILL MAKE YOU PROUD.
... JUST COME FIND ME WHEN IT'S OVER.
UKKK!
THE SEED IS NOTHING BUT THE TREE IN THEORY.
SO FROM FAR, FAR AWAY, AN INTERLOPER REPLACES THE THEORY OF THE TREE WITH THE THEORY OF HER.
SKLCH
NO...
THAPP
PLTCH

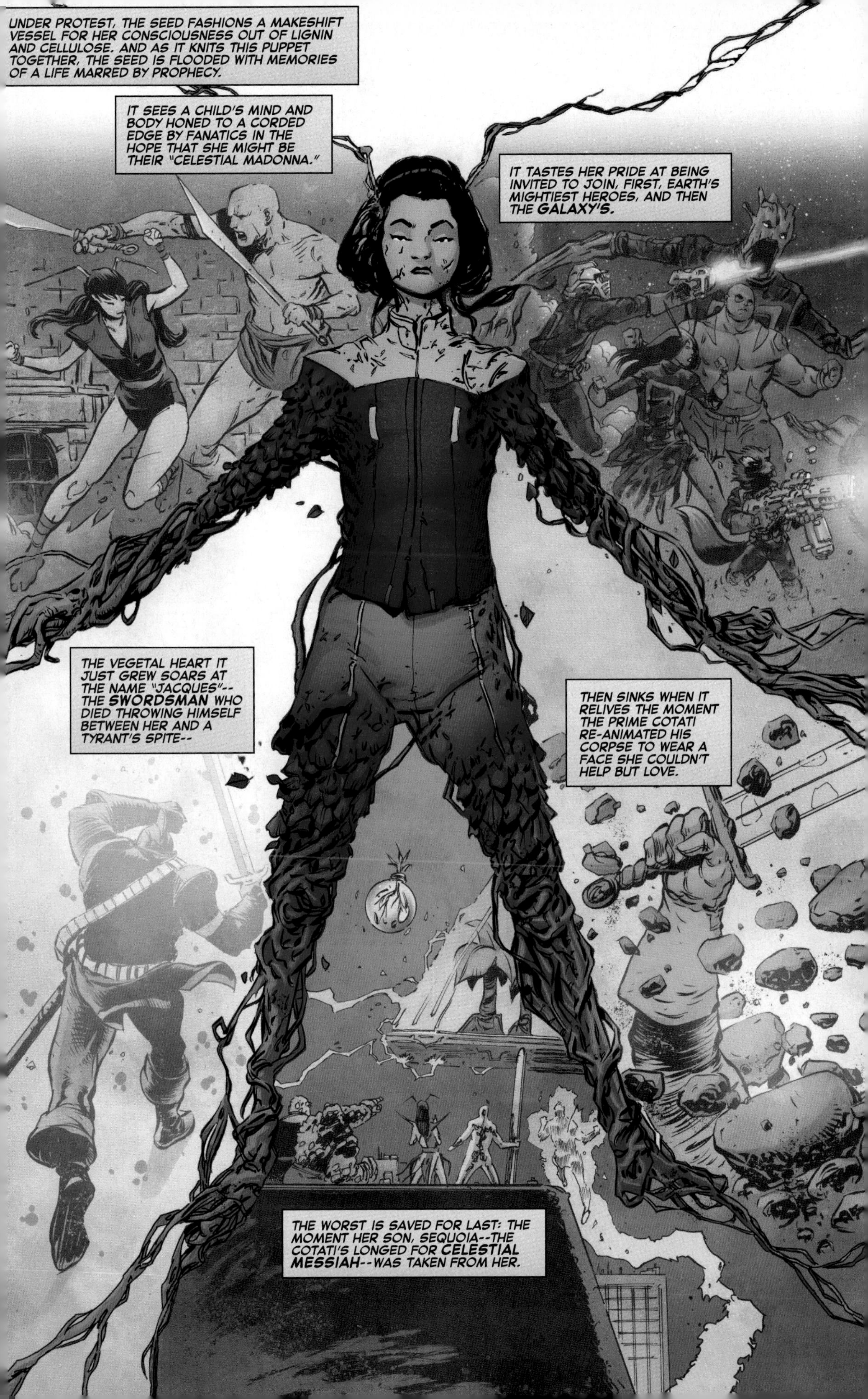
UNDER PROTEST, THE SEED FASHIONS A MAKESHIFT VESSEL FOR HER CONSCIOUSNESS OUT OF LIGNIN AND CELLULOSE. AND AS IT KNITS THIS PUPPET TOGETHER, THE SEED IS FLOODED WITH MEMORIES OF A LIFE MARRED BY PROPHECY.
IT SEES A CHILD'S MIND AND BODY HONED TO A CORDED EDGE BY FANATICS IN THE HOPE THAT SHE MIGHT BE THEIR "CELESTIAL MADONNA."
IT TASTES HER PRIDE AT BEING INVITED TO JOIN, FIRST, EARTH'S MIGHTIEST HEROES, AND THEN THE **GALAXY'S.**
THE VEGETAL HEART IT JUST GREW SOARS AT THE NAME "JACQUES"--THE **SWORDSMAN** WHO DIED THROWING HIMSELF BETWEEN HER AND A TYRANT'S SPITE--
THEN SINKS WHEN IT RELIVES THE MOMENT THE PRIME COTATI RE-ANIMATED HIS CORPSE TO WEAR A FACE SHE COULDN'T HELP BUT LOVE.
THE WORST IS SAVED FOR LAST: THE MOMENT HER SON, SEQUOIA--THE COTATI'S LONGED FOR **CELESTIAL MESSIAH**--WAS TAKEN FROM HER.

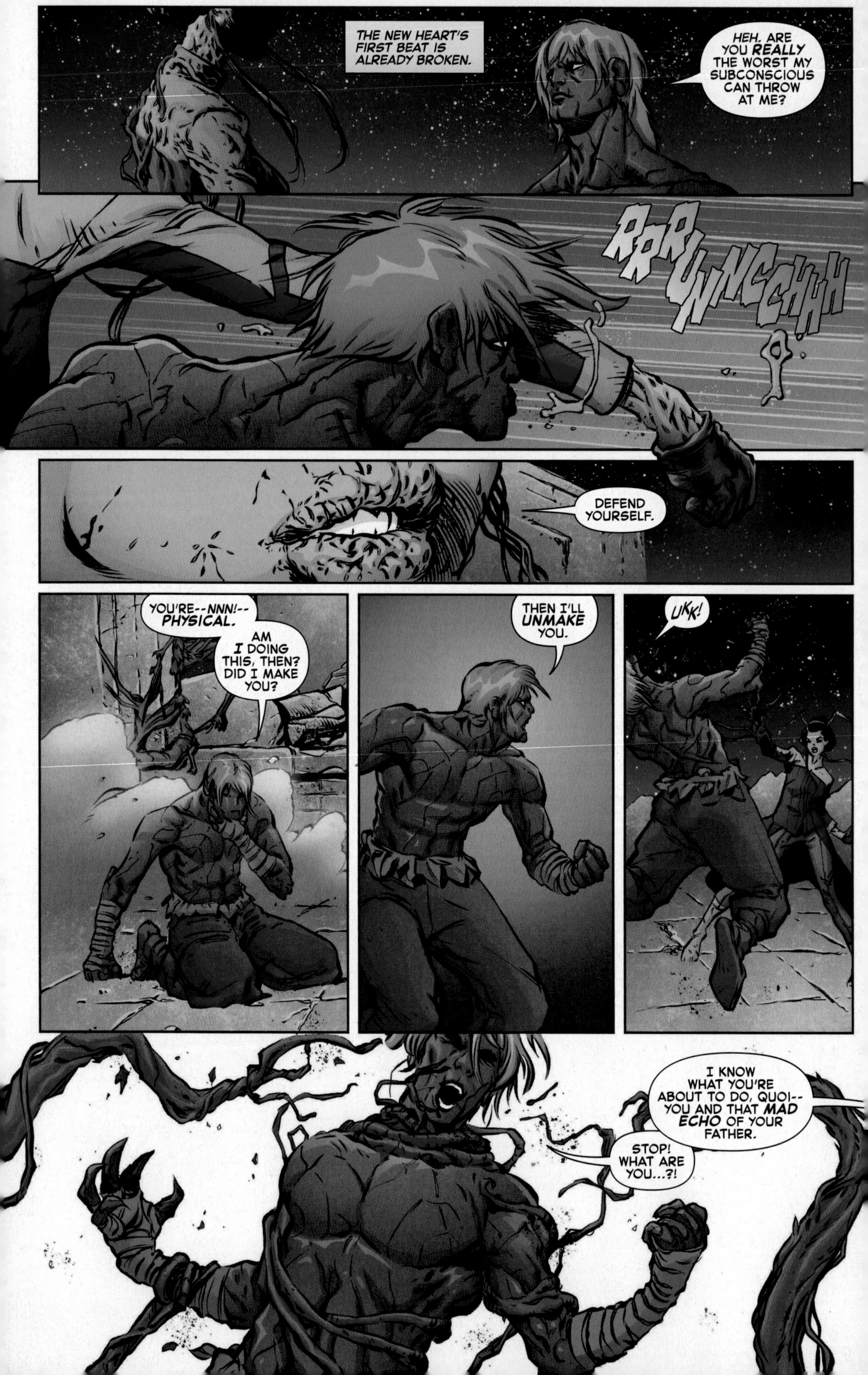
THE NEW HEART'S FIRST BEAT IS ALREADY BROKEN.
HEH. ARE YOU **REALLY** THE WORST MY SUBCONSCIOUS CAN THROW AT ME?
RRRUNNCCHHH
DEFEND YOURSELF.
YOU'RE--NNN!--**PHYSICAL.**
AM **I** DOING THIS, THEN? DID I MAKE YOU?
THEN I'LL **UNMAKE** YOU.
UKK!
I KNOW WHAT YOU'RE ABOUT TO DO, QUOI--YOU AND THAT **MAD ECHO** OF YOUR FATHER.
STOP! WHAT ARE YOU...?!

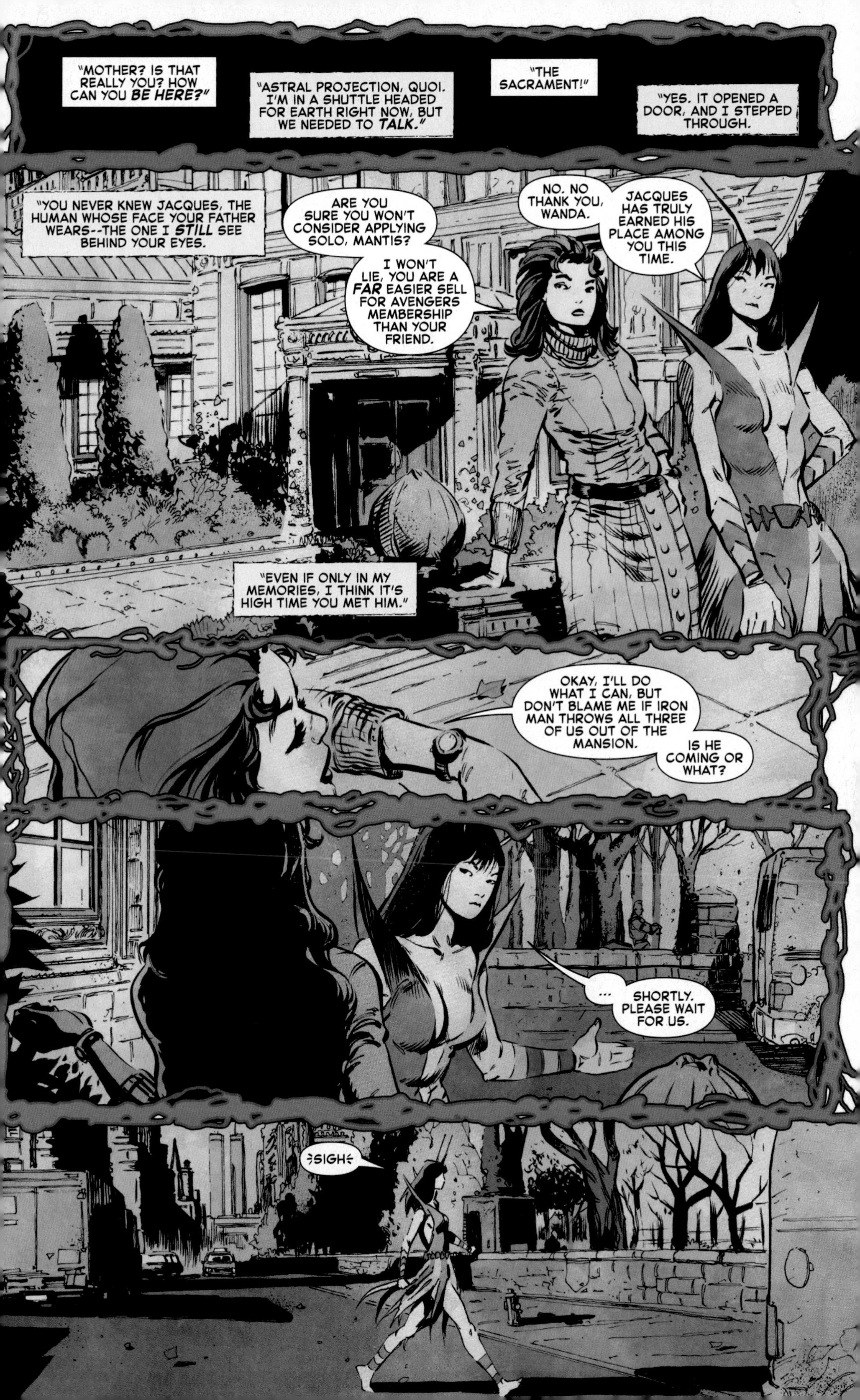
"MOTHER? IS THAT REALLY YOU? HOW CAN YOU BE HERE?"
"ASTRAL PROJECTION, QUOI. I'M IN A SHUTTLE HEADED FOR EARTH RIGHT NOW, BUT WE NEEDED TO TALK."
"THE SACRAMENT!"
"YES. IT OPENED A DOOR, AND I STEPPED THROUGH.
"YOU NEVER KNEW JACQUES, THE HUMAN WHOSE FACE YOUR FATHER WEARS--THE ONE I STILL SEE BEHIND YOUR EYES.
ARE YOU SURE YOU WON'T CONSIDER APPLYING SOLO, MANTIS?
I WON'T LIE, YOU ARE A FAR EASIER SELL FOR AVENGERS MEMBERSHIP THAN YOUR FRIEND.
NO. NO THANK YOU, WANDA.
JACQUES HAS TRULY EARNED HIS PLACE AMONG YOU THIS TIME.
"EVEN IF ONLY IN MY MEMORIES, I THINK IT'S HIGH TIME YOU MET HIM."
OKAY, I'LL DO WHAT I CAN, BUT DON'T BLAME ME IF IRON MAN THROWS ALL THREE OF US OUT OF THE MANSION.
IS HE COMING OR WHAT?
... SHORTLY. PLEASE WAIT FOR US.
SIGH

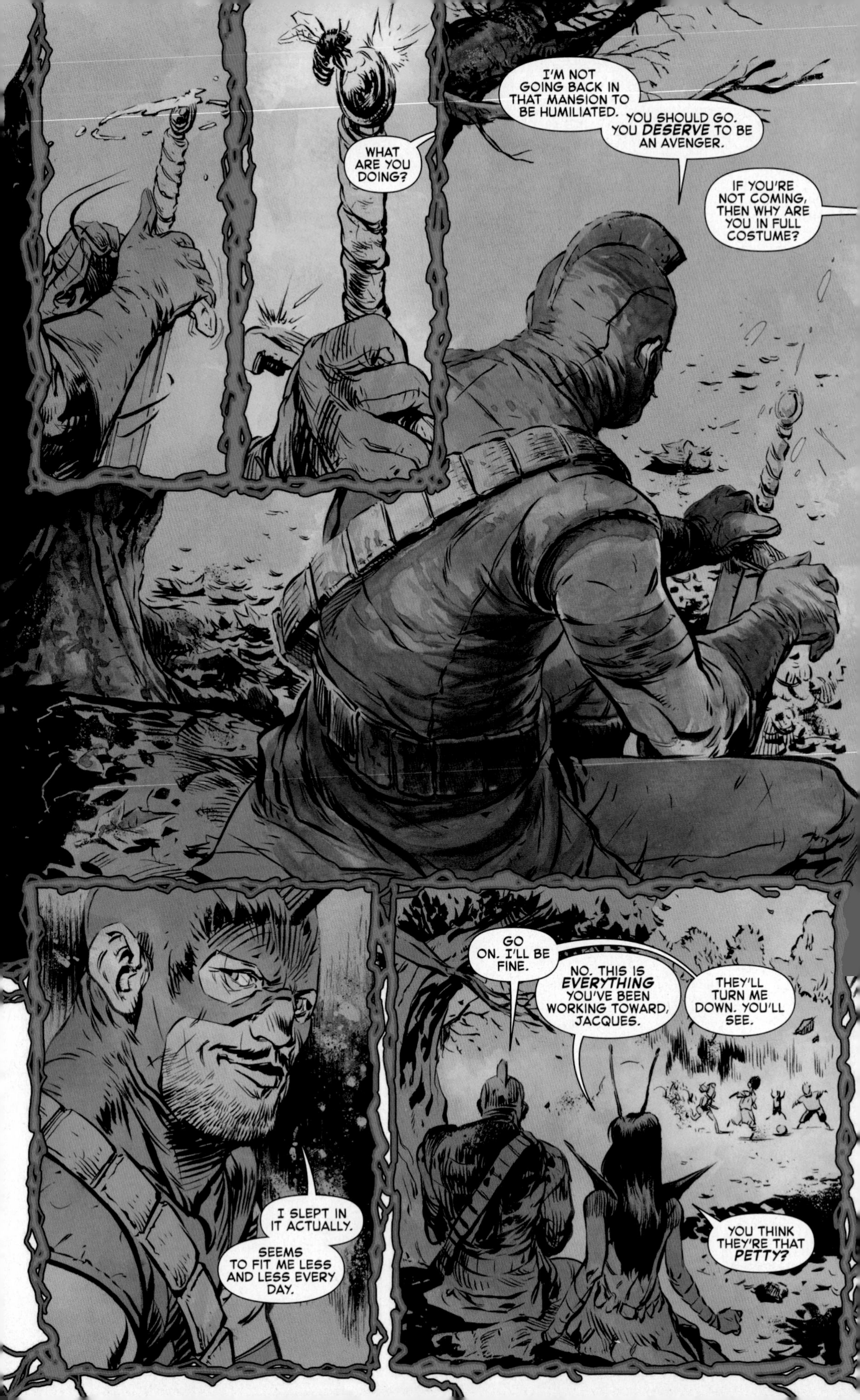
WHAT ARE YOU DOING?
I'M NOT GOING BACK IN THAT MANSION TO BE HUMILIATED.
YOU SHOULD GO. YOU DESERVE TO BE AN AVENGER.
IF YOU'RE NOT COMING, THEN WHY ARE YOU IN FULL COSTUME?
I SLEPT IN IT ACTUALLY.
SEEMS TO FIT ME LESS AND LESS EVERY DAY.
GO ON. I'LL BE FINE.
NO. THIS IS EVERYTHING YOU'VE BEEN WORKING TOWARD, JACQUES.
THEY'LL TURN ME DOWN. YOU'LL SEE.
YOU THINK THEY'RE THAT PETTY?

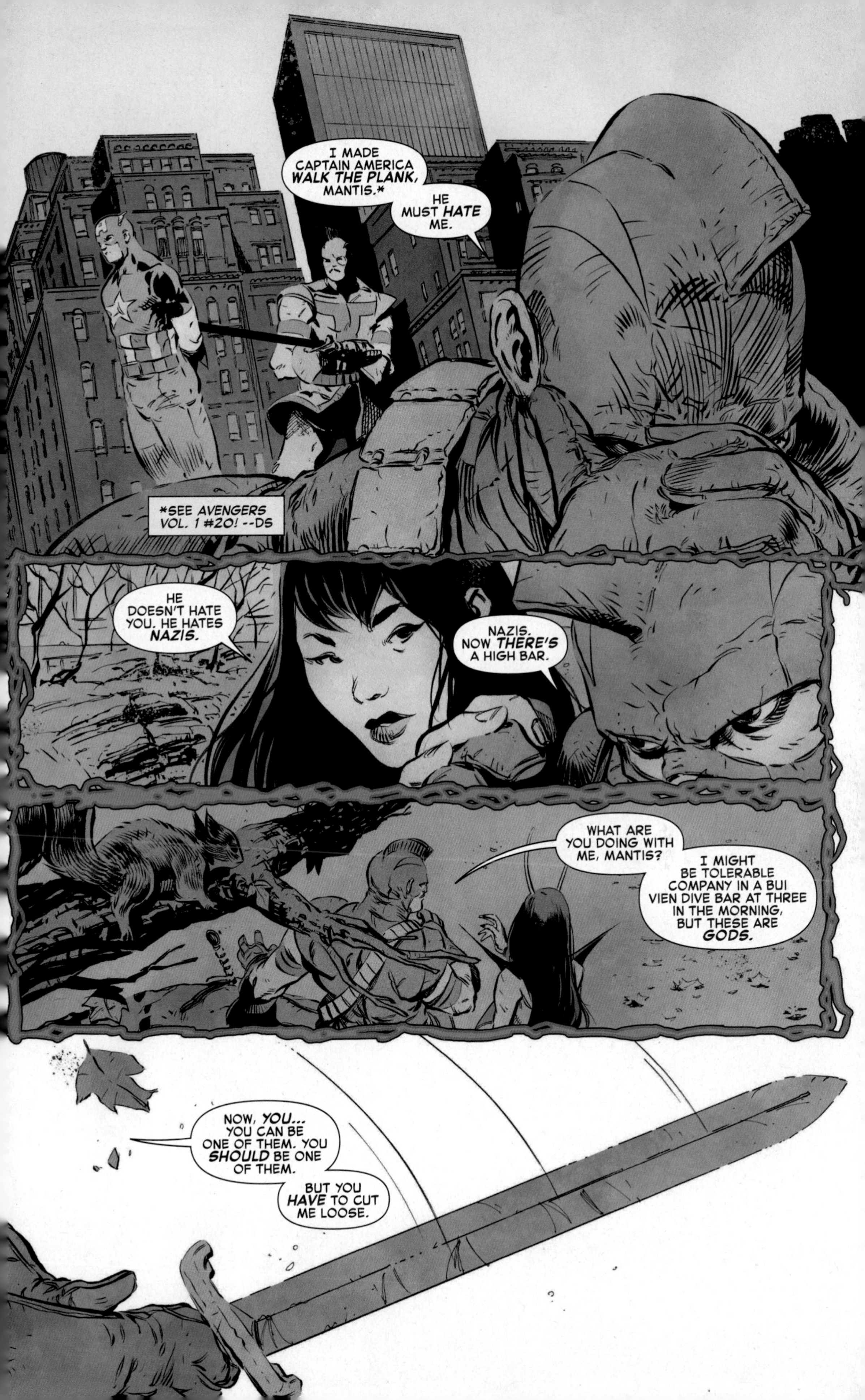
I MADE CAPTAIN AMERICA WALK THE PLANK, MANTIS.*
HE MUST HATE ME.
*SEE AVENGERS VOL. 1 #20! --DS
HE DOESN'T HATE YOU. HE HATES NAZIS.
NAZIS. NOW THERE'S A HIGH BAR.
WHAT ARE YOU DOING WITH ME, MANTIS?
I MIGHT BE TOLERABLE COMPANY IN A BUI VIEN DIVE BAR AT THREE IN THE MORNING, BUT THESE ARE GODS.
NOW, YOU... YOU CAN BE ONE OF THEM. YOU SHOULD BE ONE OF THEM.
BUT YOU HAVE TO CUT ME LOOSE.

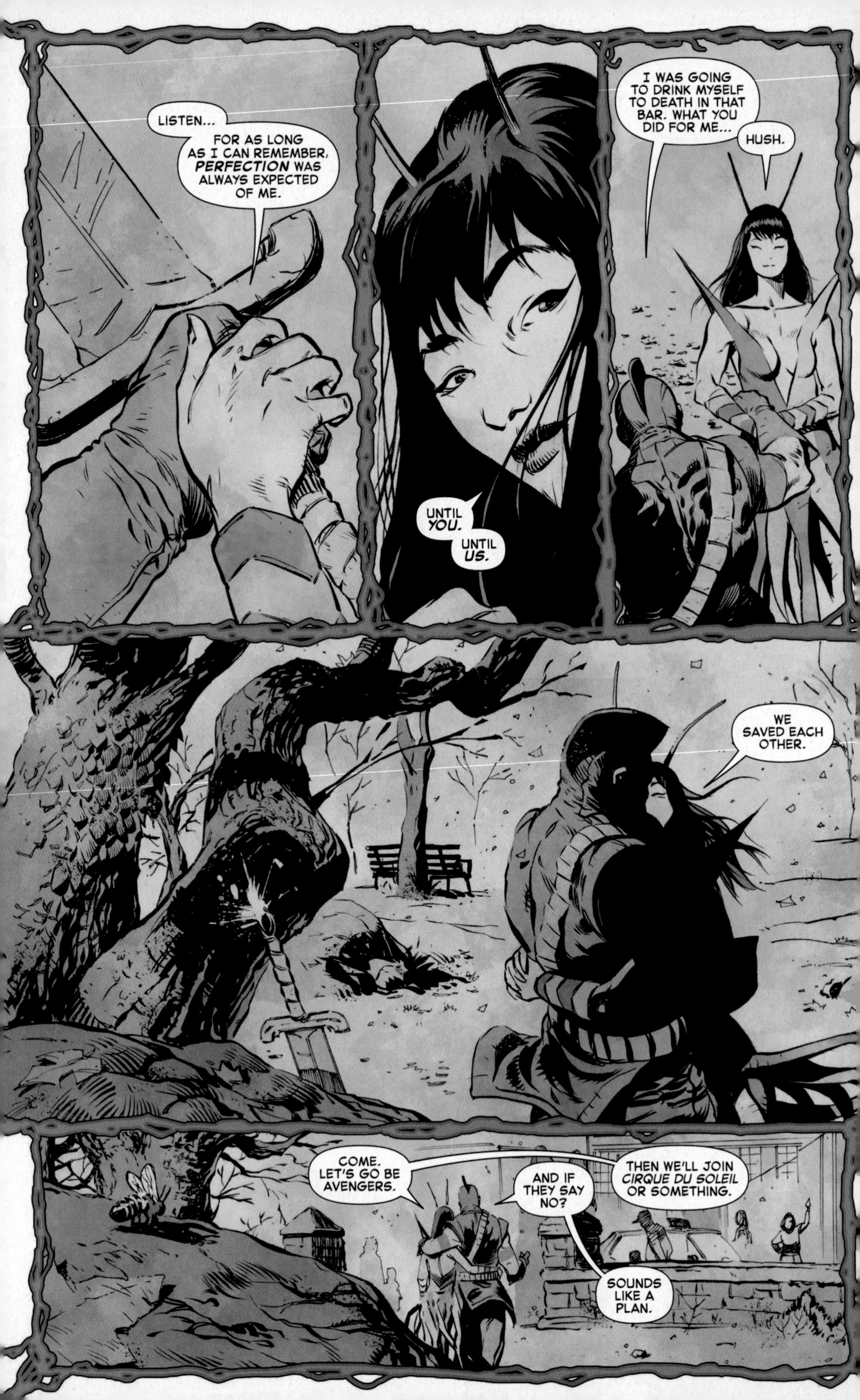
LISTEN...
FOR AS LONG AS I CAN REMEMBER, PERFECTION WAS ALWAYS EXPECTED OF ME.
UNTIL YOU.
UNTIL US.
I WAS GOING TO DRINK MYSELF TO DEATH IN THAT BAR. WHAT YOU DID FOR ME...
HUSH.
WE SAVED EACH OTHER.
COME. LET'S GO BE AVENGERS.
AND IF THEY SAY NO?
THEN WE'LL JOIN CIRQUE DU SOLEIL OR SOMETHING.
SOUNDS LIKE A PLAN.

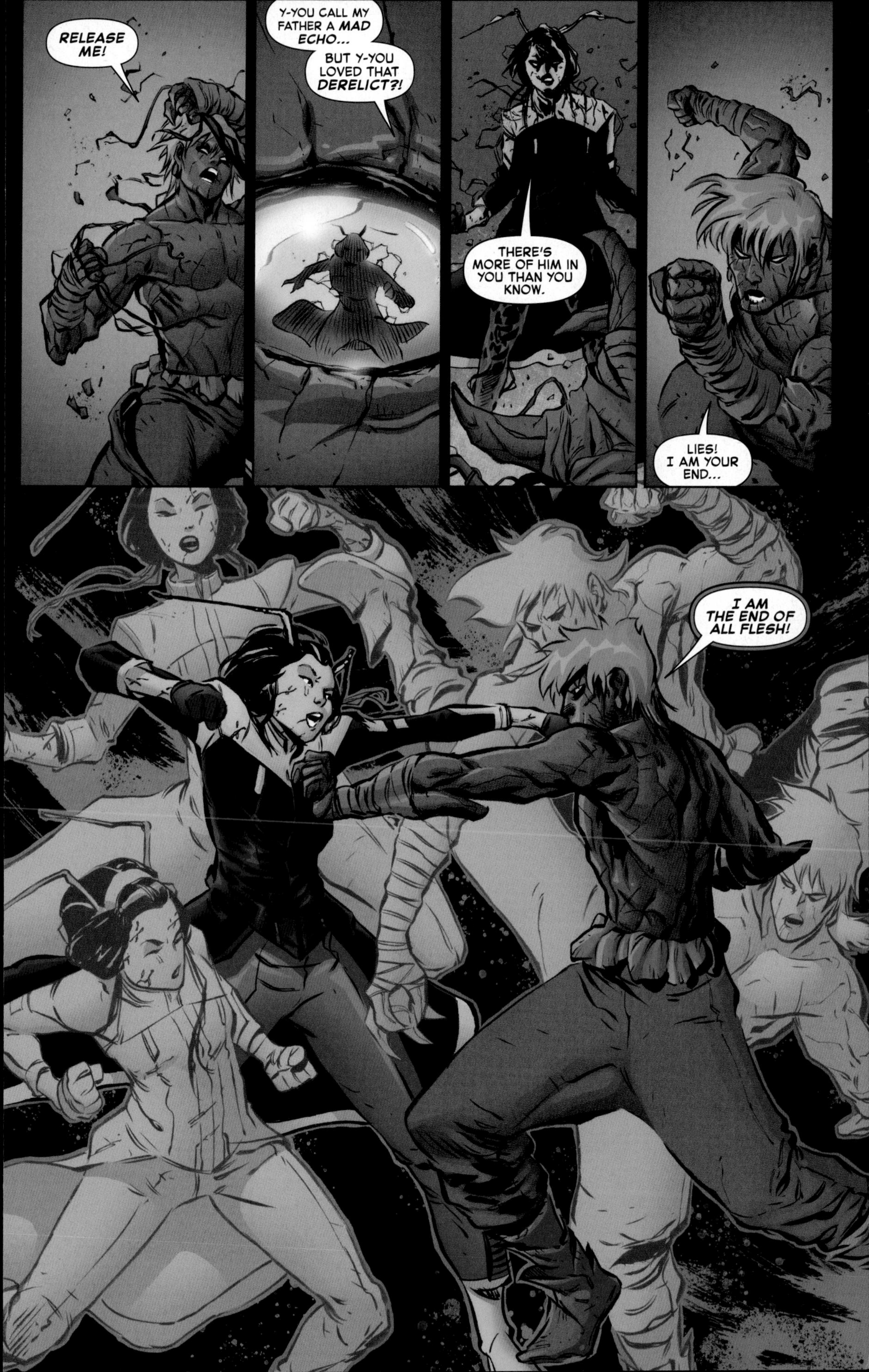
RELEASE ME!
Y-YOU CALL MY FATHER A MAD ECHO...
BUT Y-YOU LOVED THAT DERELICT?!
THERE'S MORE OF HIM IN YOU THAN YOU KNOW.
LIES! I AM YOUR END...
I AM THE END OF ALL FLESH!

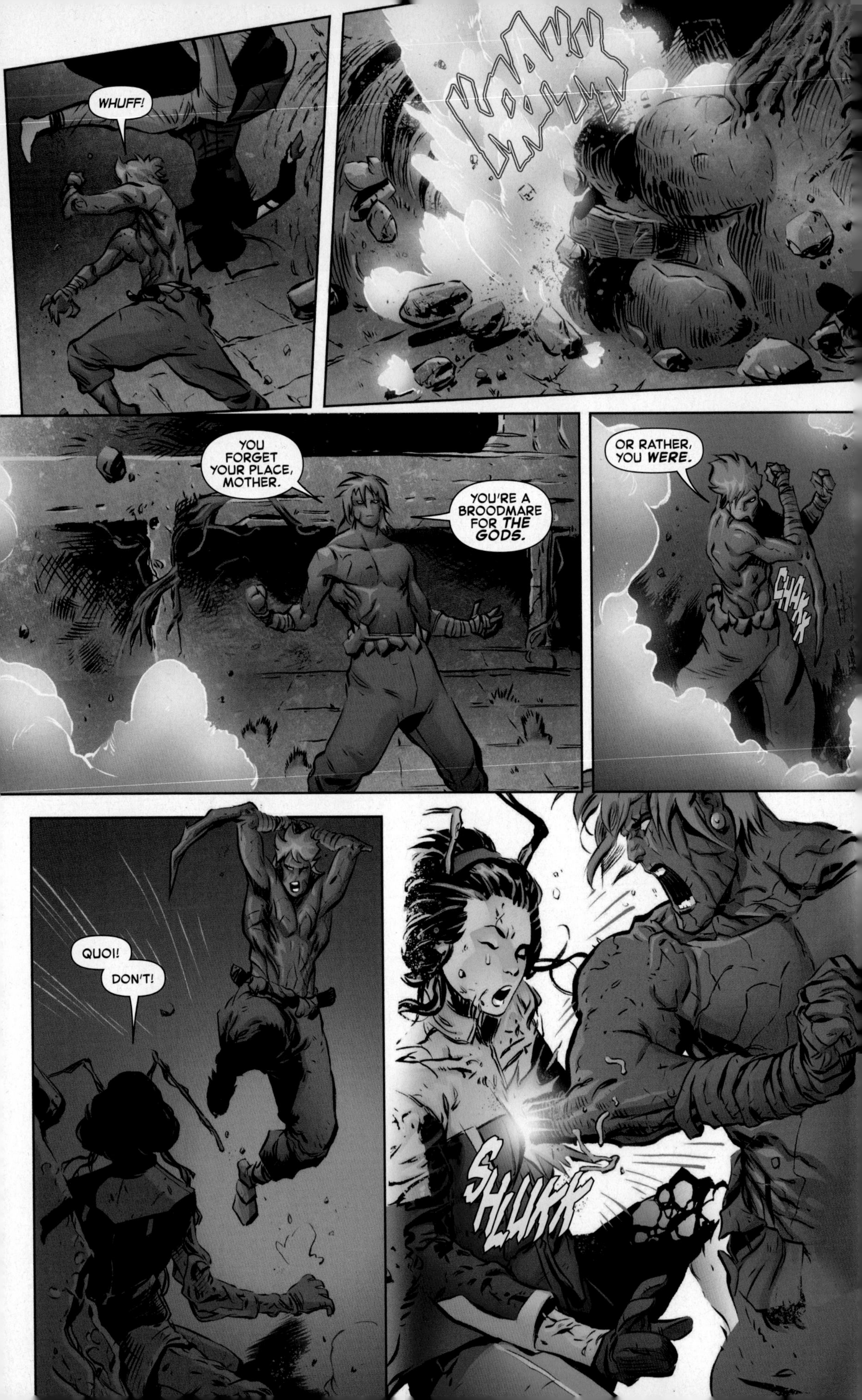

WHUFF!
CRAAAA KKOOM
YOU FORGET YOUR PLACE, MOTHER.
YOU'RE A BROODMARE FOR THE GODS.
OR RATHER, YOU WERE.
CHAKK
QUOI!
DON'T!
SHLUKK

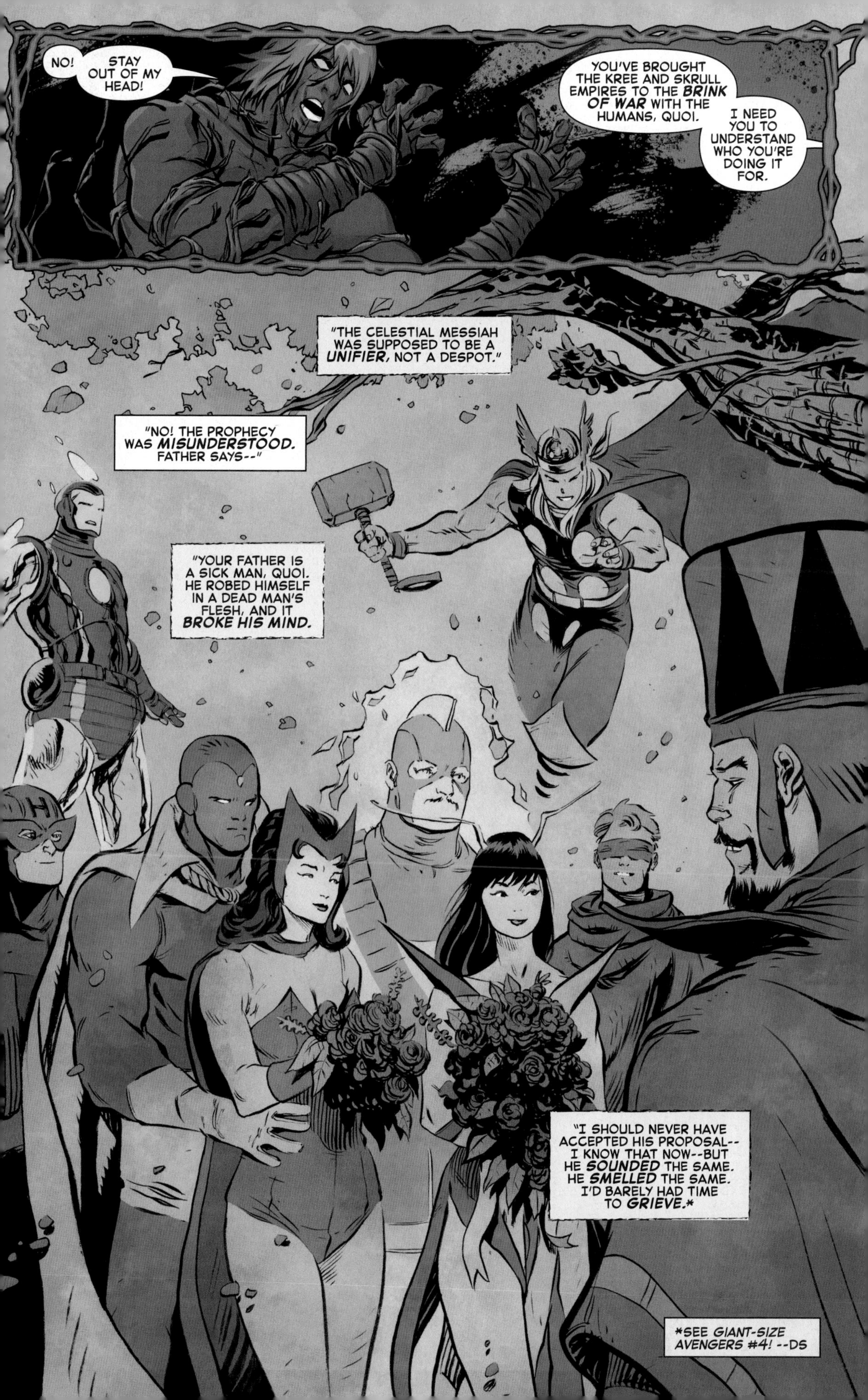

NO!
STAY OUT OF MY HEAD!
YOU'VE BROUGHT THE KREE AND SKRULL EMPIRES TO THE BRINK OF WAR WITH THE HUMANS, QUOI.
I NEED YOU TO UNDERSTAND WHO YOU'RE DOING IT FOR.
"THE CELESTIAL MESSIAH WAS SUPPOSED TO BE A UNIFIER, NOT A DESPOT."
"NO! THE PROPHECY WAS MISUNDERSTOOD. FATHER SAYS--"
"YOUR FATHER IS A SICK MAN, QUOI. HE ROBED HIMSELF IN A DEAD MAN'S FLESH, AND IT BROKE HIS MIND.
"I SHOULD NEVER HAVE ACCEPTED HIS PROPOSAL-- I KNOW THAT NOW--BUT HE SOUNDED THE SAME. HE SMELLED THE SAME. I'D BARELY HAD TIME TO GRIEVE.*
*SEE GIANT-SIZE AVENGERS #4! --DS

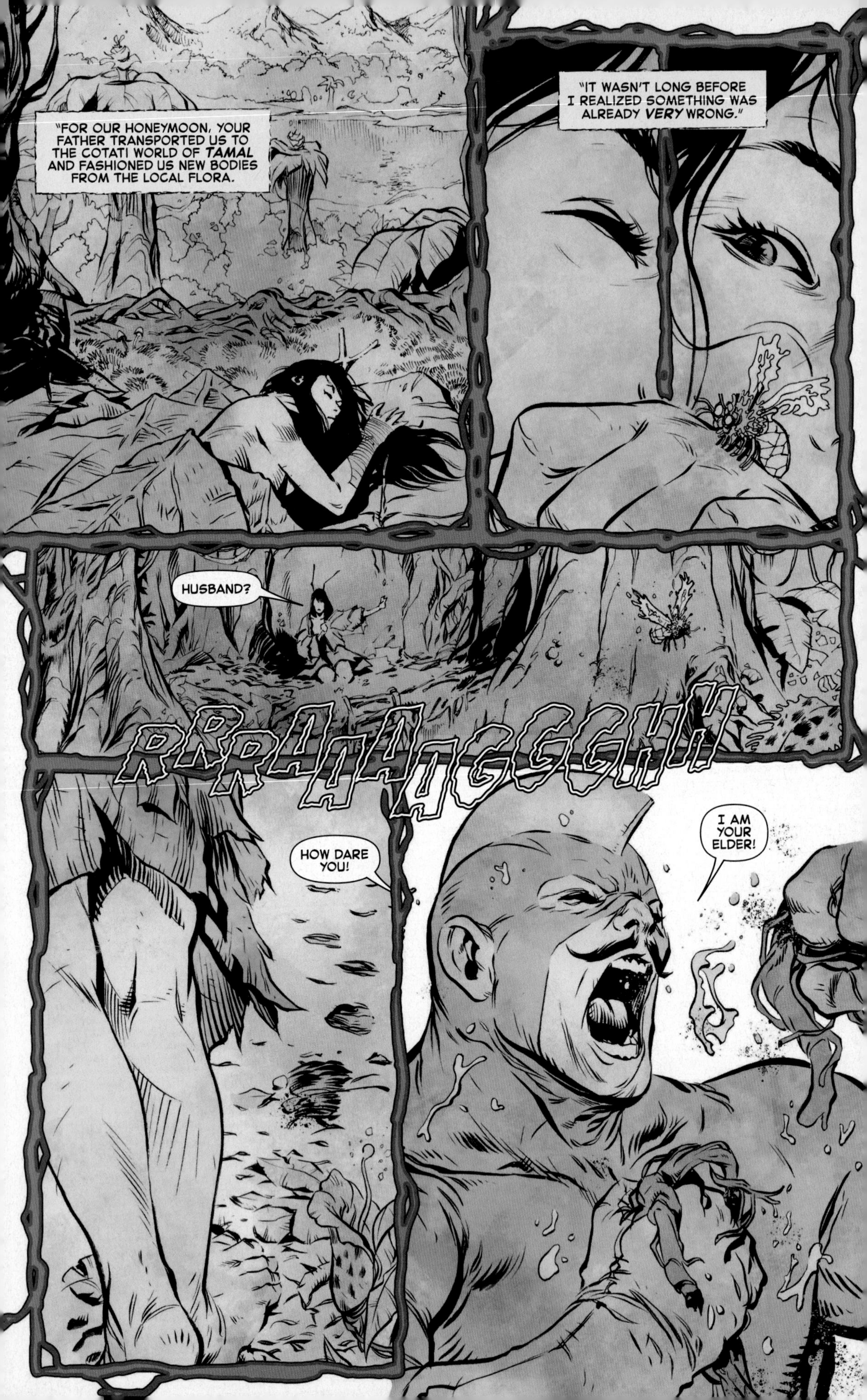

"FOR OUR HONEYMOON, YOUR FATHER TRANSPORTED US TO THE COTATI WORLD OF *TAMAL* AND FASHIONED US NEW BODIES FROM THE LOCAL FLORA.
"IT WASN'T LONG BEFORE I REALIZED SOMETHING WAS ALREADY *VERY* WRONG."
HUSBAND?
RRRAAAAGGGGHH
HOW DARE YOU!
I AM YOUR ELDER!

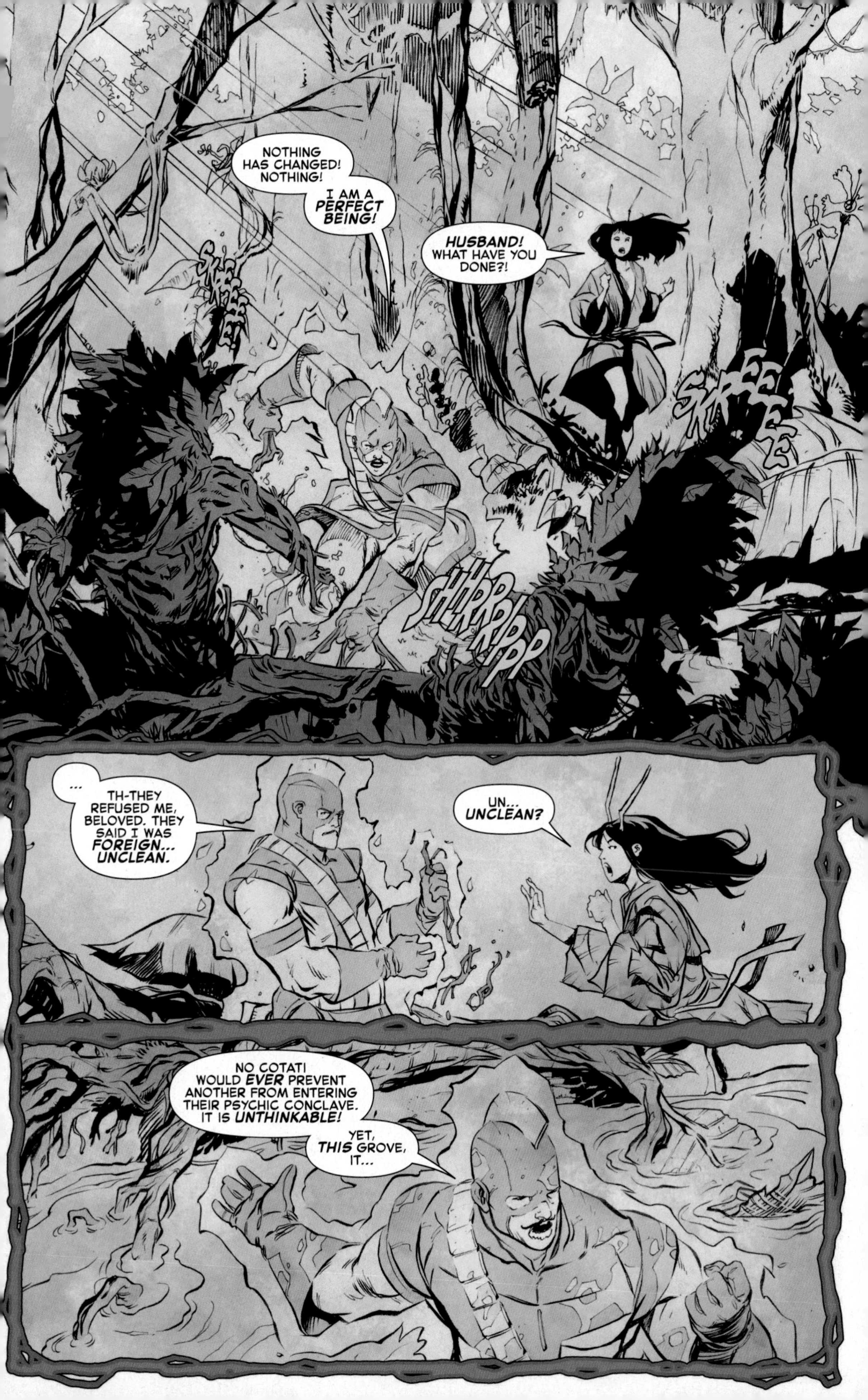
NOTHING HAS CHANGED! NOTHING!
I AM A PERFECT BEING!
HUSBAND! WHAT HAVE YOU DONE?!
SKREE
SKREEE
SHHRRIPP
... TH-THEY REFUSED ME, BELOVED. THEY SAID I WAS FOREIGN... UNCLEAN.
UN... UNCLEAN?
NO COTATI WOULD EVER PREVENT ANOTHER FROM ENTERING THEIR PSYCHIC CONCLAVE. IT IS UNTHINKABLE!
YET, THIS GROVE, IT...

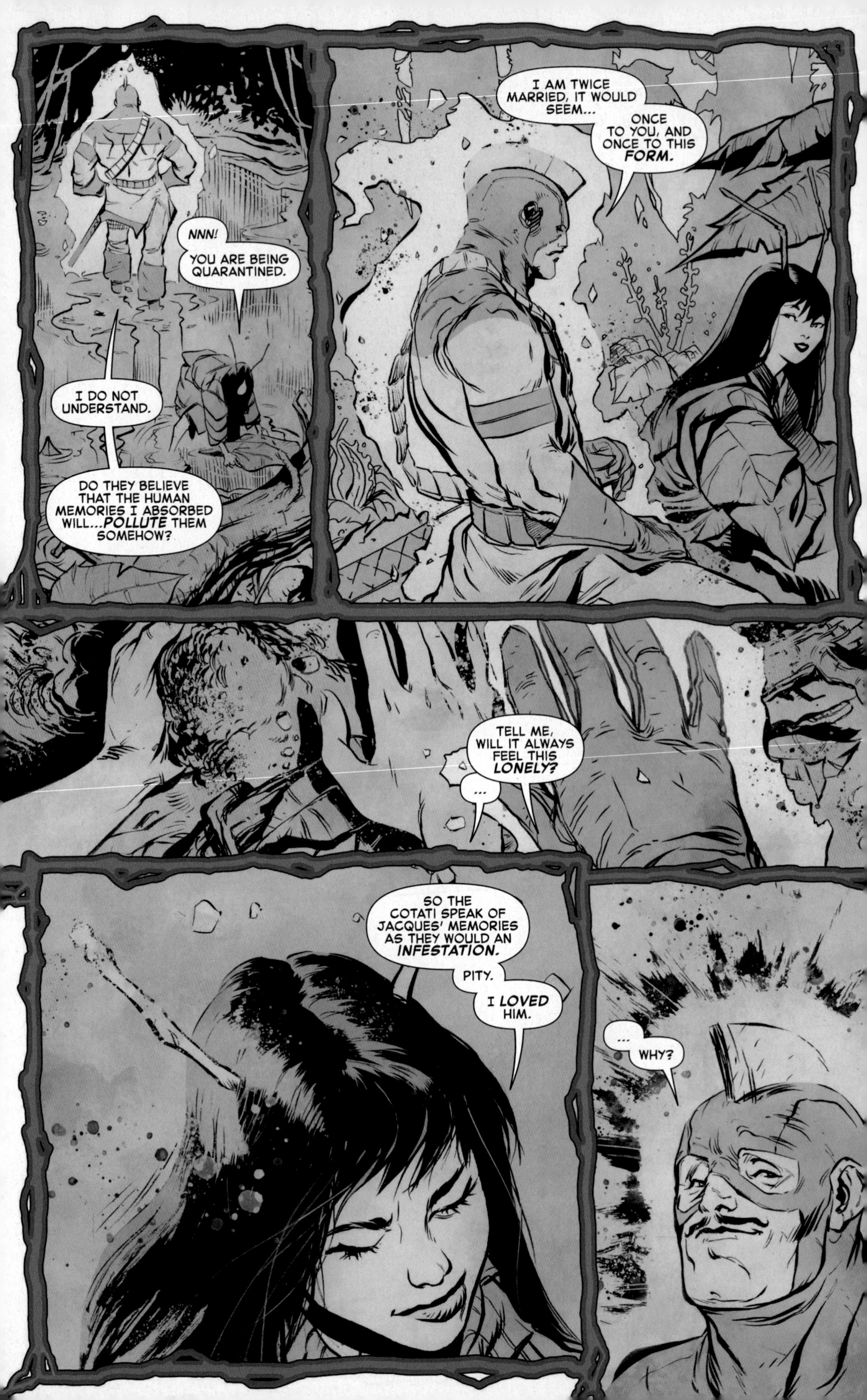
NNN!
YOU ARE BEING QUARANTINED.
I DO NOT UNDERSTAND.
DO THEY BELIEVE THAT THE HUMAN MEMORIES I ABSORBED WILL...POLLUTE THEM SOMEHOW?
I AM TWICE MARRIED, IT WOULD SEEM...
ONCE TO YOU, AND ONCE TO THIS FORM.
TELL ME, WILL IT ALWAYS FEEL THIS LONELY?
...
SO THE COTATI SPEAK OF JACQUES' MEMORIES AS THEY WOULD AN INFESTATION.
PITY.
I LOVED HIM.
...
WHY?

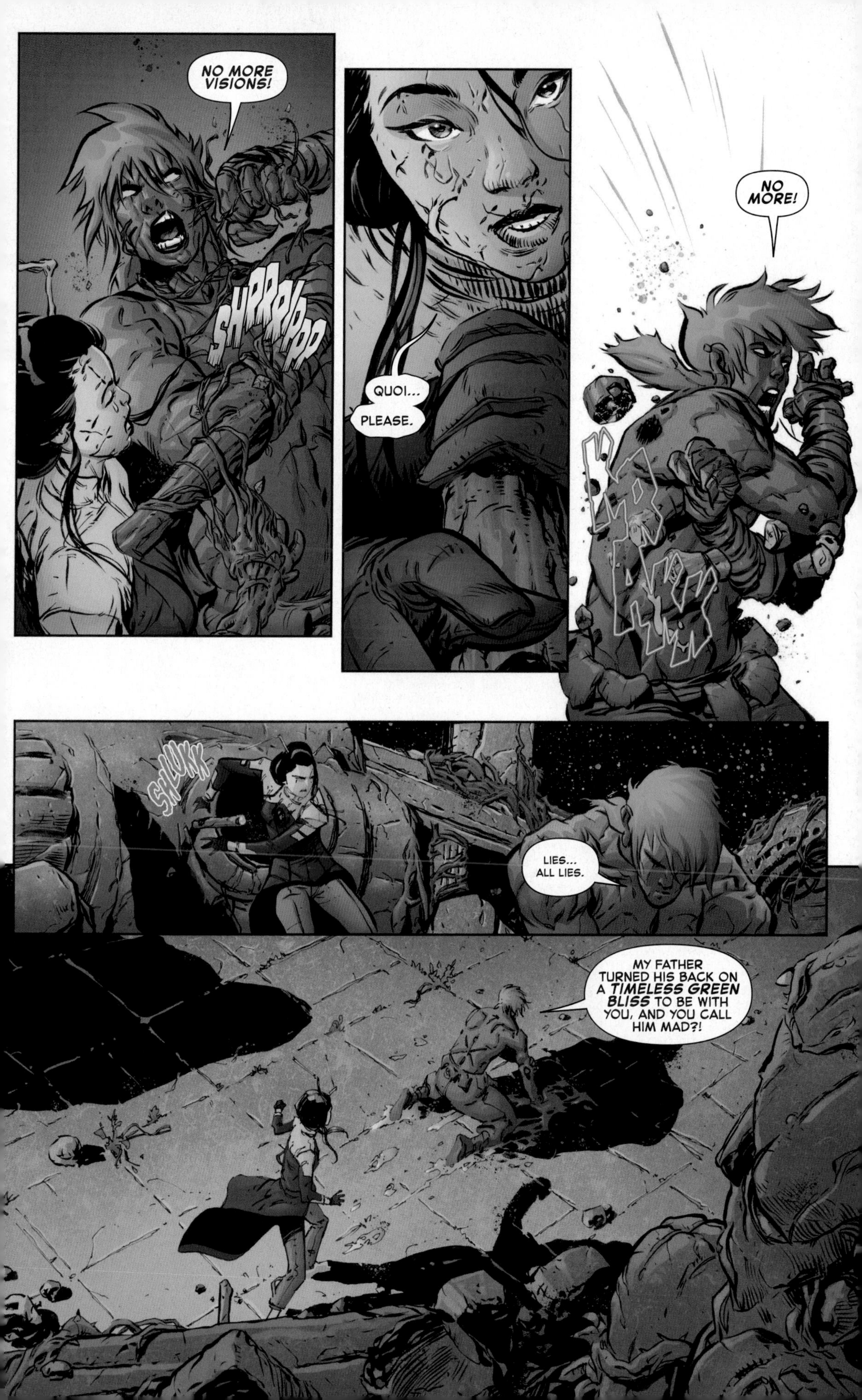
NO MORE VISIONS!
SHRRRIPP
QUOI...
PLEASE.
NO MORE!
KRAKK
SHLUKK
LIES... ALL LIES.
MY FATHER TURNED HIS BACK ON A *TIMELESS GREEN BLISS* TO BE WITH YOU, AND YOU CALL HIM MAD?!

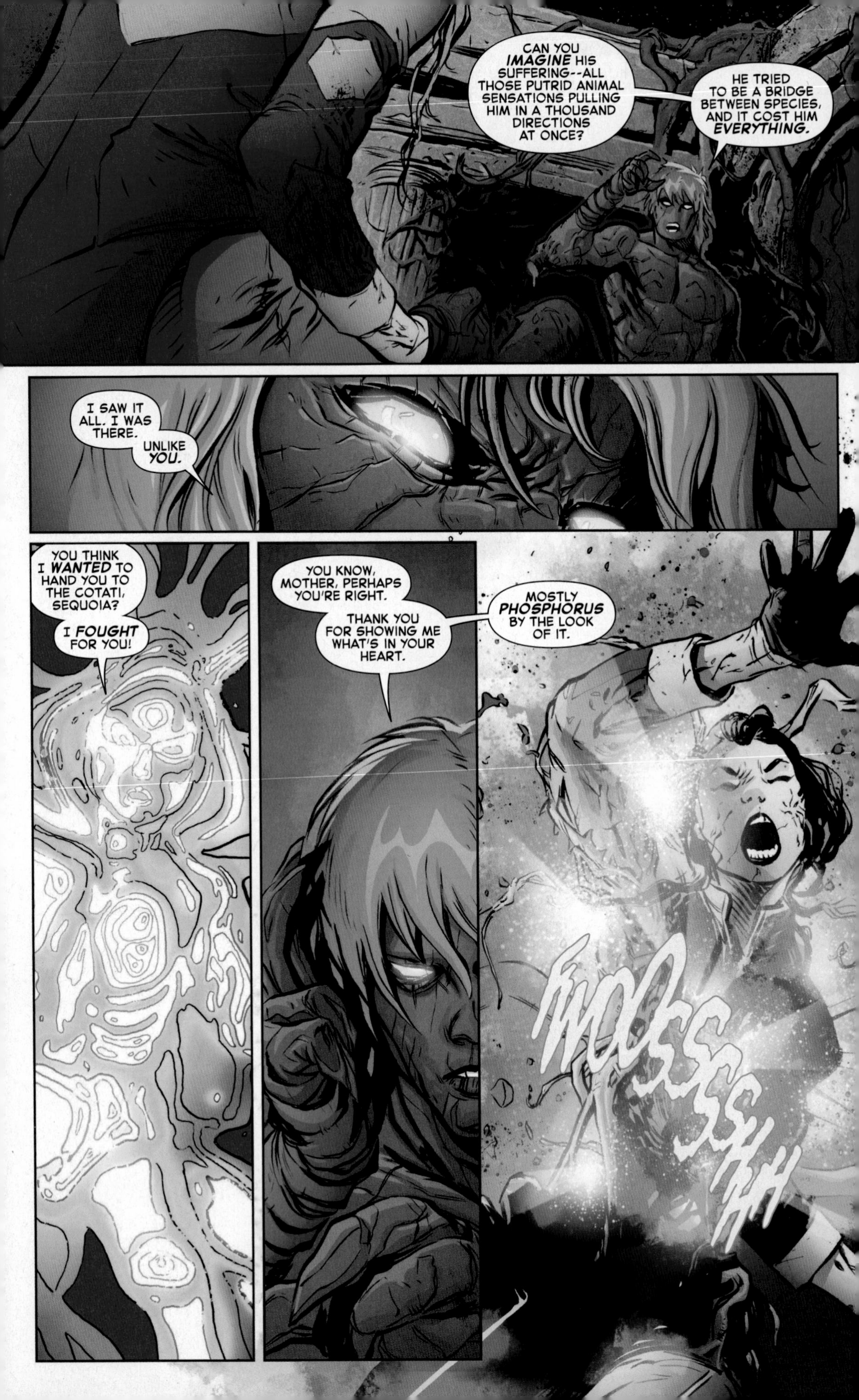
CAN YOU IMAGINE HIS SUFFERING--ALL THOSE PUTRID ANIMAL SENSATIONS PULLING HIM IN A THOUSAND DIRECTIONS AT ONCE?
HE TRIED TO BE A BRIDGE BETWEEN SPECIES, AND IT COST HIM EVERYTHING.
I SAW IT ALL. I WAS THERE.
UNLIKE YOU.
YOU THINK I WANTED TO HAND YOU TO THE COTATI, SEQUOIA?
I FOUGHT FOR YOU!
YOU KNOW, MOTHER, PERHAPS YOU'RE RIGHT.
THANK YOU FOR SHOWING ME WHAT'S IN YOUR HEART.
MOSTLY PHOSPHORUS BY THE LOOK OF IT.
FWOOSSSHH

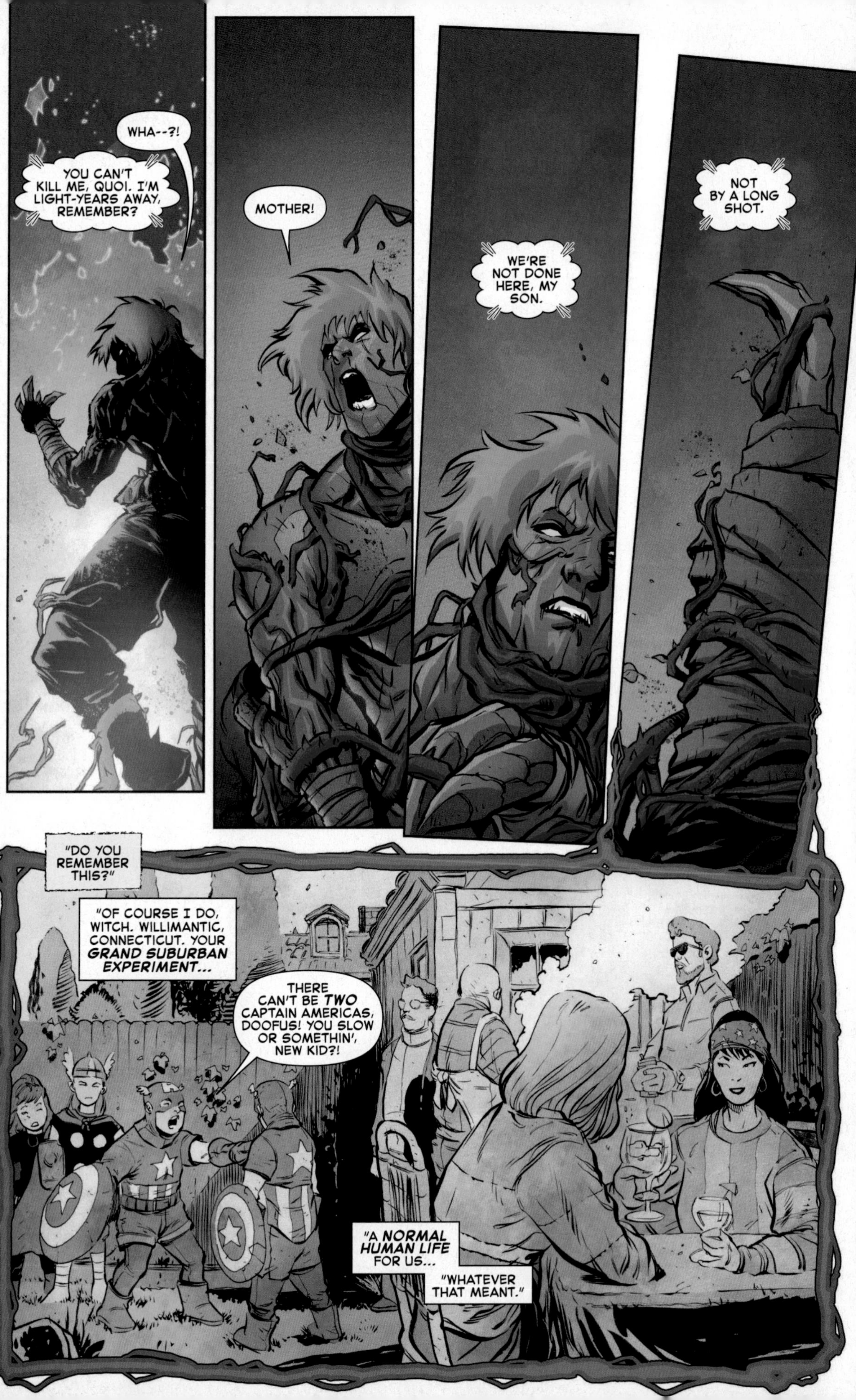
WHA--?!
YOU CAN'T KILL ME, QUOI. I'M LIGHT-YEARS AWAY, REMEMBER?
MOTHER!
WE'RE NOT DONE HERE, MY SON.
NOT BY A LONG SHOT.
"DO YOU REMEMBER THIS?"
"OF COURSE I DO, WITCH. WILLIMANTIC, CONNECTICUT. YOUR GRAND SUBURBAN EXPERIMENT...
THERE CAN'T BE TWO CAPTAIN AMERICAS, DOOFUS! YOU SLOW OR SOMETHIN', NEW KID?!
"A NORMAL HUMAN LIFE FOR US...
"WHATEVER THAT MEANT."

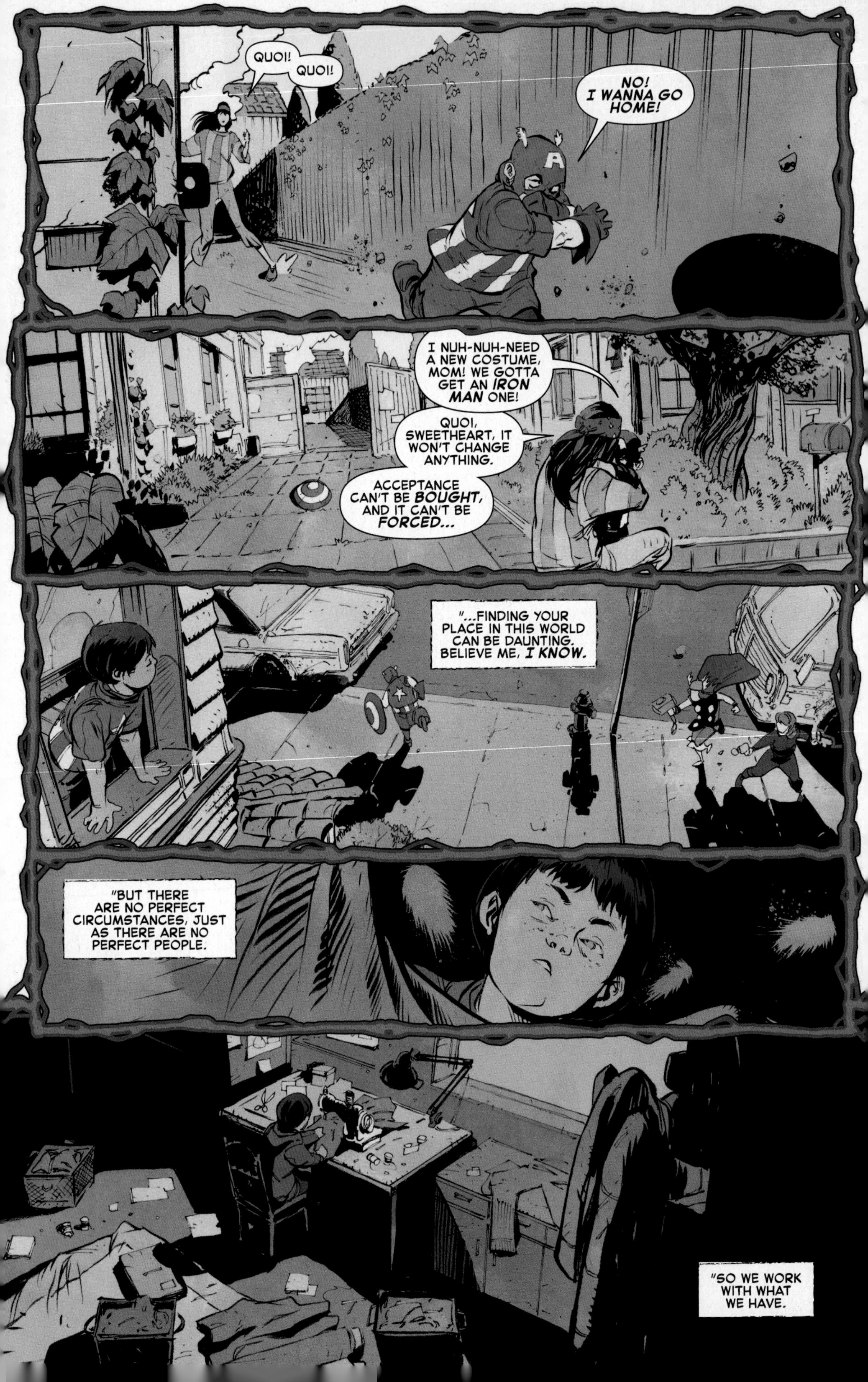
QUOI! QUOI!
NO! I WANNA GO HOME!
I NUH-NUH-NEED A NEW COSTUME, MOM! WE GOTTA GET AN *IRON MAN* ONE!
QUOI, SWEETHEART, IT WON'T CHANGE ANYTHING.
ACCEPTANCE CAN'T BE *BOUGHT,* AND IT CAN'T BE *FORCED...*
"...FINDING YOUR PLACE IN THIS WORLD CAN BE DAUNTING. BELIEVE ME, *I KNOW.*
"BUT THERE ARE NO PERFECT CIRCUMSTANCES, JUST AS THERE ARE NO PERFECT PEOPLE.
"SO WE WORK WITH WHAT WE HAVE.

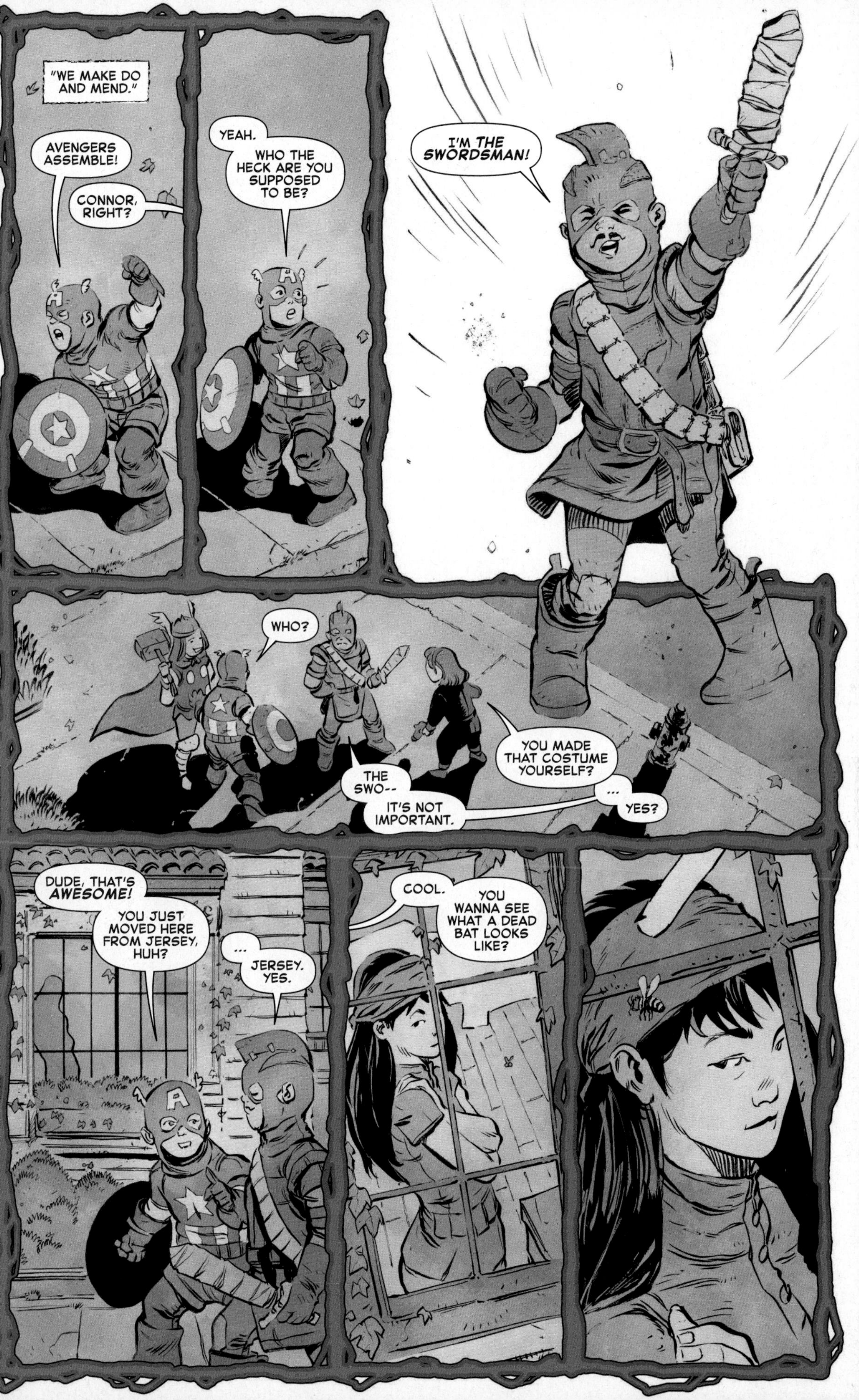
"WE MAKE DO AND MEND."
AVENGERS ASSEMBLE!
CONNOR, RIGHT?
YEAH.
WHO THE HECK ARE YOU SUPPOSED TO BE?
I'M THE SWORDSMAN!
WHO?
THE SWO-- IT'S NOT IMPORTANT.
YOU MADE THAT COSTUME YOURSELF?
... YES?
DUDE, THAT'S AWESOME!
YOU JUST MOVED HERE FROM JERSEY, HUH?
... JERSEY. YES.
COOL.
YOU WANNA SEE WHAT A DEAD BAT LOOKS LIKE?

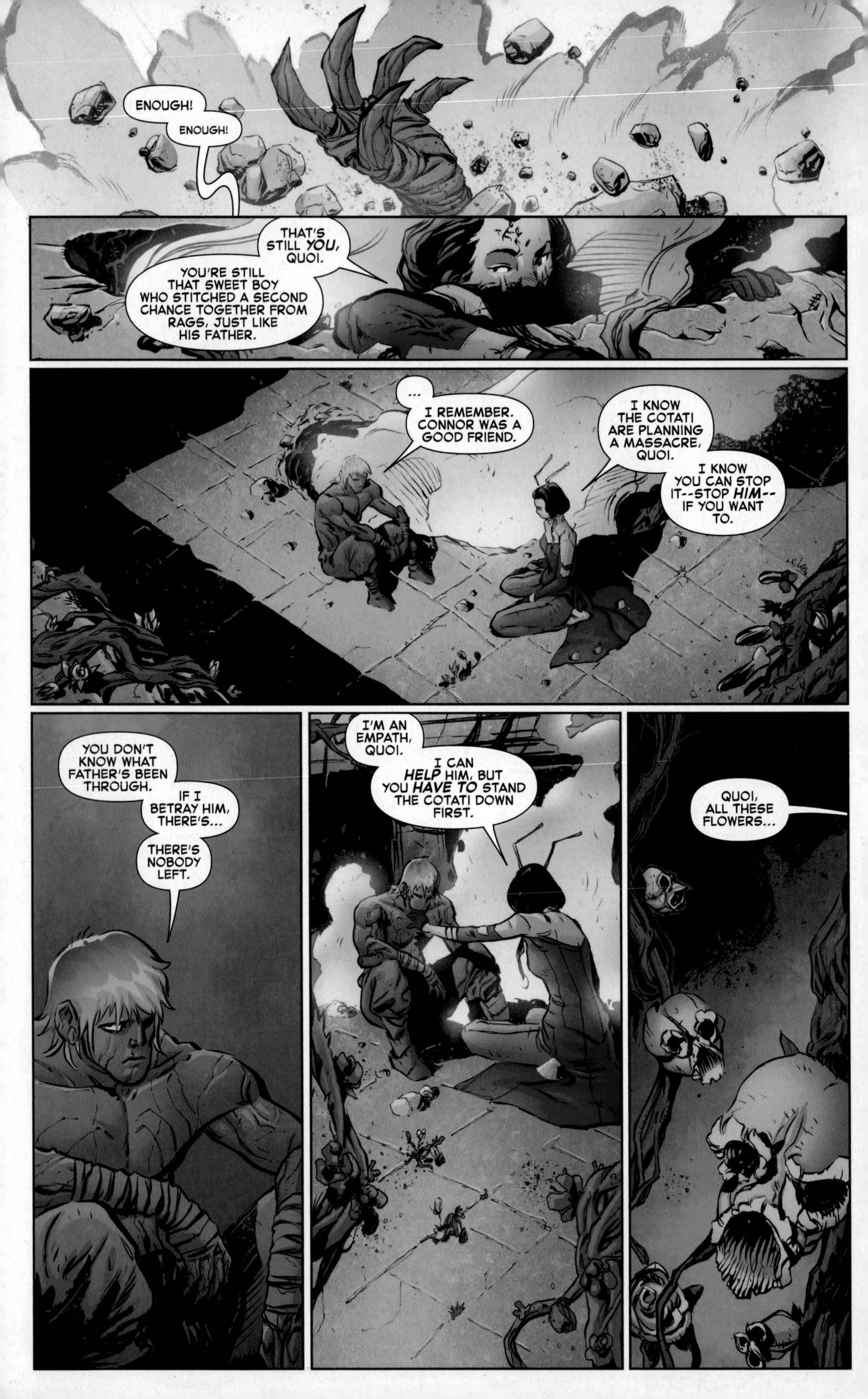
ENOUGH!
ENOUGH!
THAT'S STILL YOU, QUOI.
YOU'RE STILL THAT SWEET BOY WHO STITCHED A SECOND CHANCE TOGETHER FROM RAGS, JUST LIKE HIS FATHER.
...
I REMEMBER. CONNOR WAS A GOOD FRIEND.
I KNOW THE COTATI ARE PLANNING A MASSACRE, QUOI.
I KNOW YOU CAN STOP IT--STOP HIM--IF YOU WANT TO.
YOU DON'T KNOW WHAT FATHER'S BEEN THROUGH.
IF I BETRAY HIM, THERE'S...
THERE'S NOBODY LEFT.
I'M AN EMPATH, QUOI.
I CAN HELP HIM, BUT YOU HAVE TO STAND THE COTATI DOWN FIRST.
QUOI, ALL THESE FLOWERS...

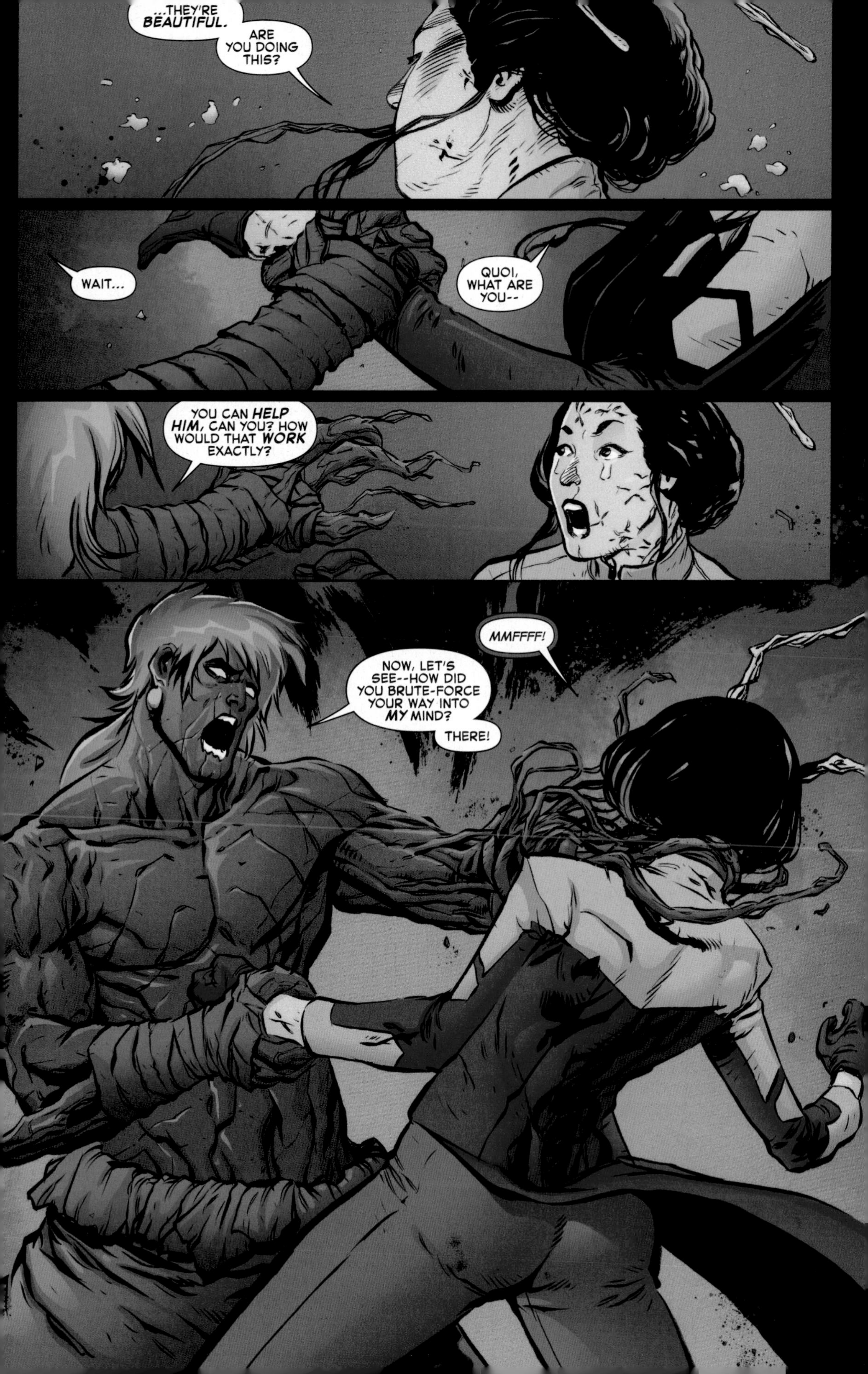
...THEY'RE BEAUTIFUL.
ARE YOU DOING THIS?
WAIT...
QUOI, WHAT ARE YOU--
YOU CAN HELP HIM, CAN YOU? HOW WOULD THAT WORK EXACTLY?
MMFFFF!
NOW, LET'S SEE--HOW DID YOU BRUTE-FORCE YOUR WAY INTO MY MIND?
THERE!

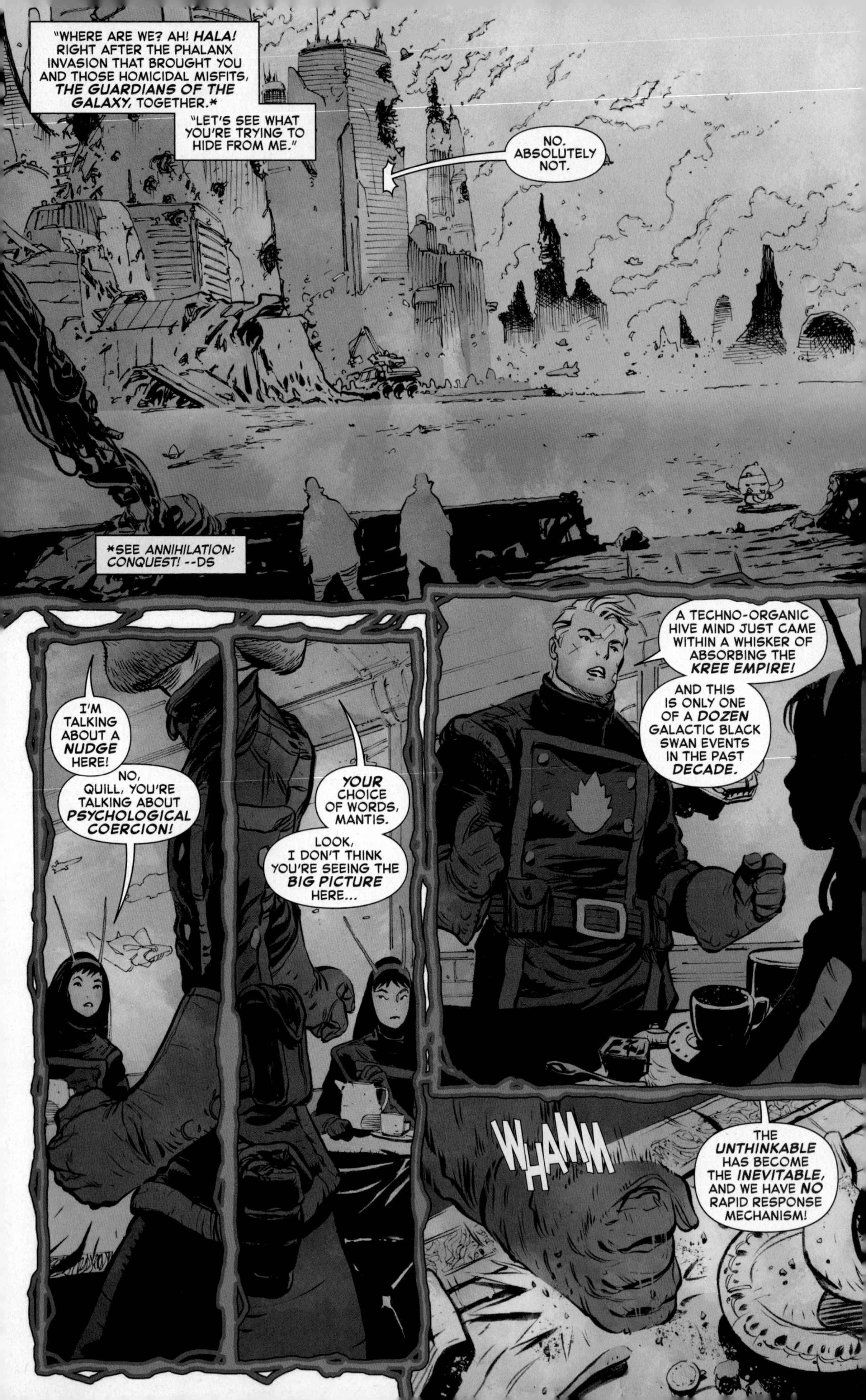
"WHERE ARE WE? AH! HALA! RIGHT AFTER THE PHALANX INVASION THAT BROUGHT YOU AND THOSE HOMICIDAL MISFITS, THE GUARDIANS OF THE GALAXY, TOGETHER.*
"LET'S SEE WHAT YOU'RE TRYING TO HIDE FROM ME."
NO. ABSOLUTELY NOT.
*SEE ANNIHILATION: CONQUEST! --DS
I'M TALKING ABOUT A NUDGE HERE!
NO, QUILL, YOU'RE TALKING ABOUT PSYCHOLOGICAL COERCION!
YOUR CHOICE OF WORDS, MANTIS.
LOOK, I DON'T THINK YOU'RE SEEING THE BIG PICTURE HERE...
A TECHNO-ORGANIC HIVE MIND JUST CAME WITHIN A WHISKER OF ABSORBING THE KREE EMPIRE!
AND THIS IS ONLY ONE OF A DOZEN GALACTIC BLACK SWAN EVENTS IN THE PAST DECADE.
WHAMM
THE UNTHINKABLE HAS BECOME THE INEVITABLE, AND WE HAVE NO RAPID RESPONSE MECHANISM!

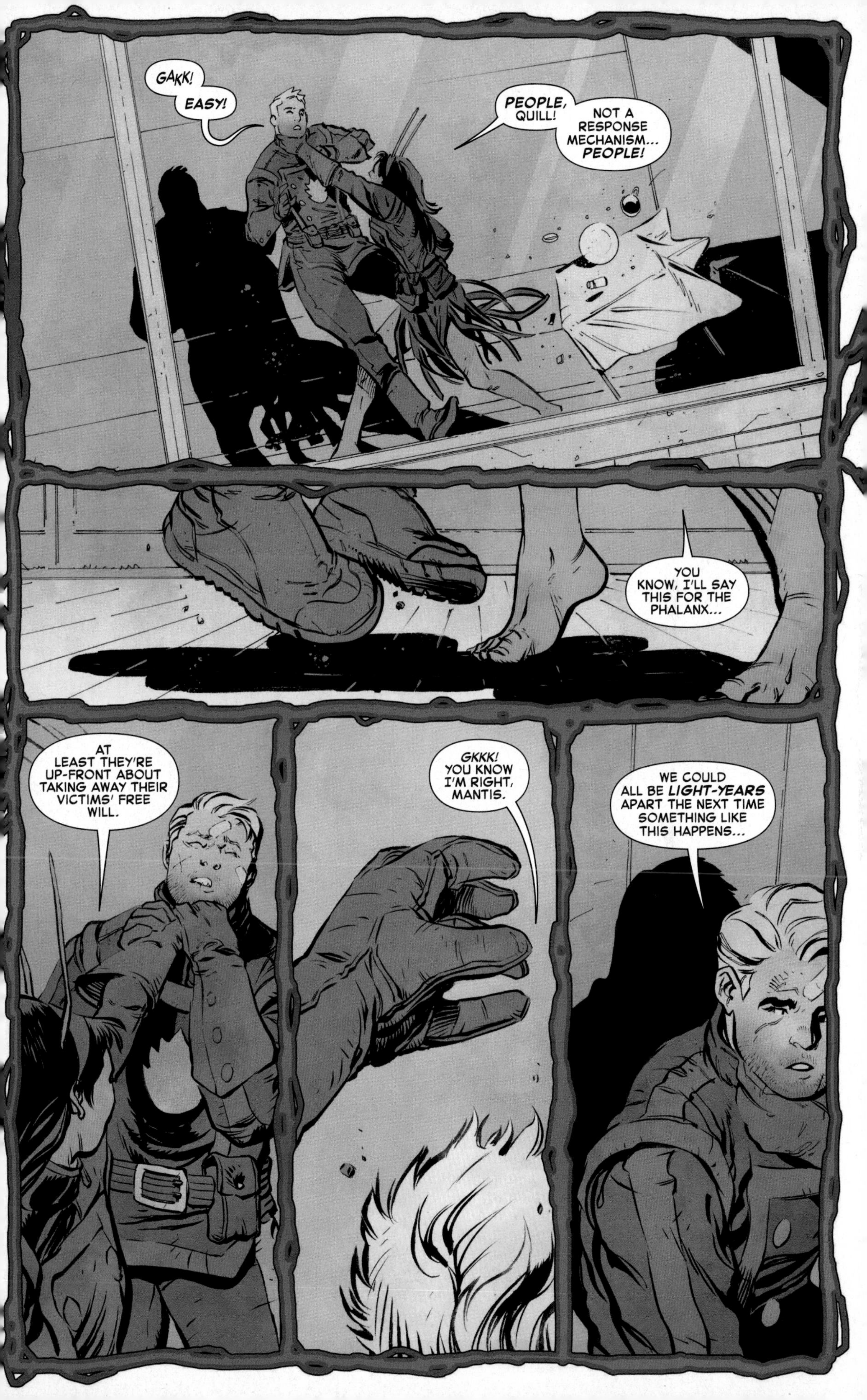
GAKK!
EASY!
PEOPLE, QUILL!
NOT A RESPONSE MECHANISM... PEOPLE!
YOU KNOW, I'LL SAY THIS FOR THE PHALANX...
AT LEAST THEY'RE UP-FRONT ABOUT TAKING AWAY THEIR VICTIMS' FREE WILL.
GKKK! YOU KNOW I'M RIGHT, MANTIS.
WE COULD ALL BE LIGHT-YEARS APART THE NEXT TIME SOMETHING LIKE THIS HAPPENS...

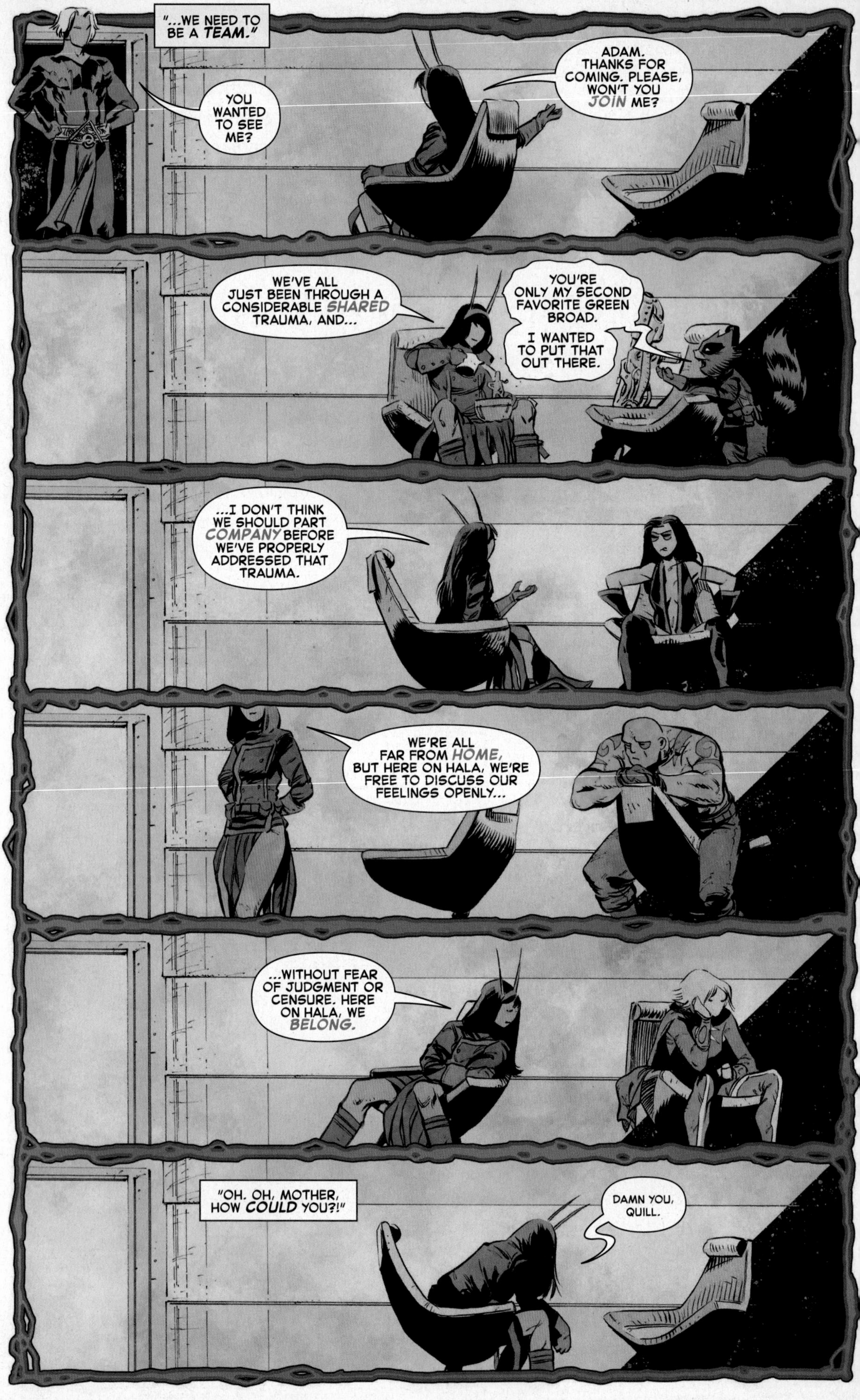
"...WE NEED TO BE A TEAM."
YOU WANTED TO SEE ME?
ADAM. THANKS FOR COMING. PLEASE, WON'T YOU JOIN ME?
WE'VE ALL JUST BEEN THROUGH A CONSIDERABLE SHARED TRAUMA, AND...
YOU'RE ONLY MY SECOND FAVORITE GREEN BROAD.
I WANTED TO PUT THAT OUT THERE.
...I DON'T THINK WE SHOULD PART COMPANY BEFORE WE'VE PROPERLY ADDRESSED THAT TRAUMA.
WE'RE ALL FAR FROM HOME, BUT HERE ON HALA, WE'RE FREE TO DISCUSS OUR FEELINGS OPENLY...
...WITHOUT FEAR OF JUDGMENT OR CENSURE. HERE ON HALA, WE BELONG.
"OH. OH, MOTHER, HOW COULD YOU?!"
DAMN YOU, QUILL.

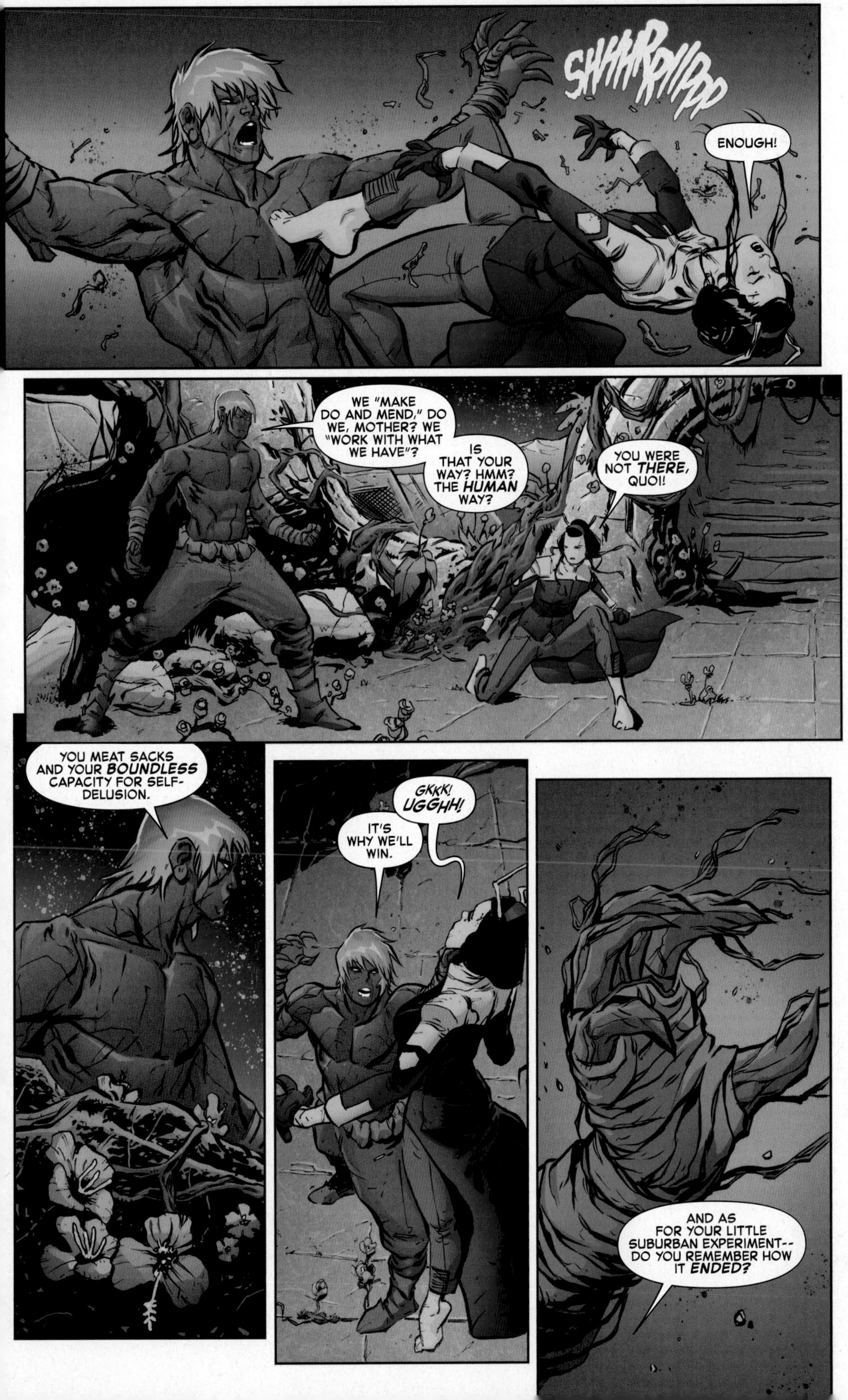
SHKKRRIIPP
ENOUGH!
WE "MAKE DO AND MEND," DO WE, MOTHER? WE "WORK WITH WHAT WE HAVE"?
IS THAT YOUR WAY? HMM? THE *HUMAN* WAY?
YOU WERE NOT *THERE,* QUOI!
YOU MEAT SACKS AND YOUR *BOUNDLESS* CAPACITY FOR SELF-DELUSION.
IT'S WHY WE'LL WIN.
GKKK! UGGHH!
AND AS FOR YOUR LITTLE SUBURBAN EXPERIMENT-- DO YOU REMEMBER HOW IT *ENDED?*

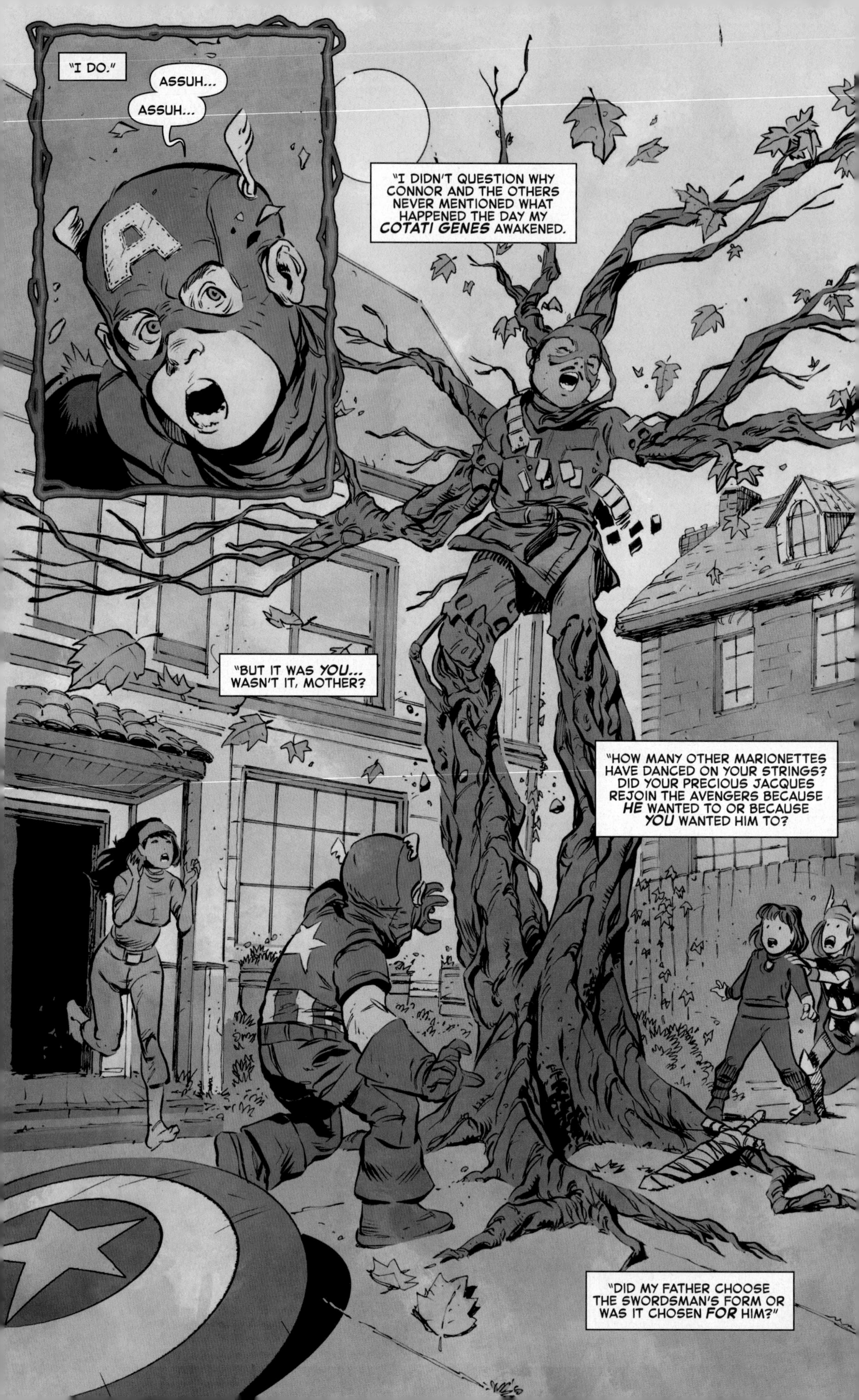
"I DO."
ASSUH...
ASSUH...
"I DIDN'T QUESTION WHY CONNOR AND THE OTHERS NEVER MENTIONED WHAT HAPPENED THE DAY MY COTATI GENES AWAKENED.
"BUT IT WAS YOU... WASN'T IT, MOTHER?
"HOW MANY OTHER MARIONETTES HAVE DANCED ON YOUR STRINGS? DID YOUR PRECIOUS JACQUES REJOIN THE AVENGERS BECAUSE HE WANTED TO OR BECAUSE YOU WANTED HIM TO?
"DID MY FATHER CHOOSE THE SWORDSMAN'S FORM OR WAS IT CHOSEN FOR HIM?"

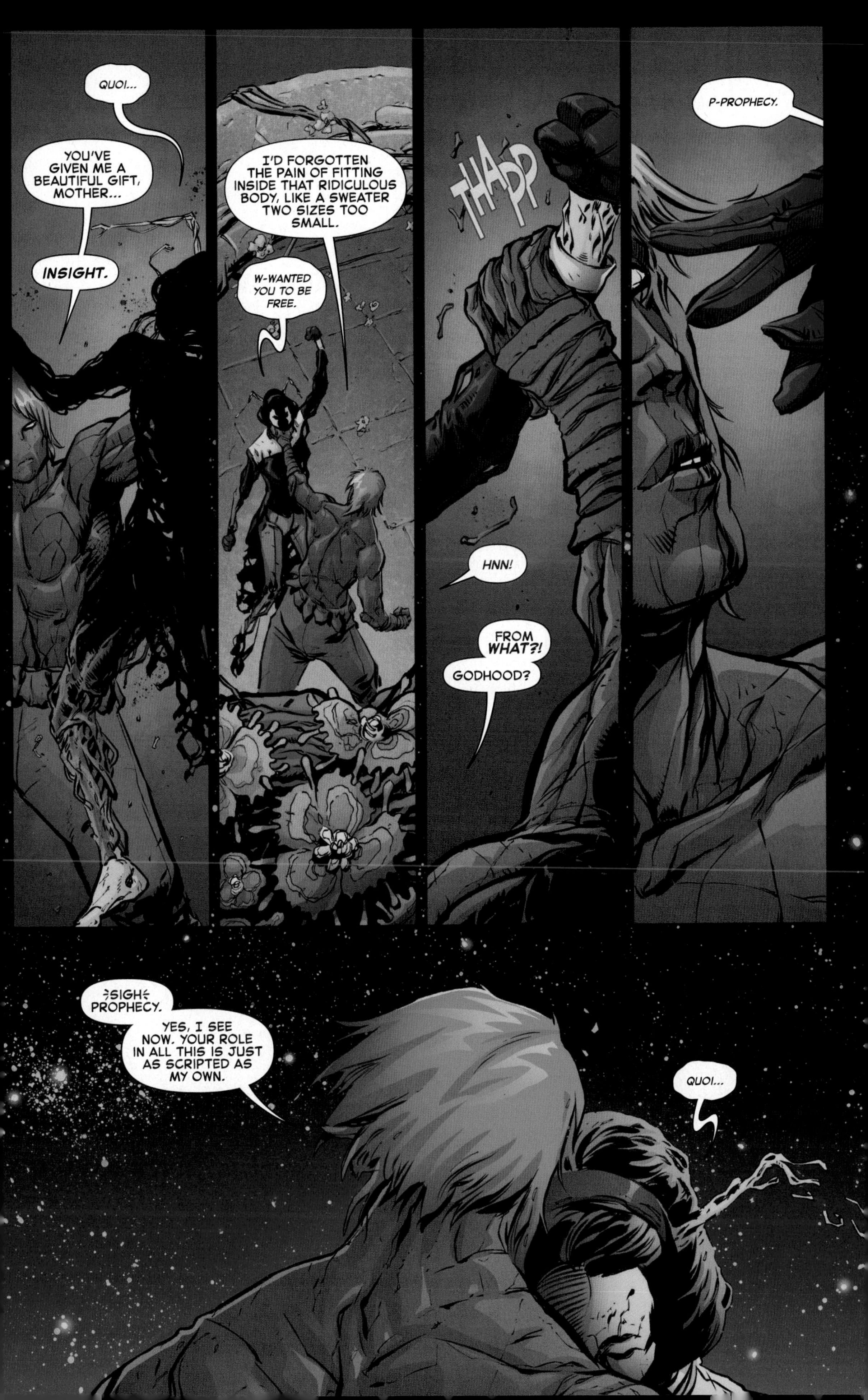
QUOI...
YOU'VE GIVEN ME A BEAUTIFUL GIFT, MOTHER...
INSIGHT.
I'D FORGOTTEN THE PAIN OF FITTING INSIDE THAT RIDICULOUS BODY, LIKE A SWEATER TWO SIZES TOO SMALL.
W-WANTED YOU TO BE FREE.
THAPP
HNN!
FROM WHAT?!
GODHOOD?
P-PROPHECY.
⋟SIGH⋞ PROPHECY.
YES, I SEE NOW. YOUR ROLE IN ALL THIS IS JUST AS SCRIPTED AS MY OWN.
QUOI...

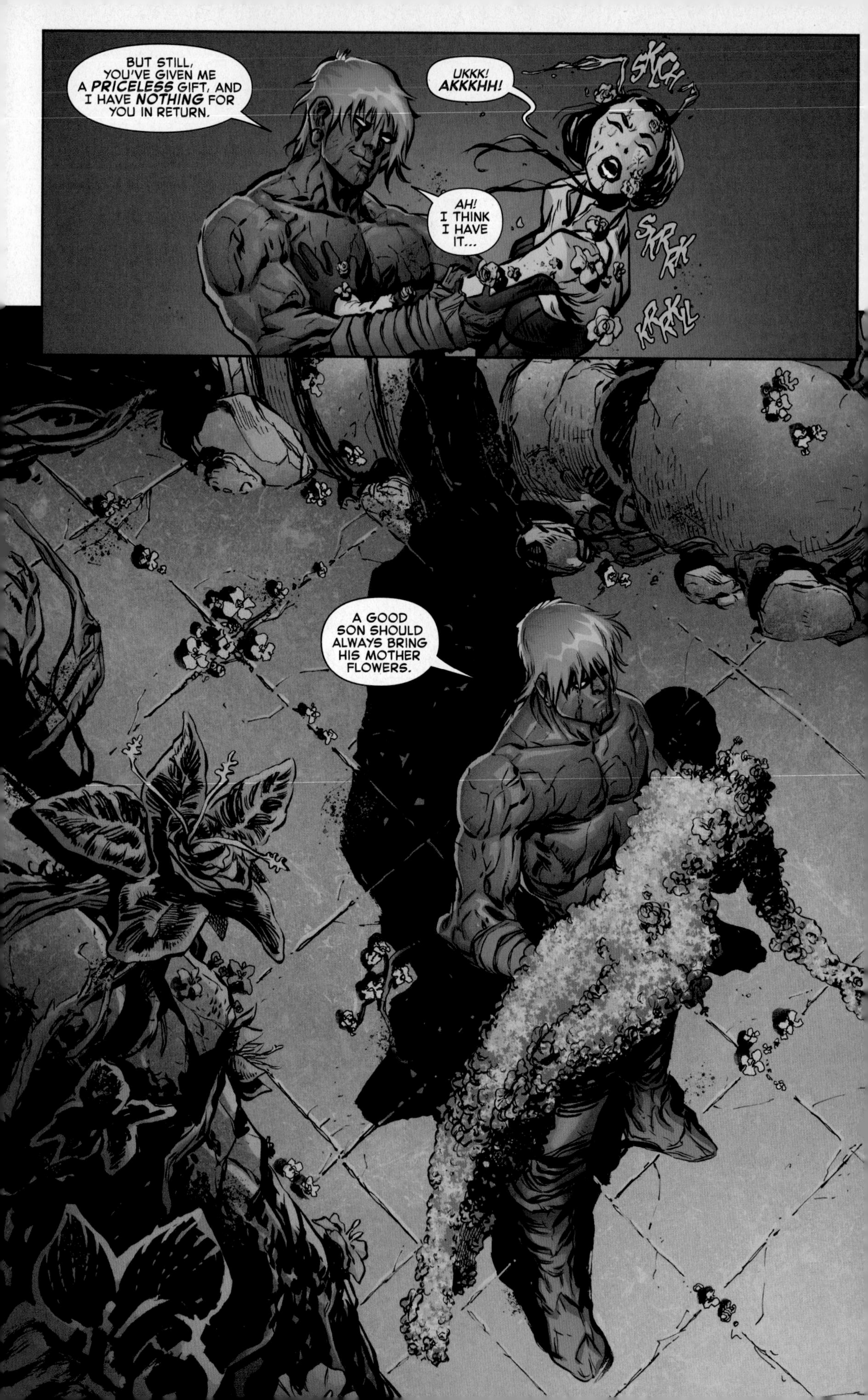
BUT STILL, YOU'VE GIVEN ME A PRICELESS GIFT, AND I HAVE NOTHING FOR YOU IN RETURN.
UKKK! AKKKHH!
SKCH
AH! I THINK I HAVE IT...
SKRRK
KRRKLL
A GOOD SON SHOULD ALWAYS BRING HIS MOTHER FLOWERS.

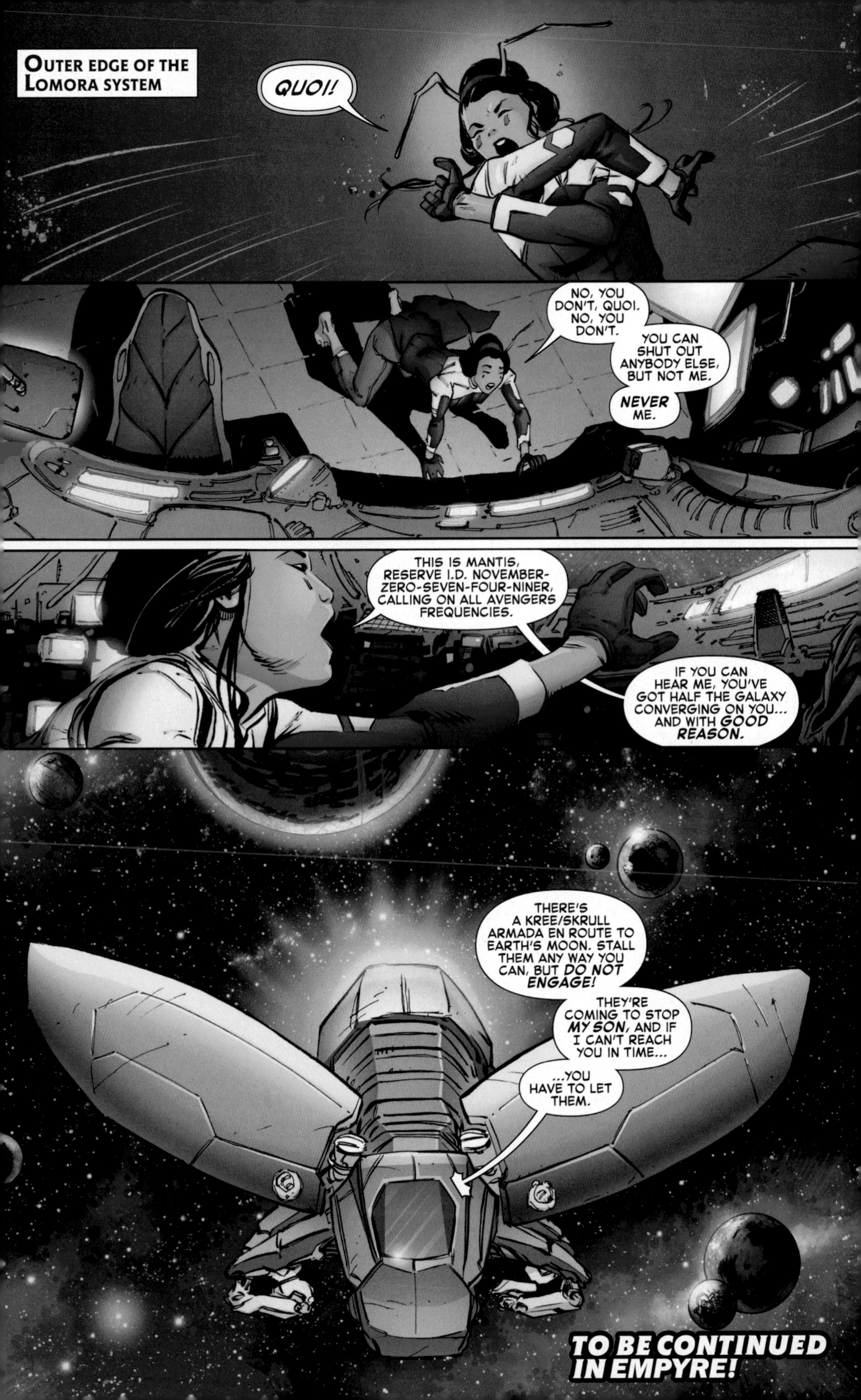

OUTER EDGE OF THE LOMORA SYSTEM
QUOI!
NO, YOU DON'T, QUOI. NO, YOU DON'T.
YOU CAN SHUT OUT ANYBODY ELSE, BUT NOT ME.
NEVER ME.
THIS IS MANTIS, RESERVE I.D. NOVEMBER-ZERO-SEVEN-FOUR-NINER, CALLING ON ALL AVENGERS FREQUENCIES.
IF YOU CAN HEAR ME, YOU'VE GOT HALF THE GALAXY CONVERGING ON YOU... AND WITH GOOD REASON.
THERE'S A KREE/SKRULL ARMADA EN ROUTE TO EARTH'S MOON. STALL THEM ANY WAY YOU CAN, BUT DO NOT ENGAGE!
THEY'RE COMING TO STOP MY SON, AND IF I CAN'T REACH YOU IN TIME...
...YOU HAVE TO LET THEM.
TO BE CONTINUED IN EMPYRE!

LORDS OF EMPYRE: SWORDSMAN

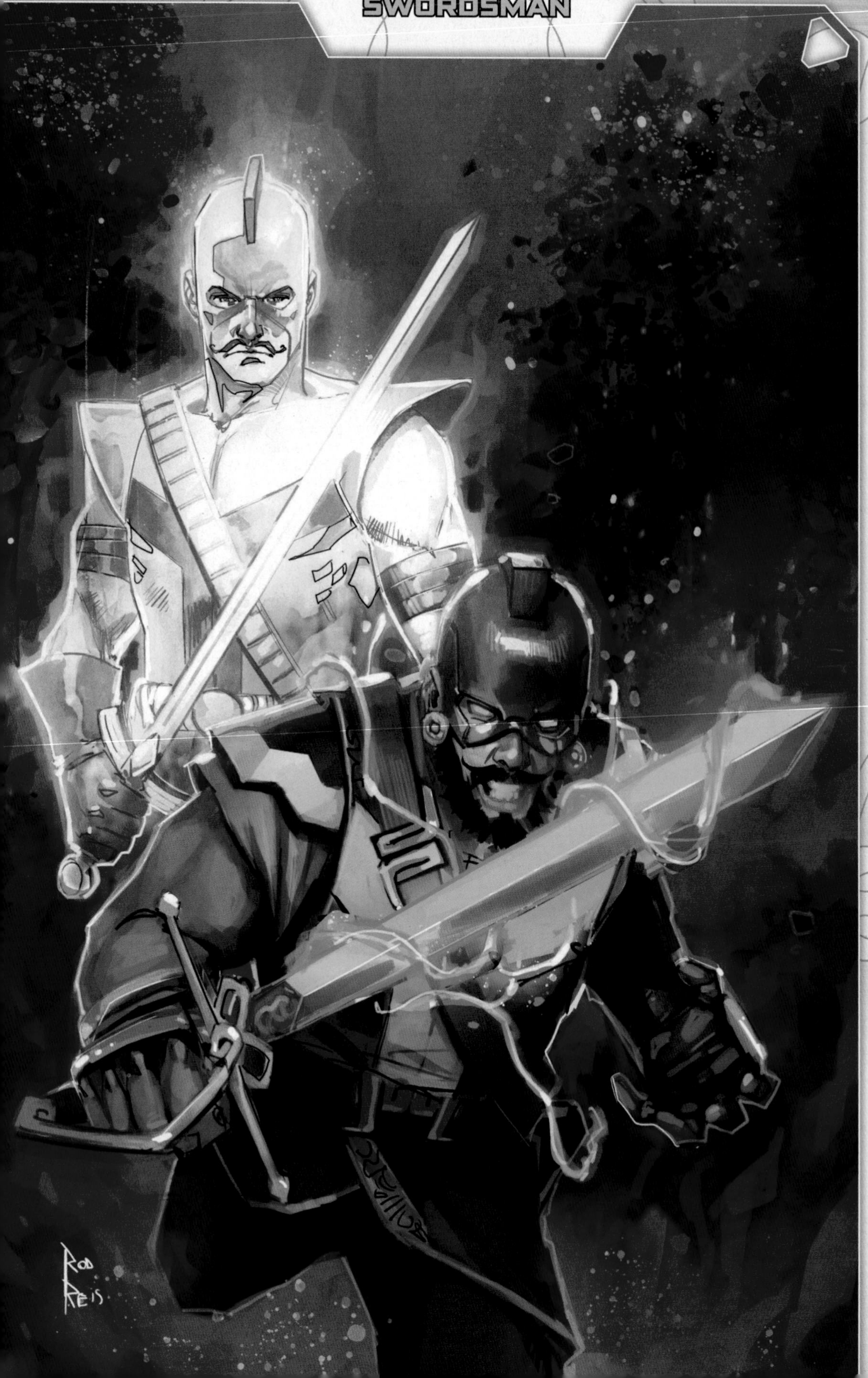
Rod Reis

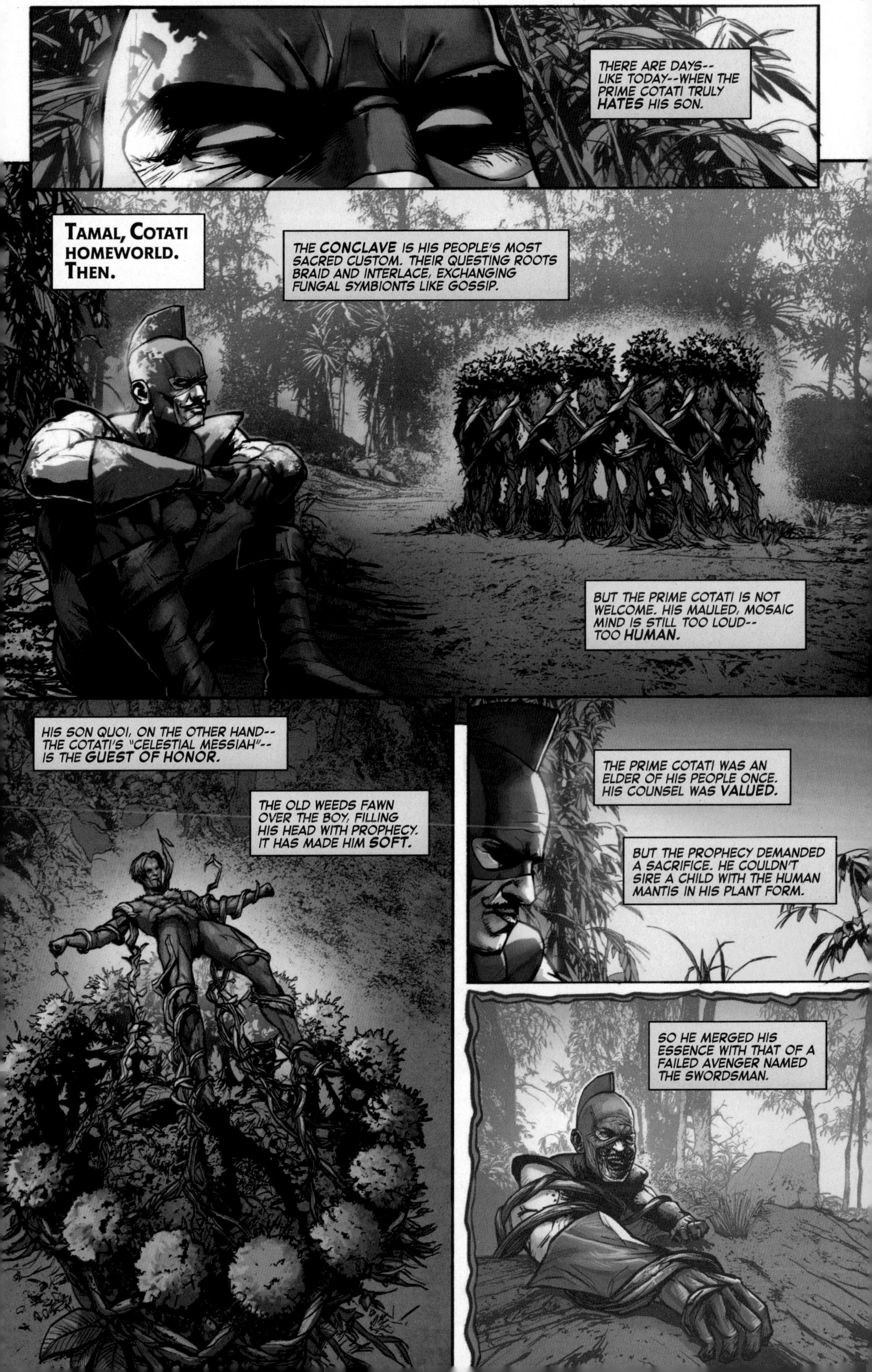
THERE ARE DAYS-- LIKE TODAY--WHEN THE PRIME COTATI TRULY HATES HIS SON.
TAMAL, COTATI HOMEWORLD. THEN.
THE CONCLAVE IS HIS PEOPLE'S MOST SACRED CUSTOM. THEIR QUESTING ROOTS BRAID AND INTERLACE, EXCHANGING FUNGAL SYMBIONTS LIKE GOSSIP.
BUT THE PRIME COTATI IS NOT WELCOME. HIS MAULED, MOSAIC MIND IS STILL TOO LOUD-- TOO HUMAN.
HIS SON QUOI, ON THE OTHER HAND-- THE COTATI'S "CELESTIAL MESSIAH"-- IS THE GUEST OF HONOR.
THE OLD WEEDS FAWN OVER THE BOY, FILLING HIS HEAD WITH PROPHECY. IT HAS MADE HIM SOFT.
THE PRIME COTATI WAS AN ELDER OF HIS PEOPLE ONCE. HIS COUNSEL WAS VALUED.
BUT THE PROPHECY DEMANDED A SACRIFICE. HE COULDN'T SIRE A CHILD WITH THE HUMAN MANTIS IN HIS PLANT FORM.
SO HE MERGED HIS ESSENCE WITH THAT OF A FAILED AVENGER NAMED THE SWORDSMAN.

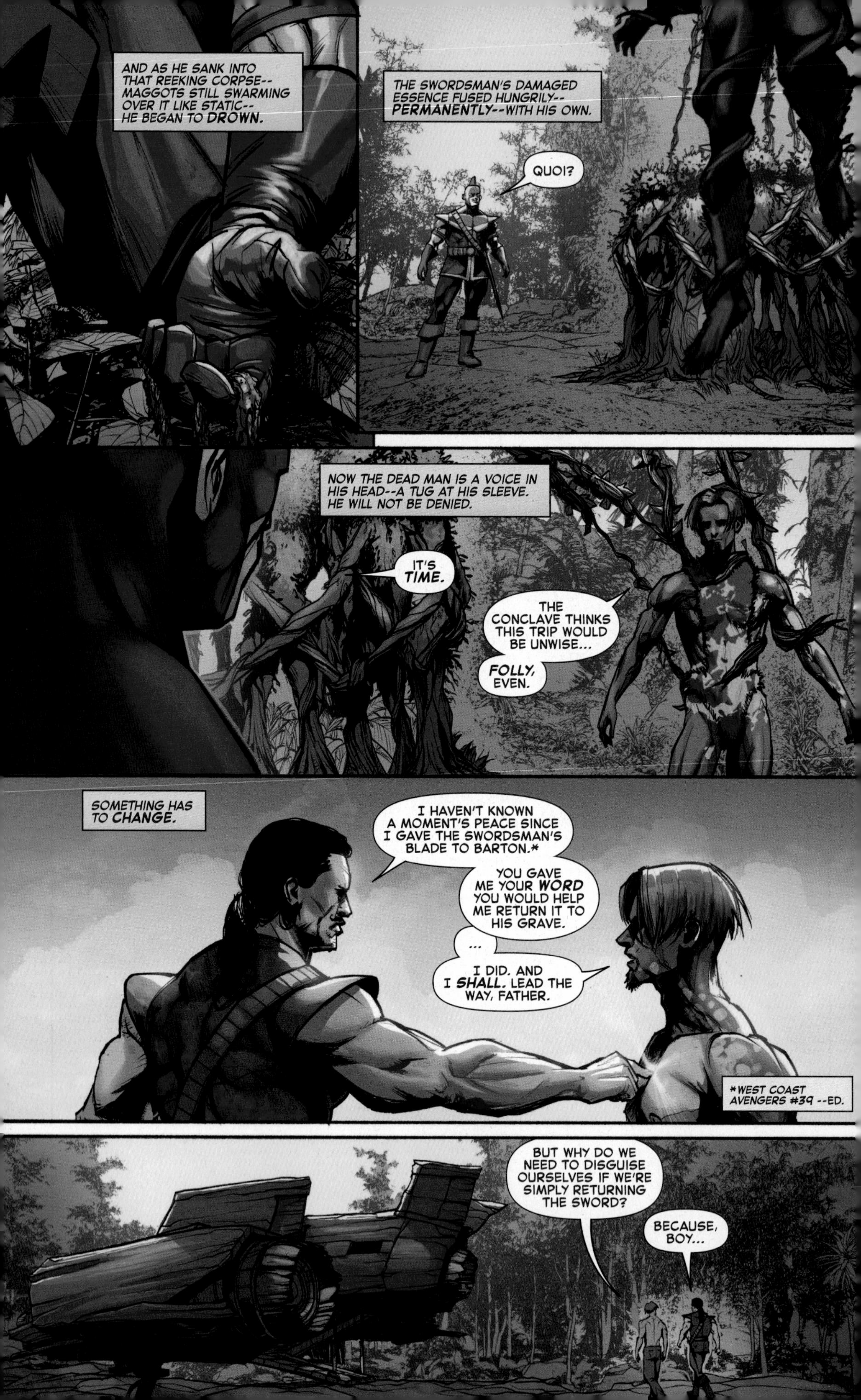

AND AS HE SANK INTO THAT REEKING CORPSE-- MAGGOTS STILL SWARMING OVER IT LIKE STATIC-- HE BEGAN TO DROWN.
THE SWORDSMAN'S DAMAGED ESSENCE FUSED HUNGRILY-- PERMANENTLY--WITH HIS OWN.
QUOI?
NOW THE DEAD MAN IS A VOICE IN HIS HEAD--A TUG AT HIS SLEEVE. HE WILL NOT BE DENIED.
IT'S TIME.
THE CONCLAVE THINKS THIS TRIP WOULD BE UNWISE...
FOLLY, EVEN.
SOMETHING HAS TO CHANGE.
I HAVEN'T KNOWN A MOMENT'S PEACE SINCE I GAVE THE SWORDSMAN'S BLADE TO BARTON.*
YOU GAVE ME YOUR WORD YOU WOULD HELP ME RETURN IT TO HIS GRAVE.
...
I DID. AND I SHALL. LEAD THE WAY, FATHER.
*WEST COAST AVENGERS #39 --ED.
BUT WHY DO WE NEED TO DISGUISE OURSELVES IF WE'RE SIMPLY RETURNING THE SWORD?
BECAUSE, BOY...

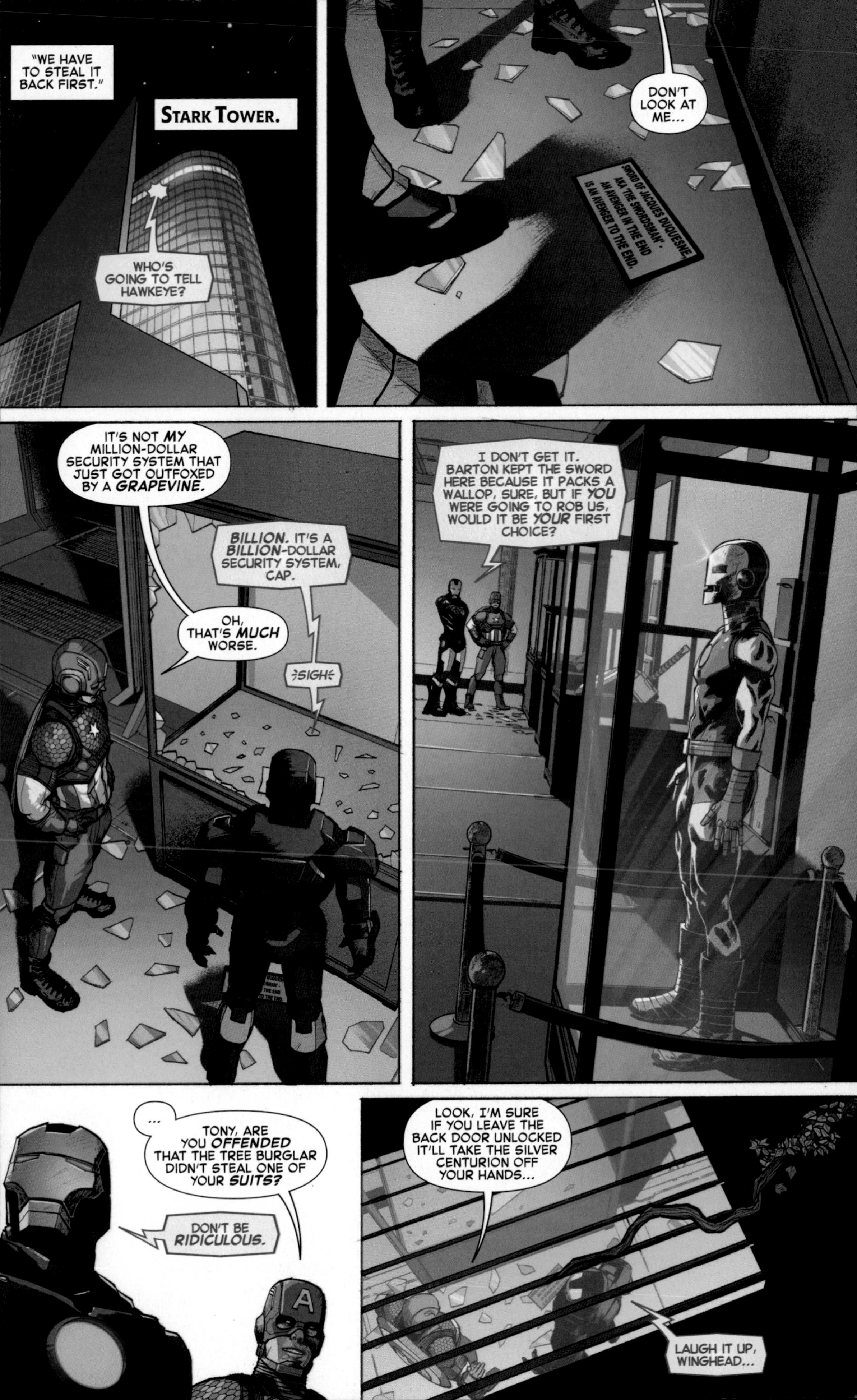
"WE HAVE TO STEAL IT BACK FIRST."
STARK TOWER.
WHO'S GOING TO TELL HAWKEYE?
DON'T LOOK AT ME...
SWORD OF JACQUES DUQUESNE, AKA 'THE SWORDSMAN'. AN AVENGER IN THE END IS AN AVENGER TO THE END.
IT'S NOT MY MILLION-DOLLAR SECURITY SYSTEM THAT JUST GOT OUTFOXED BY A GRAPEVINE.
BILLION. IT'S A BILLION-DOLLAR SECURITY SYSTEM, CAP.
OH, THAT'S MUCH WORSE.
SIGH
I DON'T GET IT. BARTON KEPT THE SWORD HERE BECAUSE IT PACKS A WALLOP, SURE, BUT IF YOU WERE GOING TO ROB US, WOULD IT BE YOUR FIRST CHOICE?
... TONY, ARE YOU OFFENDED THAT THE TREE BURGLAR DIDN'T STEAL ONE OF YOUR SUITS?
DON'T BE RIDICULOUS.
LOOK, I'M SURE IF YOU LEAVE THE BACK DOOR UNLOCKED IT'LL TAKE THE SILVER CENTURION OFF YOUR HANDS...
LAUGH IT UP, WINGHEAD...

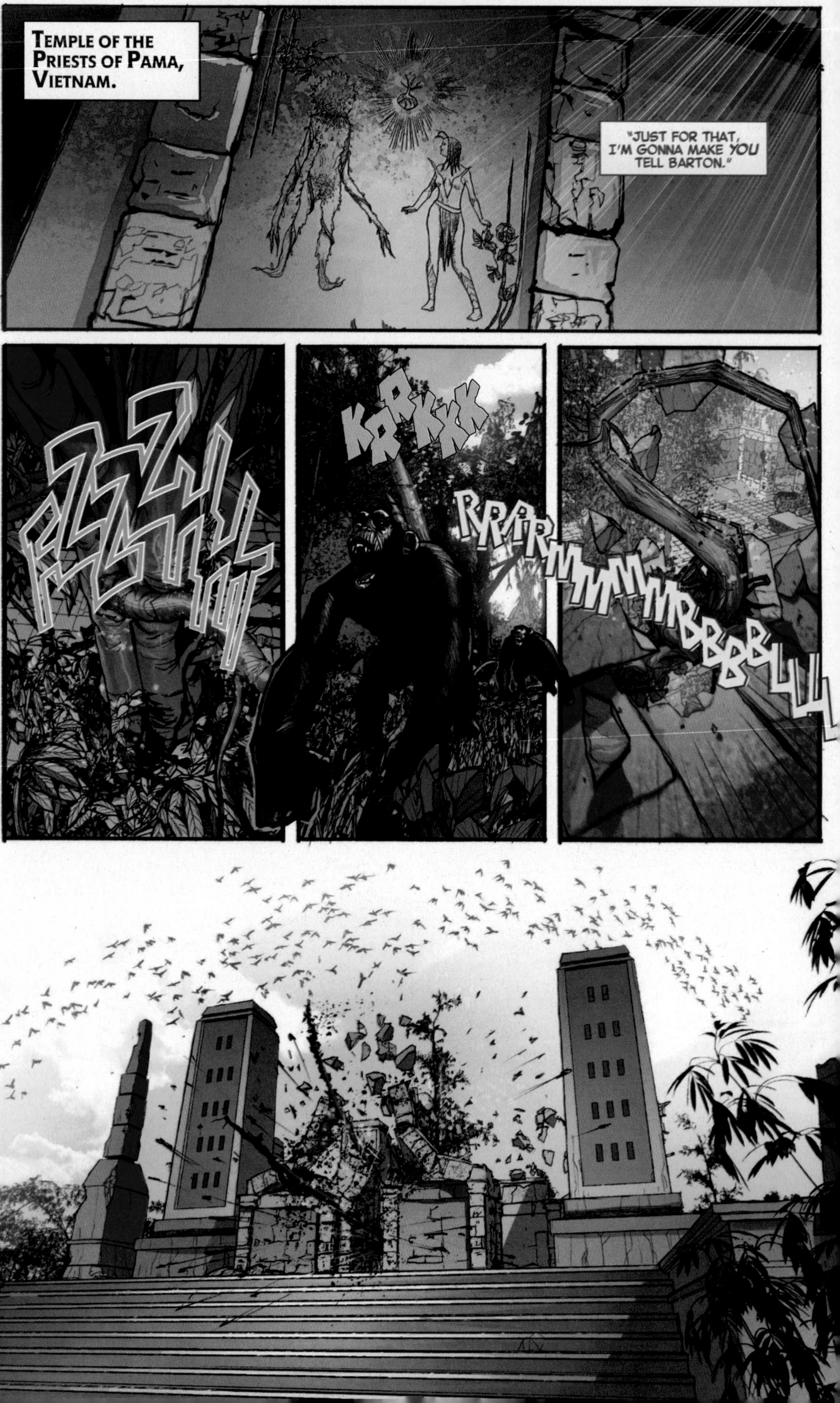
TEMPLE OF THE PRIESTS OF PAMA, VIETNAM.
"JUST FOR THAT, I'M GONNA MAKE YOU TELL BARTON."

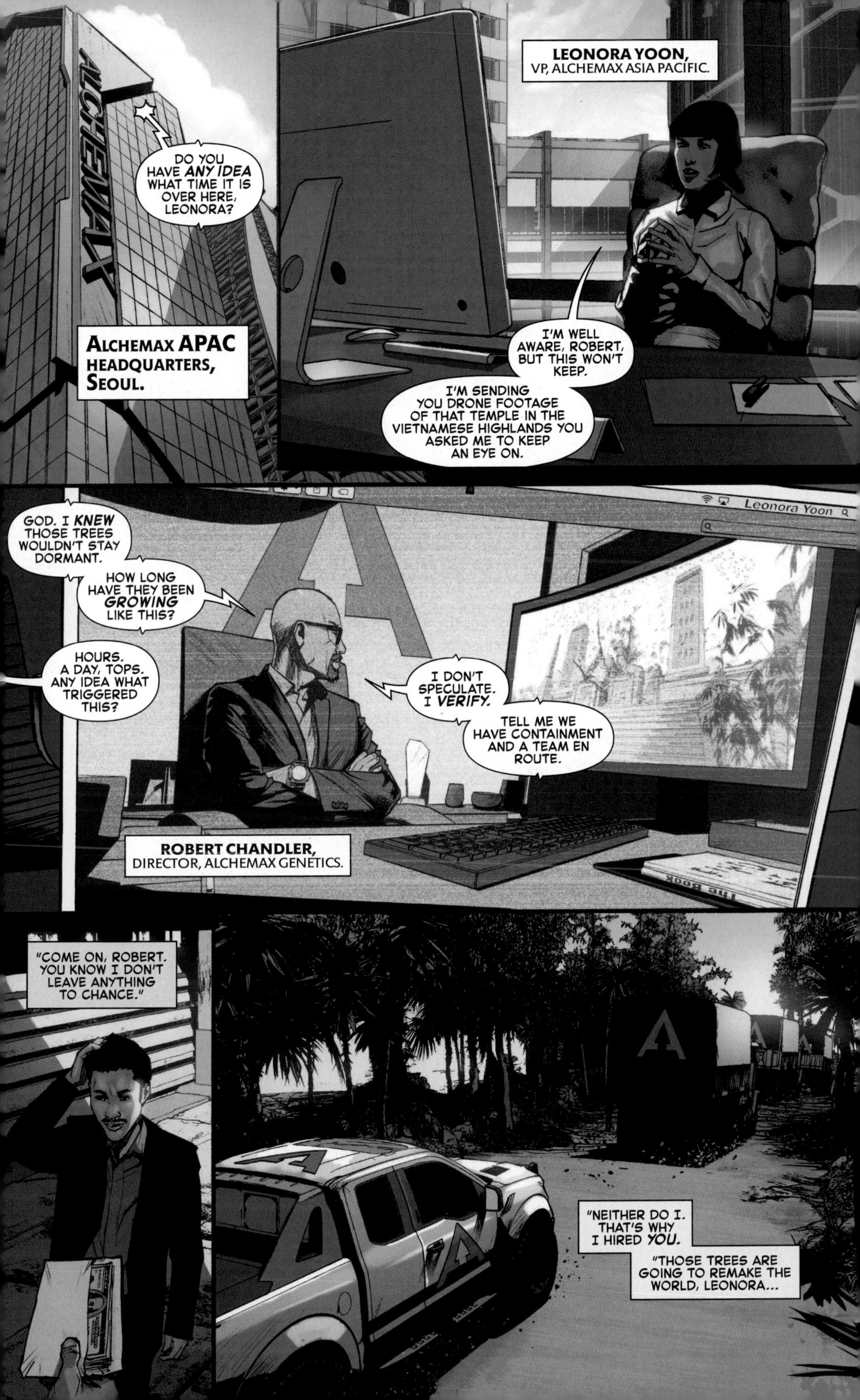
DO YOU HAVE ANY IDEA WHAT TIME IT IS OVER HERE, LEONORA?
ALCHEMAX APAC HEADQUARTERS, SEOUL.
LEONORA YOON, VP, ALCHEMAX ASIA PACIFIC.
I'M WELL AWARE, ROBERT, BUT THIS WON'T KEEP.
I'M SENDING YOU DRONE FOOTAGE OF THAT TEMPLE IN THE VIETNAMESE HIGHLANDS YOU ASKED ME TO KEEP AN EYE ON.
Leonora Yoon
GOD. I KNEW THOSE TREES WOULDN'T STAY DORMANT.
HOW LONG HAVE THEY BEEN GROWING LIKE THIS?
HOURS. A DAY, TOPS. ANY IDEA WHAT TRIGGERED THIS?
I DON'T SPECULATE. I VERIFY.
TELL ME WE HAVE CONTAINMENT AND A TEAM EN ROUTE.
ROBERT CHANDLER, DIRECTOR, ALCHEMAX GENETICS.
"COME ON, ROBERT. YOU KNOW I DON'T LEAVE ANYTHING TO CHANCE."
"NEITHER DO I. THAT'S WHY I HIRED YOU.
"THOSE TREES ARE GOING TO REMAKE THE WORLD, LEONORA...

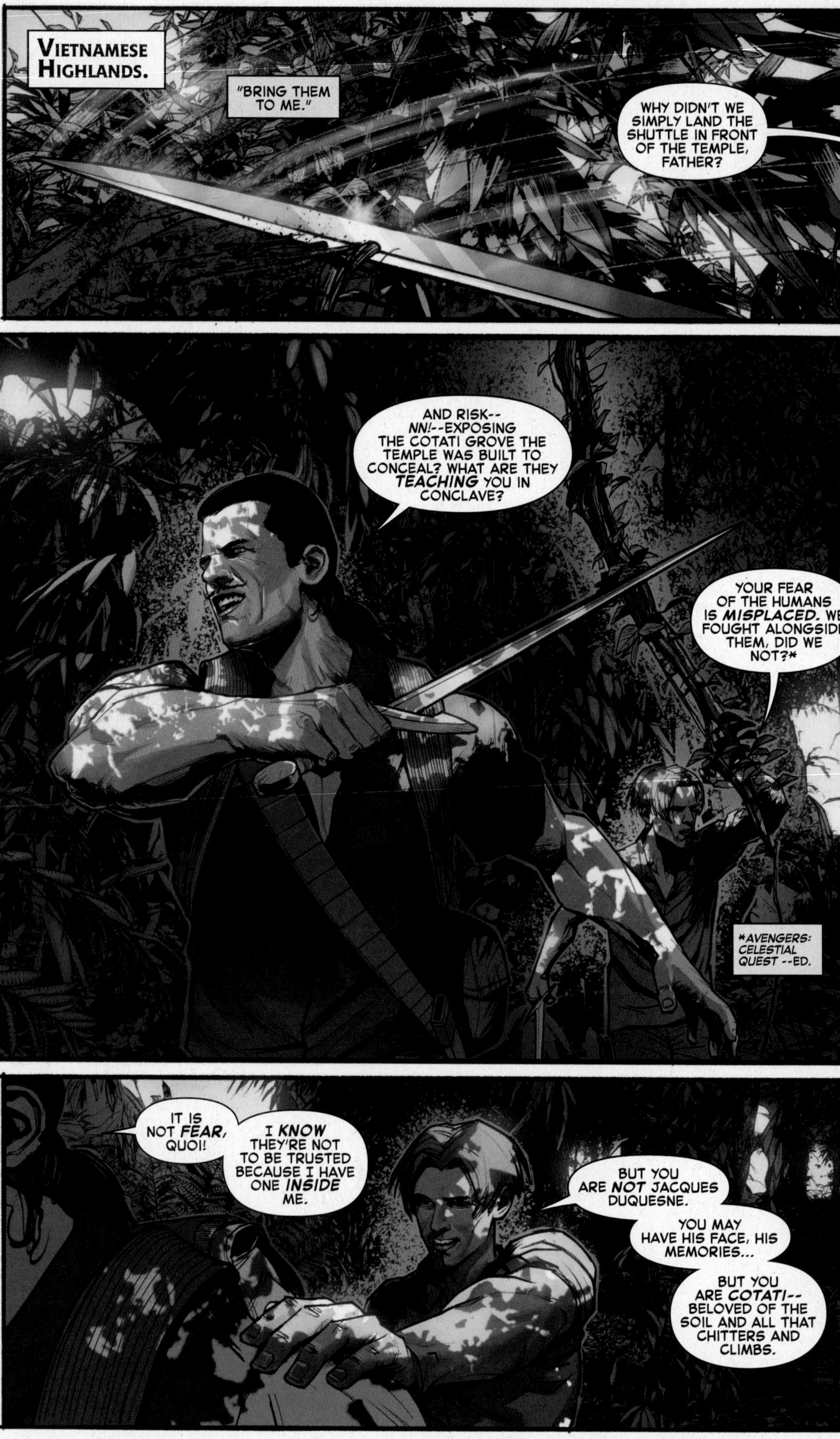
VIETNAMESE HIGHLANDS.
"BRING THEM TO ME."
WHY DIDN'T WE SIMPLY LAND THE SHUTTLE IN FRONT OF THE TEMPLE, FATHER?
AND RISK-- NN!--EXPOSING THE COTATI GROVE THE TEMPLE WAS BUILT TO CONCEAL? WHAT ARE THEY TEACHING YOU IN CONCLAVE?
YOUR FEAR OF THE HUMANS IS MISPLACED. WE FOUGHT ALONGSIDE THEM, DID WE NOT?*
*AVENGERS: CELESTIAL QUEST --ED.
IT IS NOT FEAR, QUOI!
I KNOW THEY'RE NOT TO BE TRUSTED BECAUSE I HAVE ONE INSIDE ME.
BUT YOU ARE NOT JACQUES DUQUESNE.
YOU MAY HAVE HIS FACE, HIS MEMORIES...
BUT YOU ARE COTATI-- BELOVED OF THE SOIL AND ALL THAT CHITTERS AND CLIMBS.

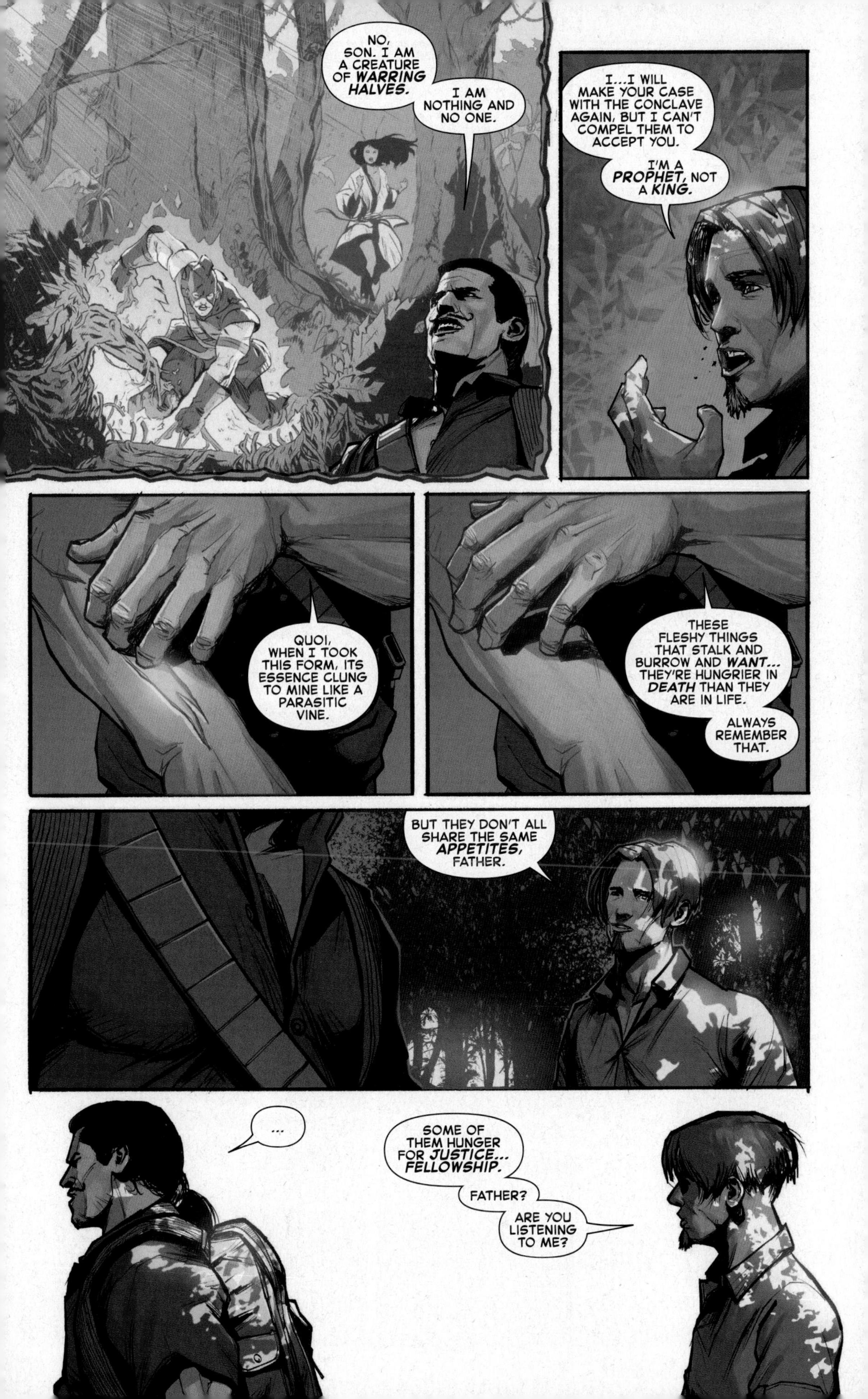
NO, SON. I AM A CREATURE OF WARRING HALVES.
I AM NOTHING AND NO ONE.
I...I WILL MAKE YOUR CASE WITH THE CONCLAVE AGAIN, BUT I CAN'T COMPEL THEM TO ACCEPT YOU.
I'M A PROPHET, NOT A KING.
QUOI, WHEN I TOOK THIS FORM, ITS ESSENCE CLUNG TO MINE LIKE A PARASITIC VINE.
THESE FLESHY THINGS THAT STALK AND BURROW AND WANT... THEY'RE HUNGRIER IN DEATH THAN THEY ARE IN LIFE.
ALWAYS REMEMBER THAT.
BUT THEY DON'T ALL SHARE THE SAME APPETITES, FATHER.
...
SOME OF THEM HUNGER FOR JUSTICE... FELLOWSHIP.
FATHER?
ARE YOU LISTENING TO ME?

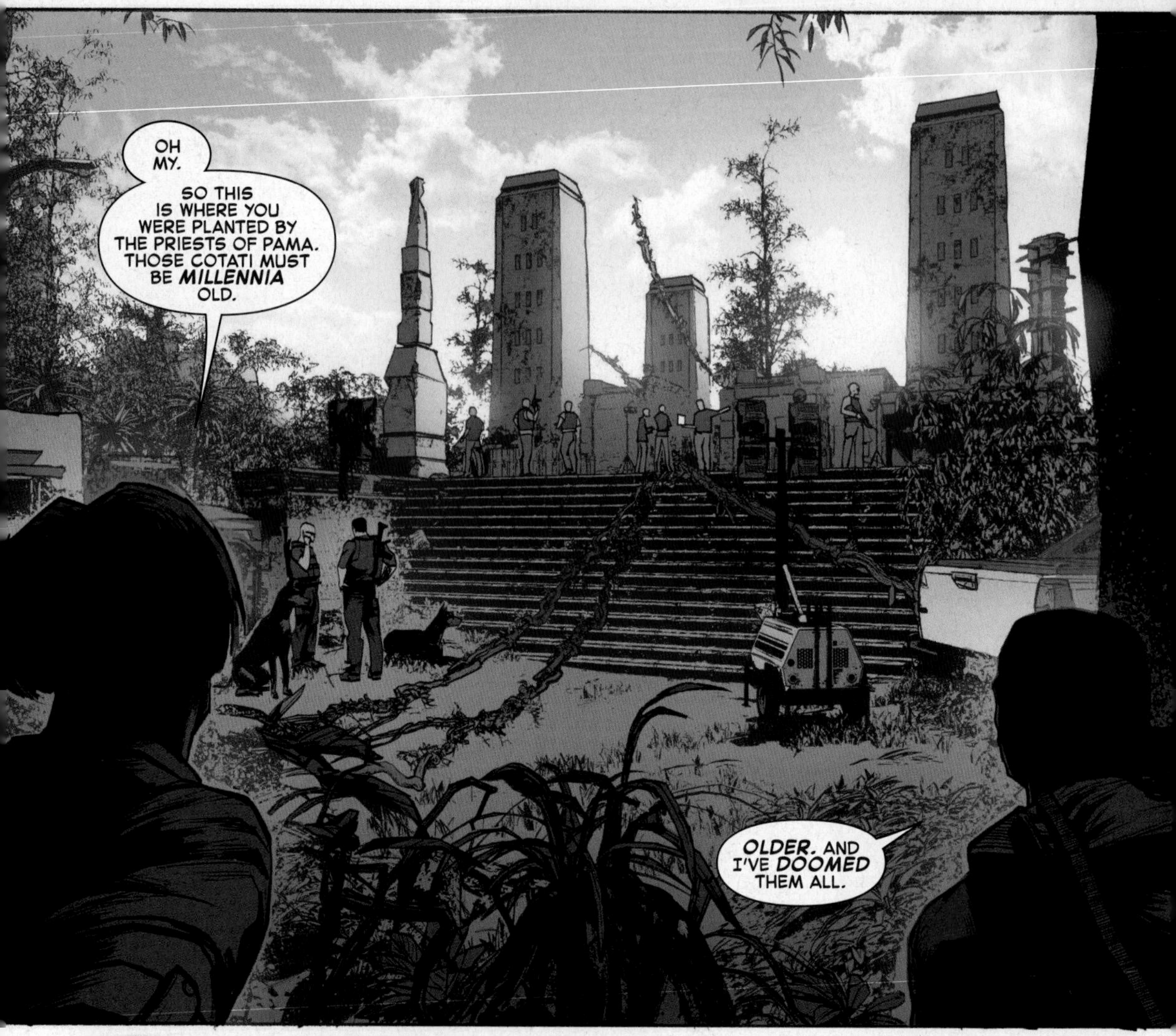
OH MY.
SO THIS IS WHERE YOU WERE PLANTED BY THE PRIESTS OF PAMA. THOSE COTATI MUST BE *MILLENNIA* OLD.
OLDER. AND I'VE *DOOMED* THEM ALL.

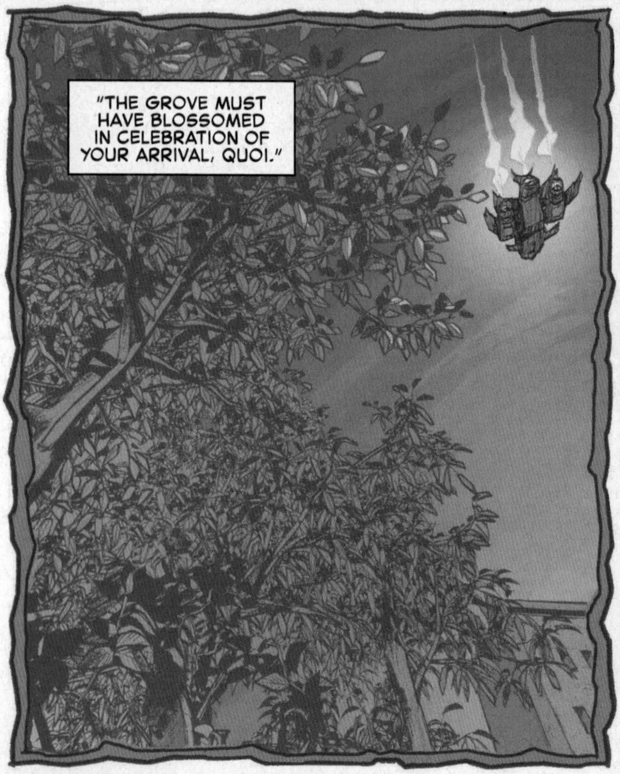
"THE GROVE MUST HAVE BLOSSOMED IN CELEBRATION OF YOUR ARRIVAL, QUOI."

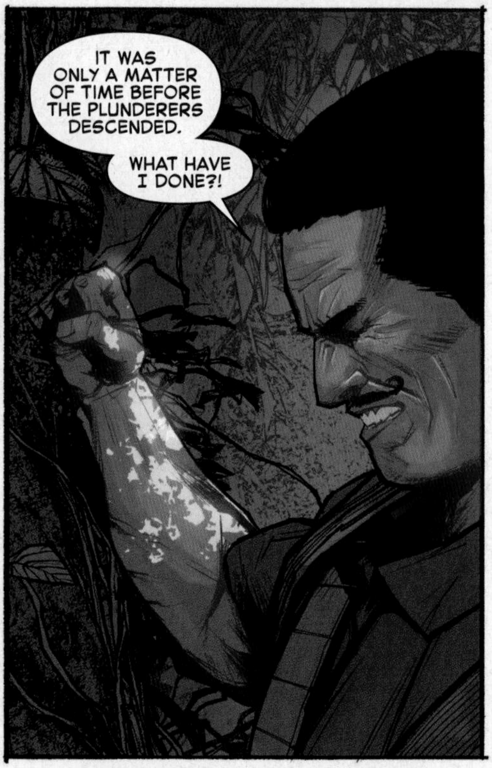
IT WAS ONLY A MATTER OF TIME BEFORE THE PLUNDERERS DESCENDED.
WHAT HAVE I DONE?!

QUOI, WHAT ARE YOU *DOING?!*

EXPLAINING THE SITUATION.

WAIT! YOU DON'T UNDERSTAND!

REASON IS A *UNIVERSAL LANGUAGE,* FATHER...

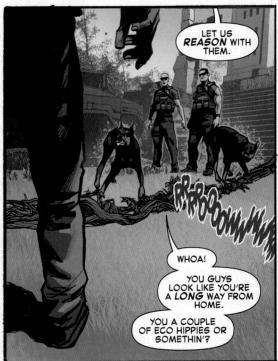

LET US *REASON* WITH THEM.

RR-RROOOWWWWWW

WHOA! YOU GUYS LOOK LIKE YOU'RE A *LONG* WAY FROM HOME.

YOU A COUPLE OF ECO HIPPIES OR SOMETHIN'?

ECO HIPPIES. YES. EXACTLY.

MAY I ASK WHAT YOUR INTENTIONS ARE REGARDING THESE... *TREES?*

QUOI, *DON'T...*

WE'RE CUTTING 'EM DOWN, KID.

WE GOT PERMITS, SO DON'T EVEN *THINK* ABOUT PROTESTING.

GENTLEMEN, THESE "TREES" HAVE CALCIUM-BASED NERVOUS SYSTEMS. THEY FEEL *PAIN.*

YOU *MUSTN'T* HARM THEM!

ALL RIGHT, THAT'S ENOUGH.

NNFFF!

YOU WANNA TALK ABOUT *PAIN,* KID? WE CAN TALK ABOUT IT *ALL DAY* IF YOU WANT.

WAIT...YOU DON'T KNOW WHAT YOU'RE DOING!

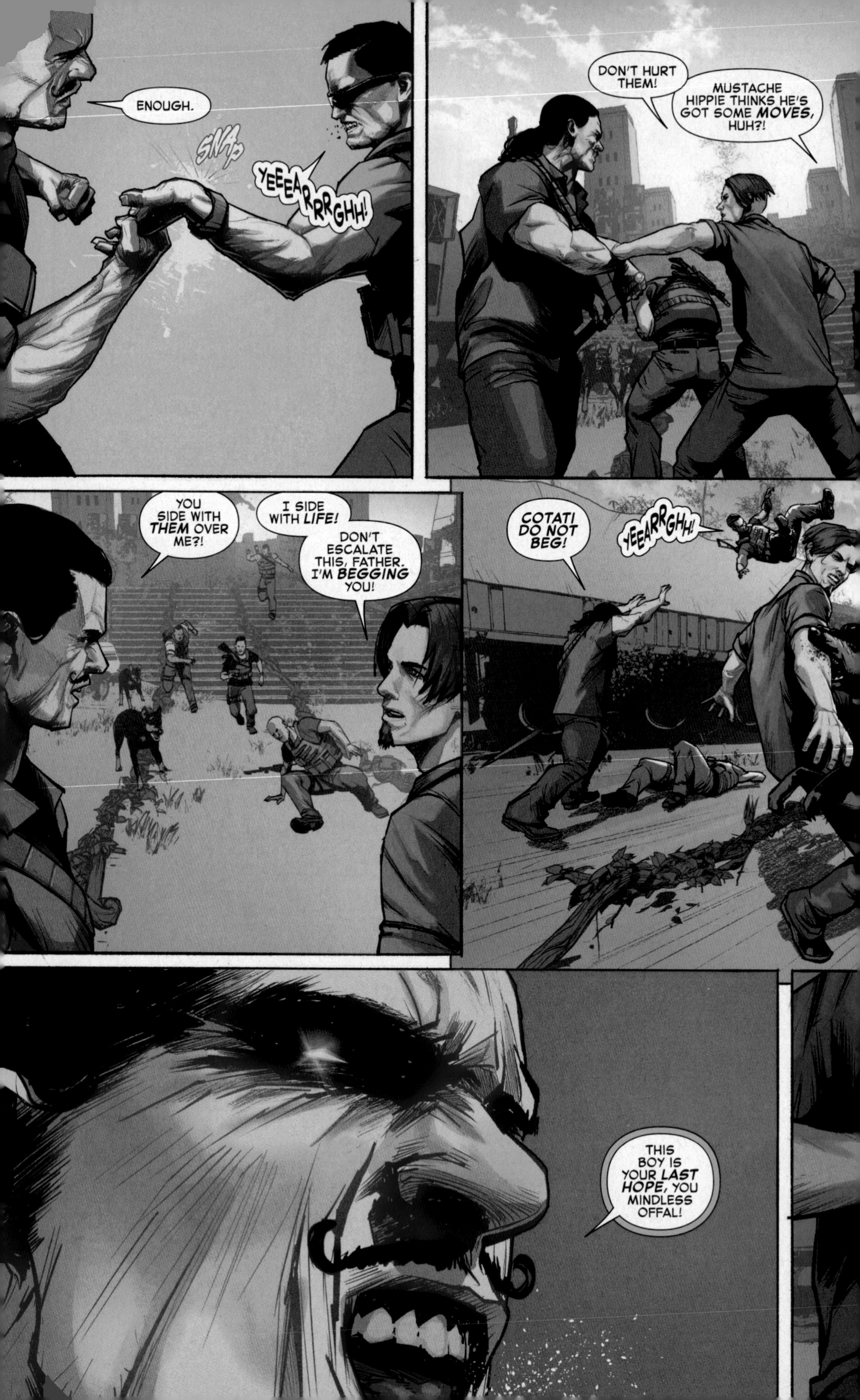
ENOUGH.
SNAP
YEEEEARRRGHH!
DON'T HURT THEM!
MUSTACHE HIPPIE THINKS HE'S GOT SOME MOVES, HUH?!
YOU SIDE WITH THEM OVER ME?!
I SIDE WITH LIFE!
DON'T ESCALATE THIS, FATHER. I'M BEGGING YOU!
COTATI DO NOT BEG!
YEEARRGHH!
THIS BOY IS YOUR LAST HOPE, YOU MINDLESS OFFAL!

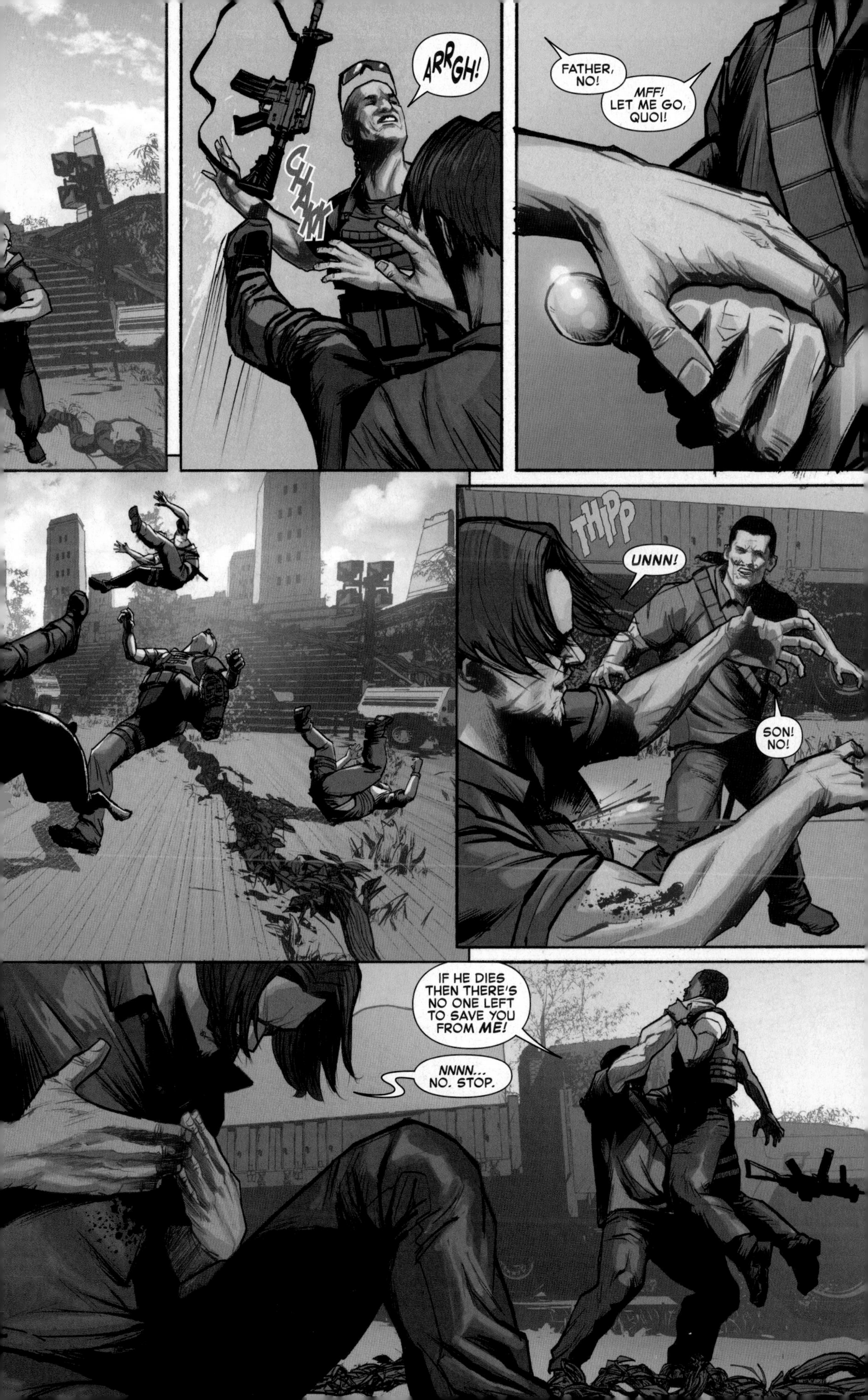
ARRGH!
CHAKK
FATHER, NO!
MFF! LET ME GO, QUOI!
THIPP
UNNN!
SON! NO!
IF HE DIES THEN THERE'S NO ONE LEFT TO SAVE YOU FROM ME!
NNNN... NO. STOP.

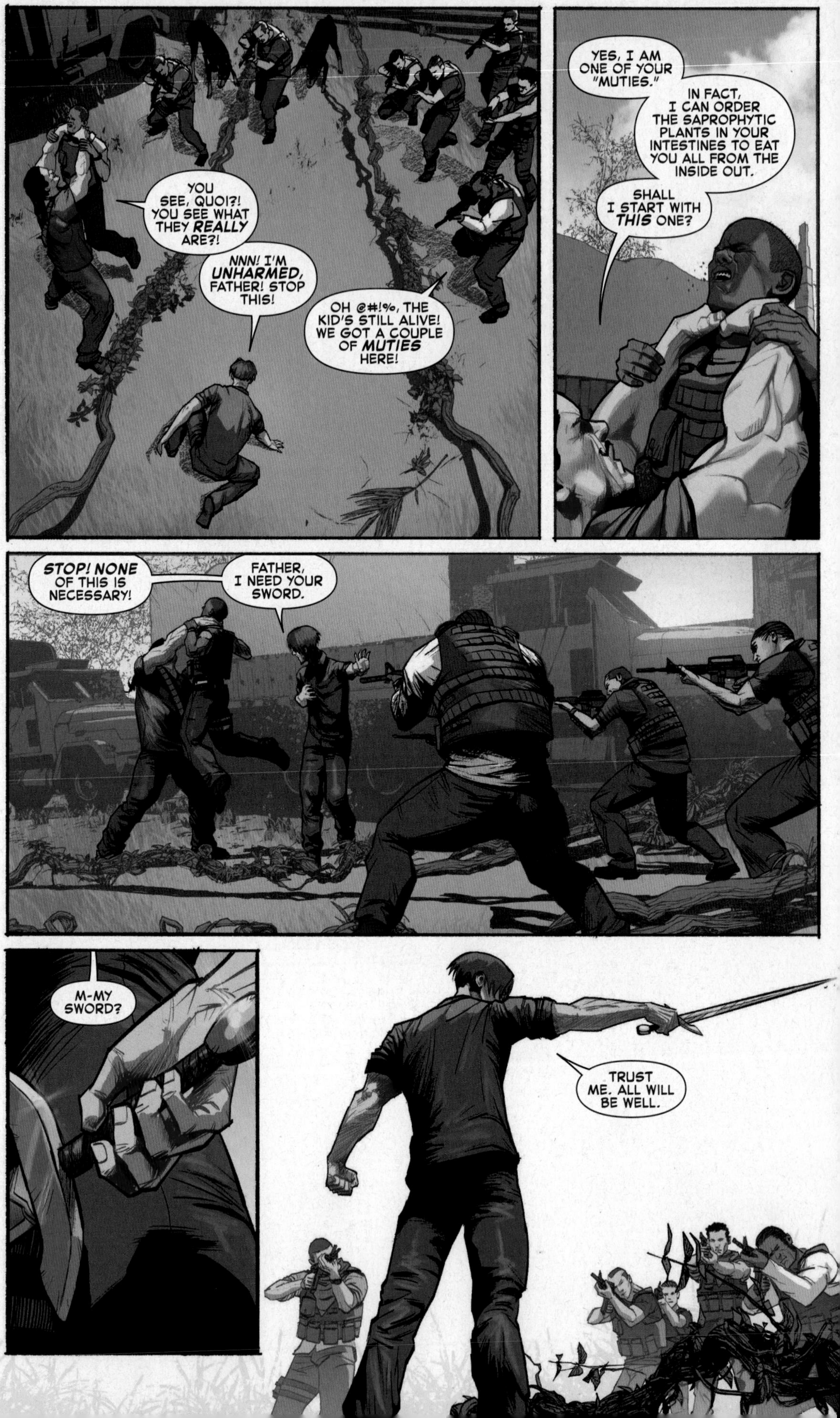
YOU SEE, QUOI?! YOU SEE WHAT THEY REALLY ARE?!
NNN! I'M UNHARMED, FATHER! STOP THIS!
OH @#!%, THE KID'S STILL ALIVE! WE GOT A COUPLE OF MUTIES HERE!
YES, I AM ONE OF YOUR "MUTIES."
IN FACT, I CAN ORDER THE SAPROPHYTIC PLANTS IN YOUR INTESTINES TO EAT YOU ALL FROM THE INSIDE OUT.
SHALL I START WITH THIS ONE?
STOP! NONE OF THIS IS NECESSARY!
FATHER, I NEED YOUR SWORD.
M-MY SWORD?
TRUST ME. ALL WILL BE WELL.

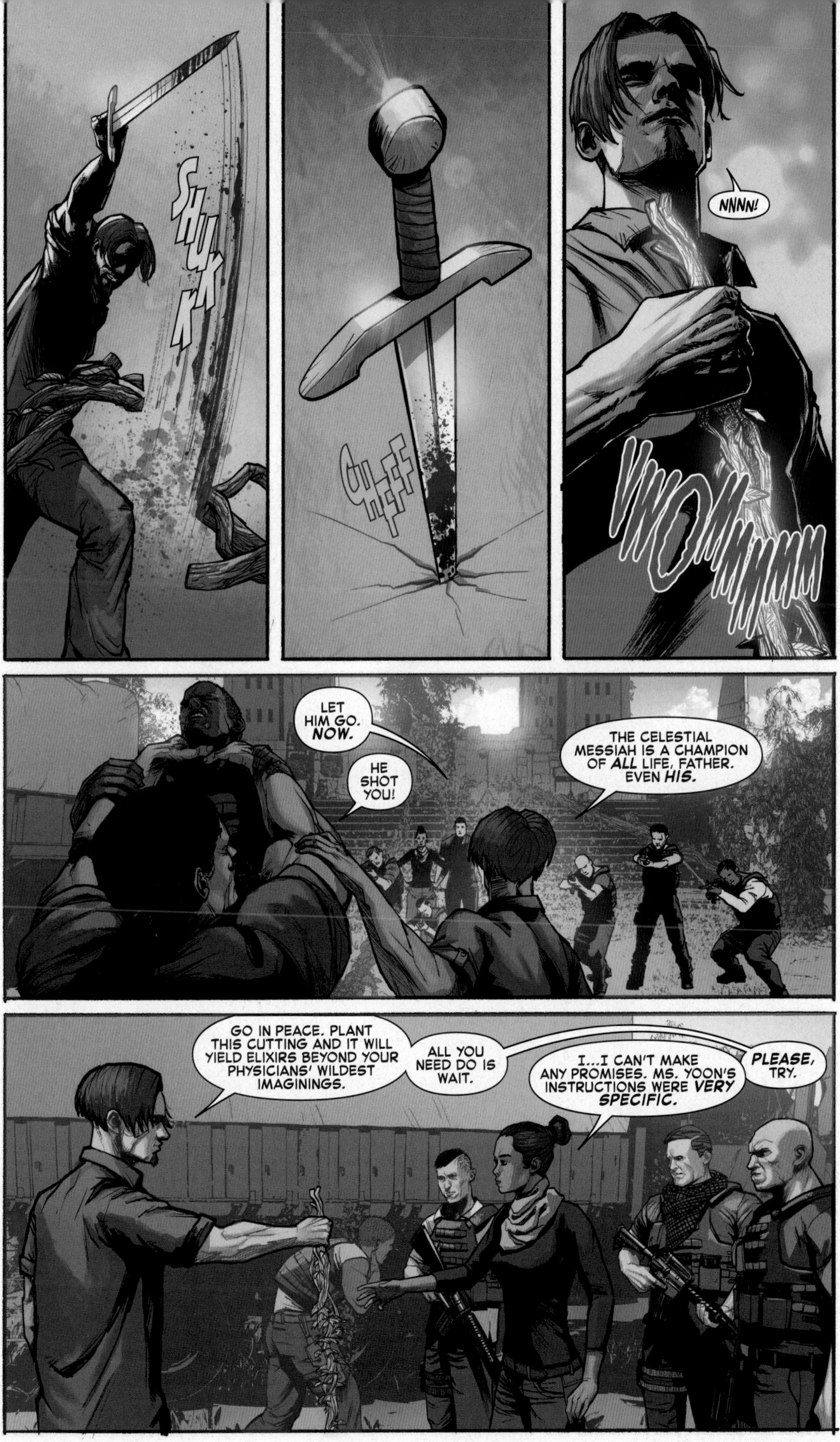
SHUKKK
CHFF
NNNN!
VWOMMMMMM
LET HIM GO. NOW.
HE SHOT YOU!
THE CELESTIAL MESSIAH IS A CHAMPION OF ALL LIFE, FATHER. EVEN HIS.
GO IN PEACE. PLANT THIS CUTTING AND IT WILL YIELD ELIXIRS BEYOND YOUR PHYSICIANS' WILDEST IMAGININGS.
ALL YOU NEED DO IS WAIT.
I...I CAN'T MAKE ANY PROMISES. MS. YOON'S INSTRUCTIONS WERE VERY SPECIFIC.
PLEASE, TRY.

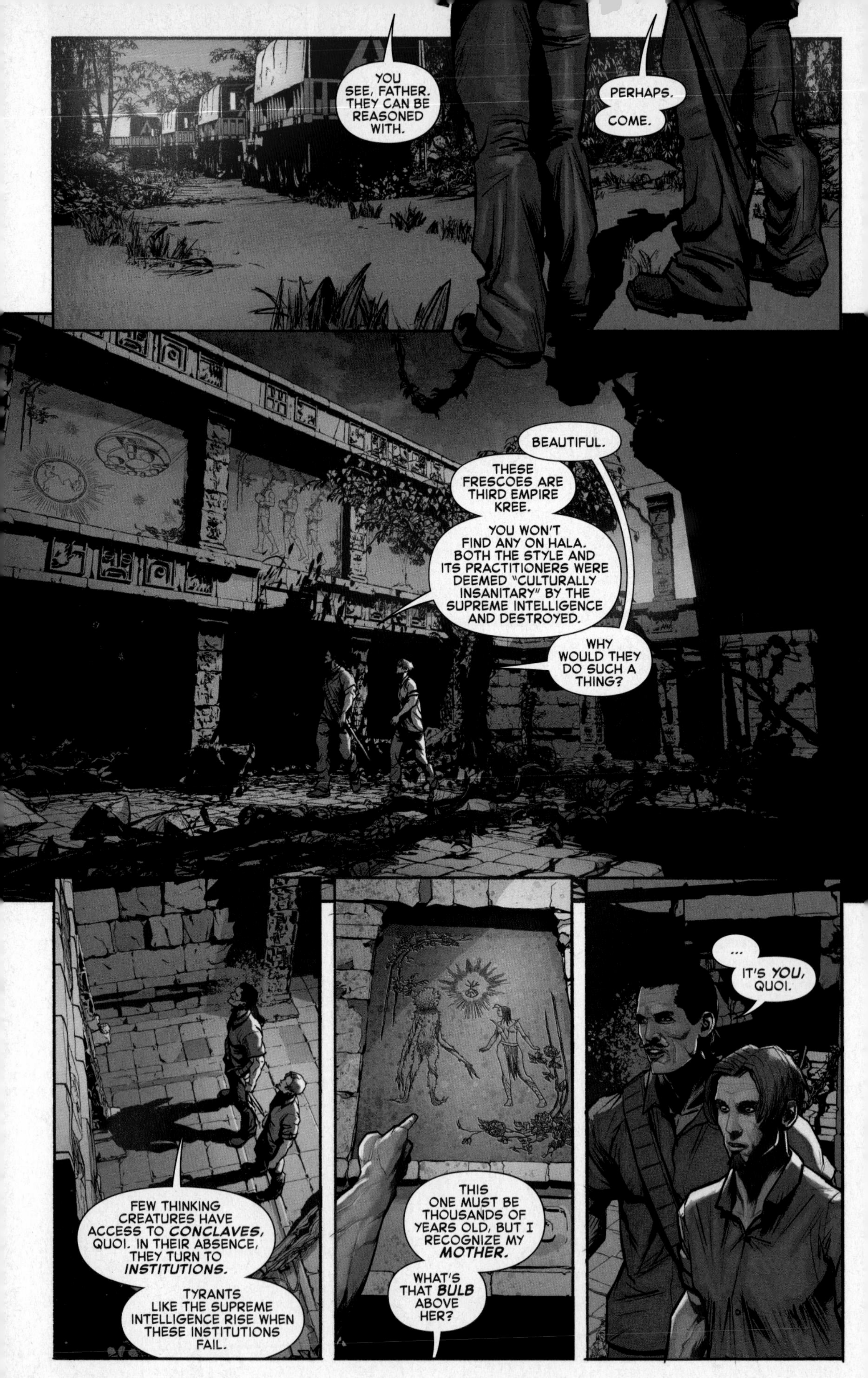
YOU SEE, FATHER. THEY CAN BE REASONED WITH.
PERHAPS.
COME.
BEAUTIFUL.
THESE FRESCOES ARE THIRD EMPIRE KREE.
YOU WON'T FIND ANY ON HALA. BOTH THE STYLE AND ITS PRACTITIONERS WERE DEEMED "CULTURALLY INSANITARY" BY THE SUPREME INTELLIGENCE AND DESTROYED.
WHY WOULD THEY DO SUCH A THING?
FEW THINKING CREATURES HAVE ACCESS TO *CONCLAVES*, QUOI. IN THEIR ABSENCE, THEY TURN TO *INSTITUTIONS.*
TYRANTS LIKE THE SUPREME INTELLIGENCE RISE WHEN THESE INSTITUTIONS FAIL.
THIS ONE MUST BE THOUSANDS OF YEARS OLD, BUT I RECOGNIZE MY *MOTHER.*
WHAT'S THAT *BULB* ABOVE HER?
...
IT'S *YOU*, QUOI.

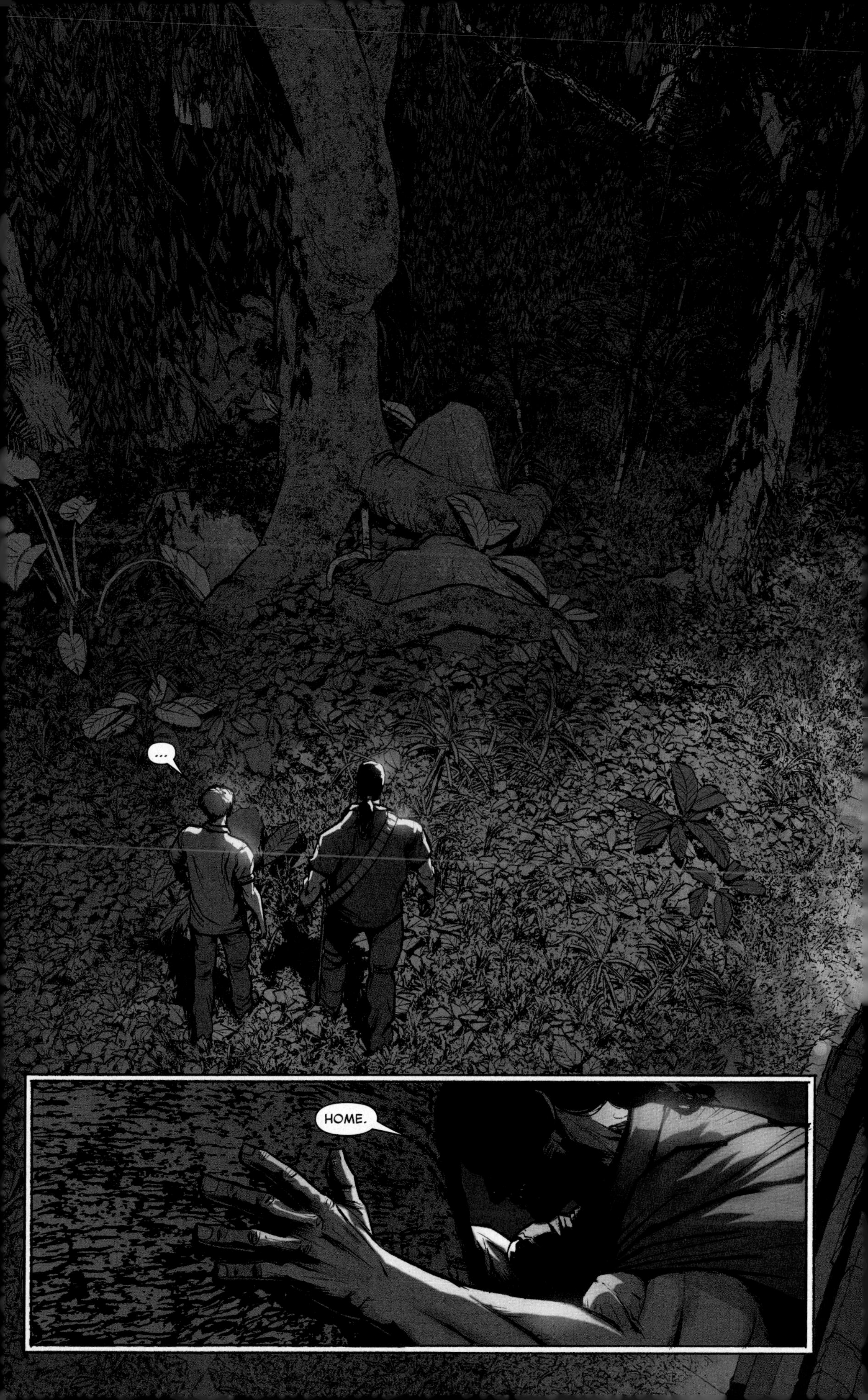
...
HOME.

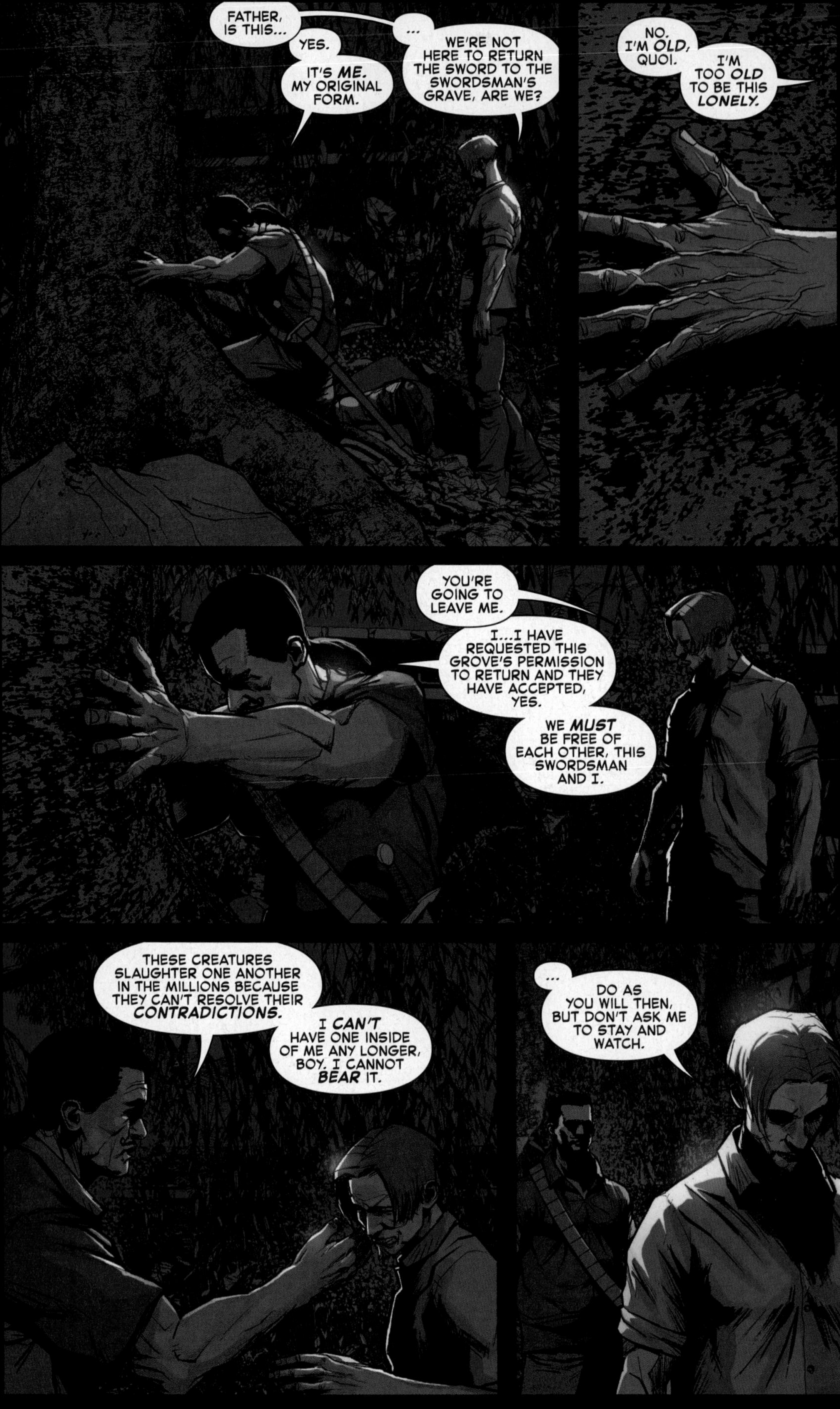
FATHER, IS THIS...
...
YES.
IT'S ME. MY ORIGINAL FORM.
WE'RE NOT HERE TO RETURN THE SWORD TO THE SWORDSMAN'S GRAVE, ARE WE?
NO. I'M OLD, QUOI.
I'M TOO OLD TO BE THIS LONELY.
YOU'RE GOING TO LEAVE ME.
I...I HAVE REQUESTED THIS GROVE'S PERMISSION TO RETURN AND THEY HAVE ACCEPTED, YES.
WE MUST BE FREE OF EACH OTHER, THIS SWORDSMAN AND I.
THESE CREATURES SLAUGHTER ONE ANOTHER IN THE MILLIONS BECAUSE THEY CAN'T RESOLVE THEIR CONTRADICTIONS.
I CAN'T HAVE ONE INSIDE OF ME ANY LONGER, BOY. I CANNOT BEAR IT.
...
DO AS YOU WILL THEN, BUT DON'T ASK ME TO STAY AND WATCH.

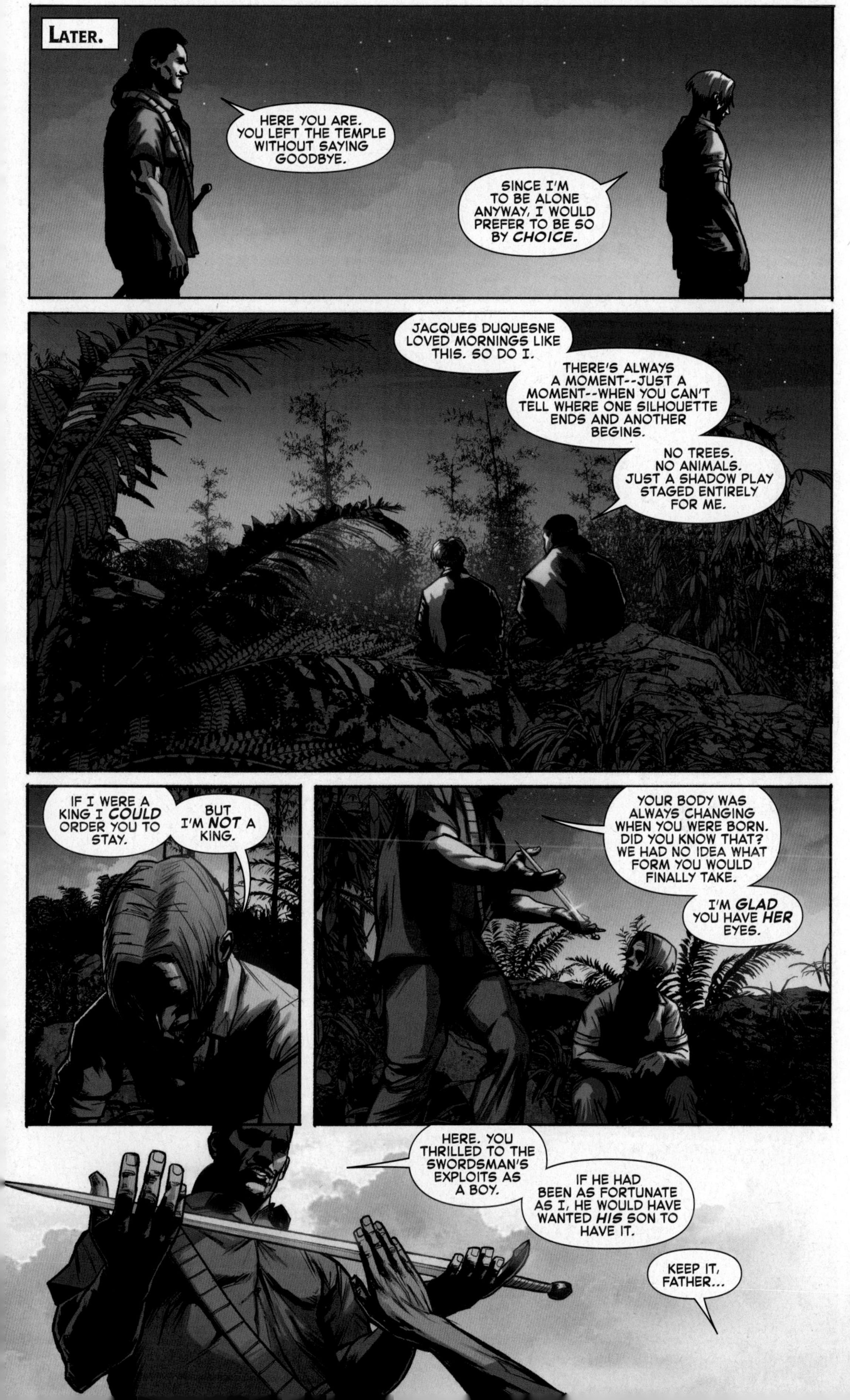
LATER.
HERE YOU ARE. YOU LEFT THE TEMPLE WITHOUT SAYING GOODBYE.
SINCE I'M TO BE ALONE ANYWAY, I WOULD PREFER TO BE SO BY CHOICE.
JACQUES DUQUESNE LOVED MORNINGS LIKE THIS. SO DO I.
THERE'S ALWAYS A MOMENT--JUST A MOMENT--WHEN YOU CAN'T TELL WHERE ONE SILHOUETTE ENDS AND ANOTHER BEGINS.
NO TREES. NO ANIMALS. JUST A SHADOW PLAY STAGED ENTIRELY FOR ME.
IF I WERE A KING I COULD ORDER YOU TO STAY.
BUT I'M NOT A KING.
YOUR BODY WAS ALWAYS CHANGING WHEN YOU WERE BORN. DID YOU KNOW THAT? WE HAD NO IDEA WHAT FORM YOU WOULD FINALLY TAKE.
I'M GLAD YOU HAVE HER EYES.
HERE. YOU THRILLED TO THE SWORDSMAN'S EXPLOITS AS A BOY.
IF HE HAD BEEN AS FORTUNATE AS I, HE WOULD HAVE WANTED HIS SON TO HAVE IT.
KEEP IT, FATHER...

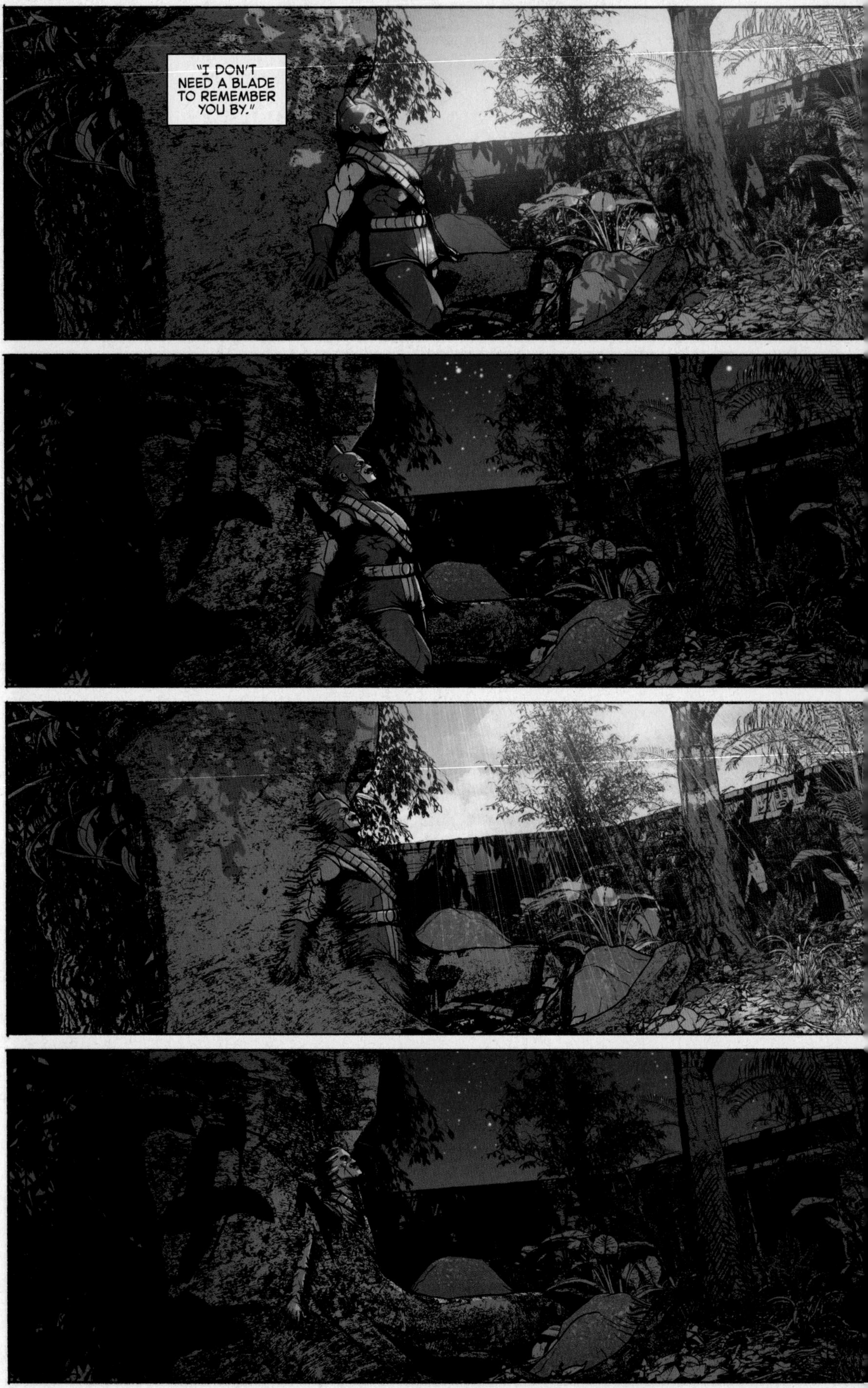
"I DON'T NEED A BLADE TO REMEMBER YOU BY."

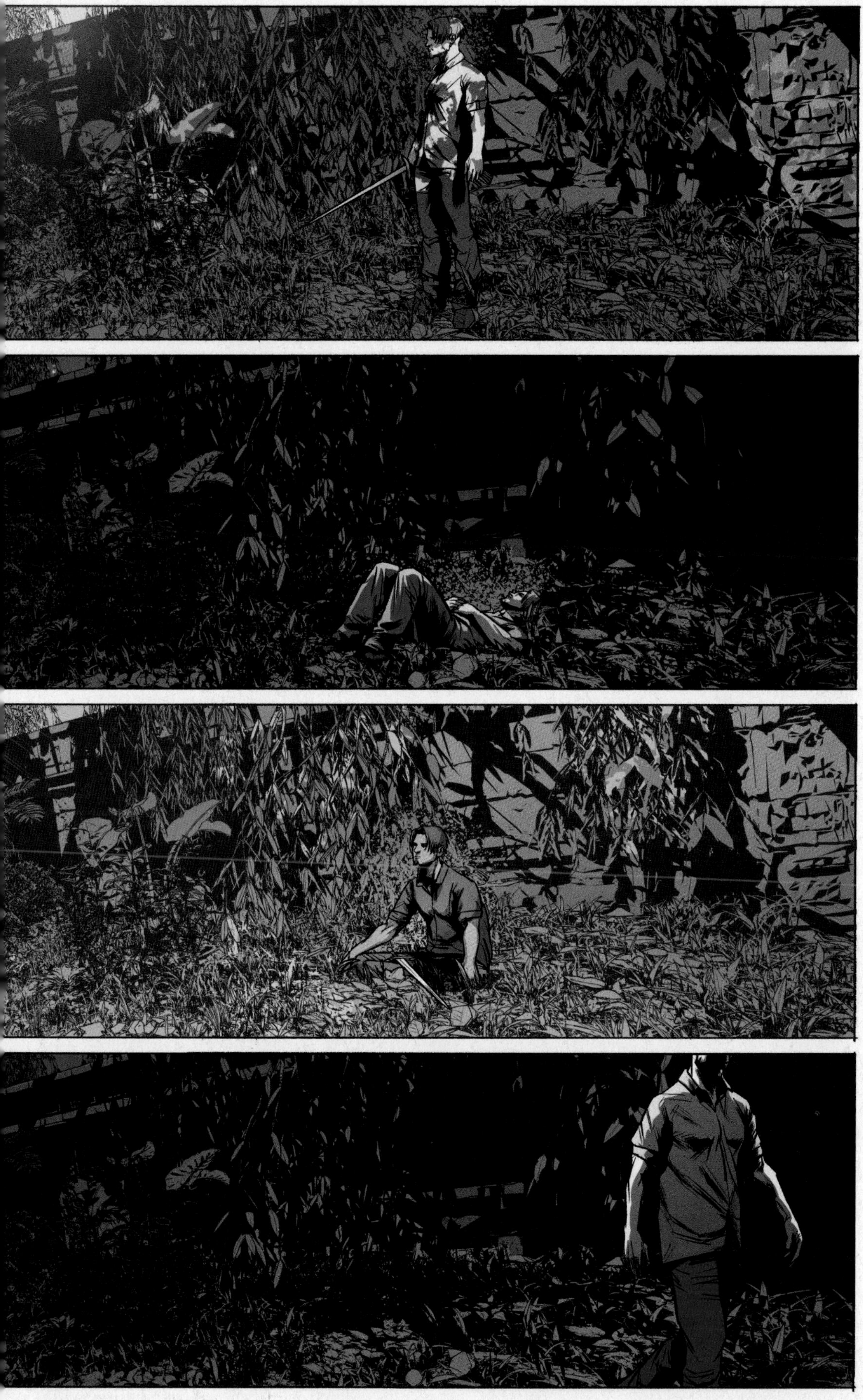

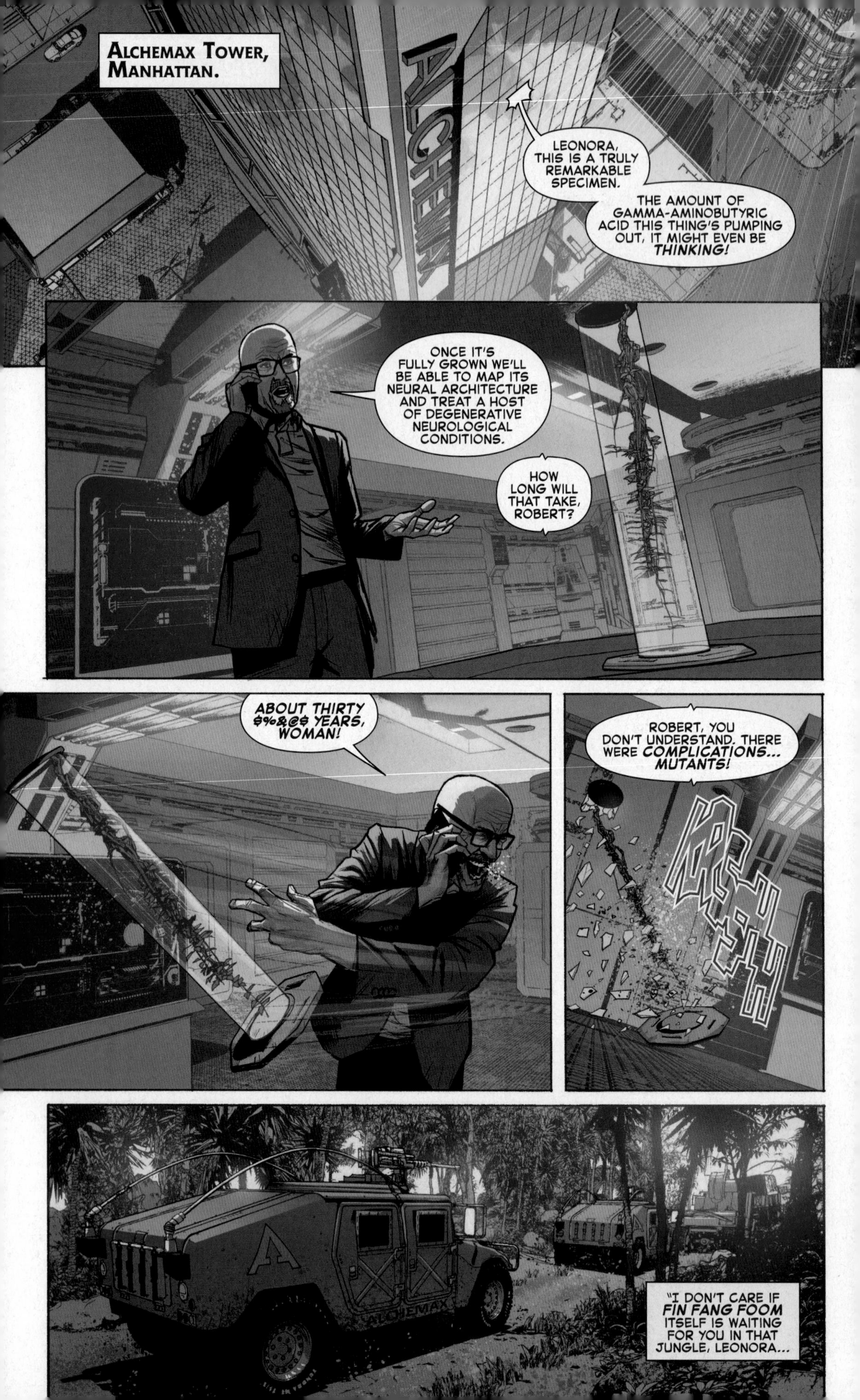
ALCHEMAX TOWER, MANHATTAN.
LEONORA, THIS IS A TRULY REMARKABLE SPECIMEN.
THE AMOUNT OF GAMMA-AMINOBUTYRIC ACID THIS THING'S PUMPING OUT, IT MIGHT EVEN BE THINKING!
ONCE IT'S FULLY GROWN WE'LL BE ABLE TO MAP ITS NEURAL ARCHITECTURE AND TREAT A HOST OF DEGENERATIVE NEUROLOGICAL CONDITIONS.
HOW LONG WILL THAT TAKE, ROBERT?
ABOUT THIRTY $%&@$ YEARS, WOMAN!
ROBERT, YOU DON'T UNDERSTAND. THERE WERE COMPLICATIONS... MUTANTS!
"I DON'T CARE IF FIN FANG FOOM ITSELF IS WAITING FOR YOU IN THAT JUNGLE, LEONORA...

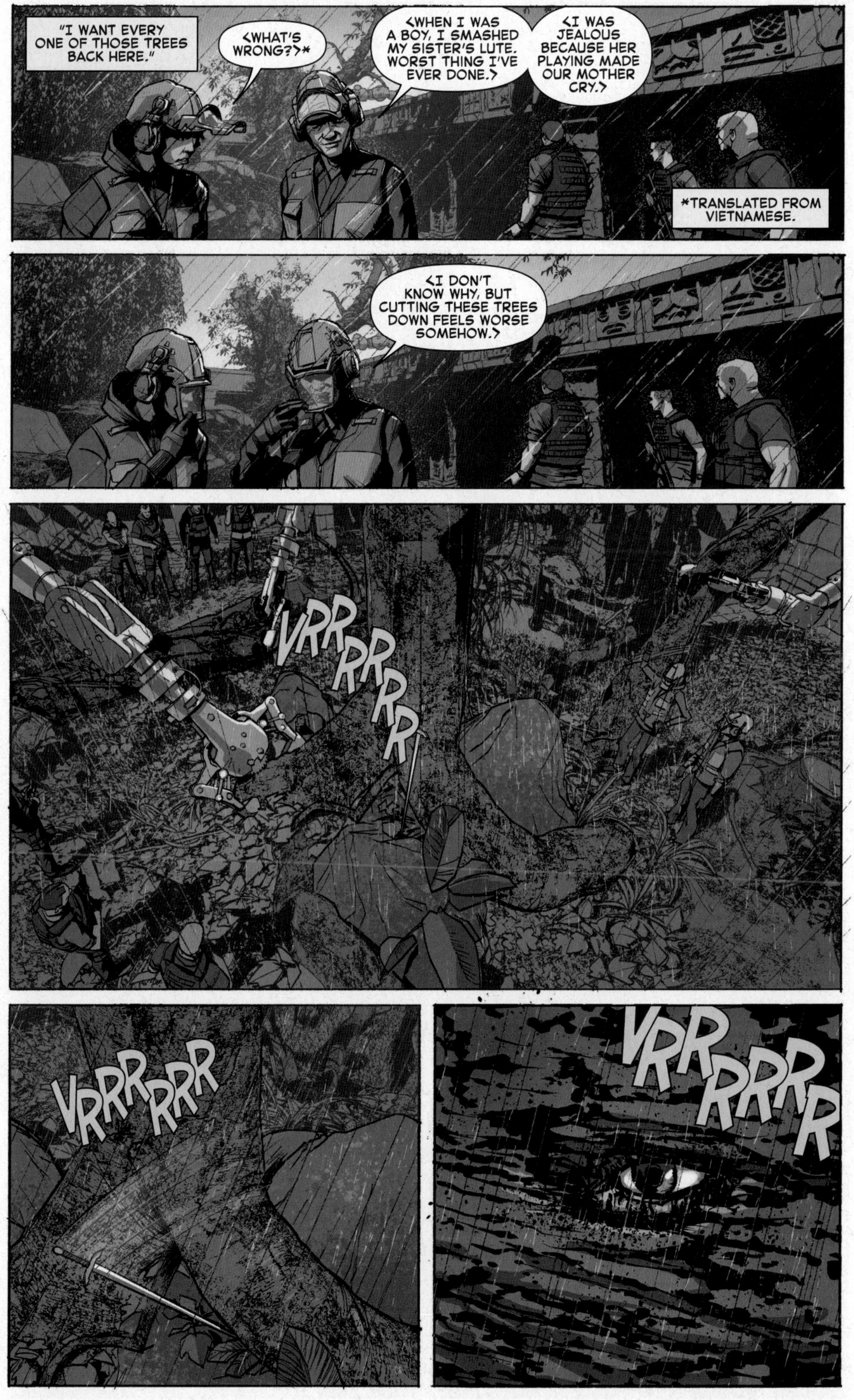
"I WANT EVERY ONE OF THOSE TREES BACK HERE."
<WHAT'S WRONG?>*
<WHEN I WAS A BOY, I SMASHED MY SISTER'S LUTE. WORST THING I'VE EVER DONE.>
<I WAS JEALOUS BECAUSE HER PLAYING MADE OUR MOTHER CRY.>
*TRANSLATED FROM VIETNAMESE.
<I DON'T KNOW WHY, BUT CUTTING THESE TREES DOWN FEELS WORSE SOMEHOW.>
VRRRRRRR
VRRRRRRR
VRRRRRRR

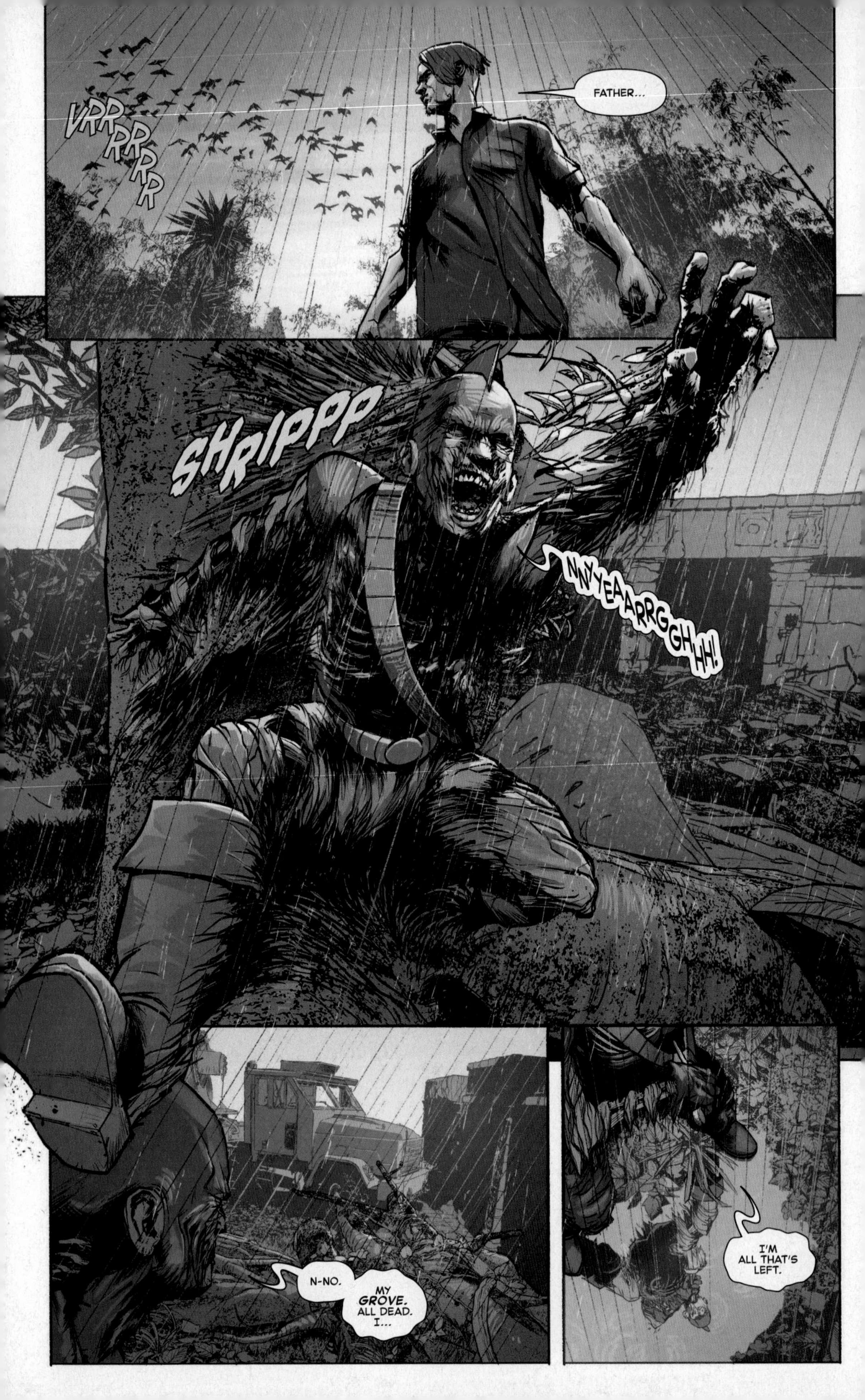
VRRRRRRR
FATHER...
SHRIPPP
NNYYEAARRGGHHH!
N-NO.
MY GROVE. ALL DEAD. I...
I'M ALL THAT'S LEFT.

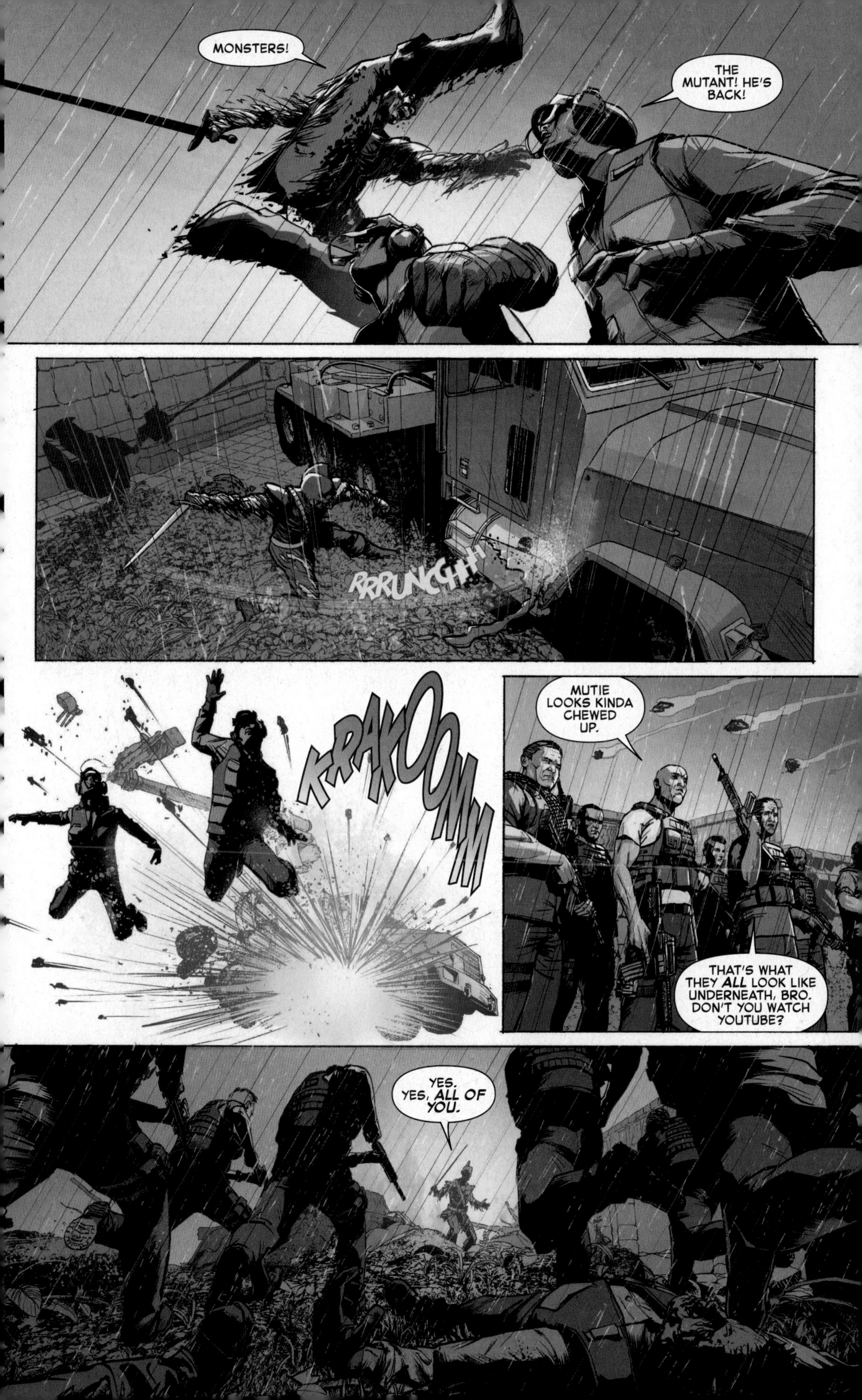
MONSTERS!
THE MUTANT! HE'S BACK!
RRRUNCHH!
K-RAKOOMM
MUTIE LOOKS KINDA CHEWED UP.
THAT'S WHAT THEY ALL LOOK LIKE UNDERNEATH, BRO. DON'T YOU WATCH YOUTUBE?
YES. YES, ALL OF YOU.

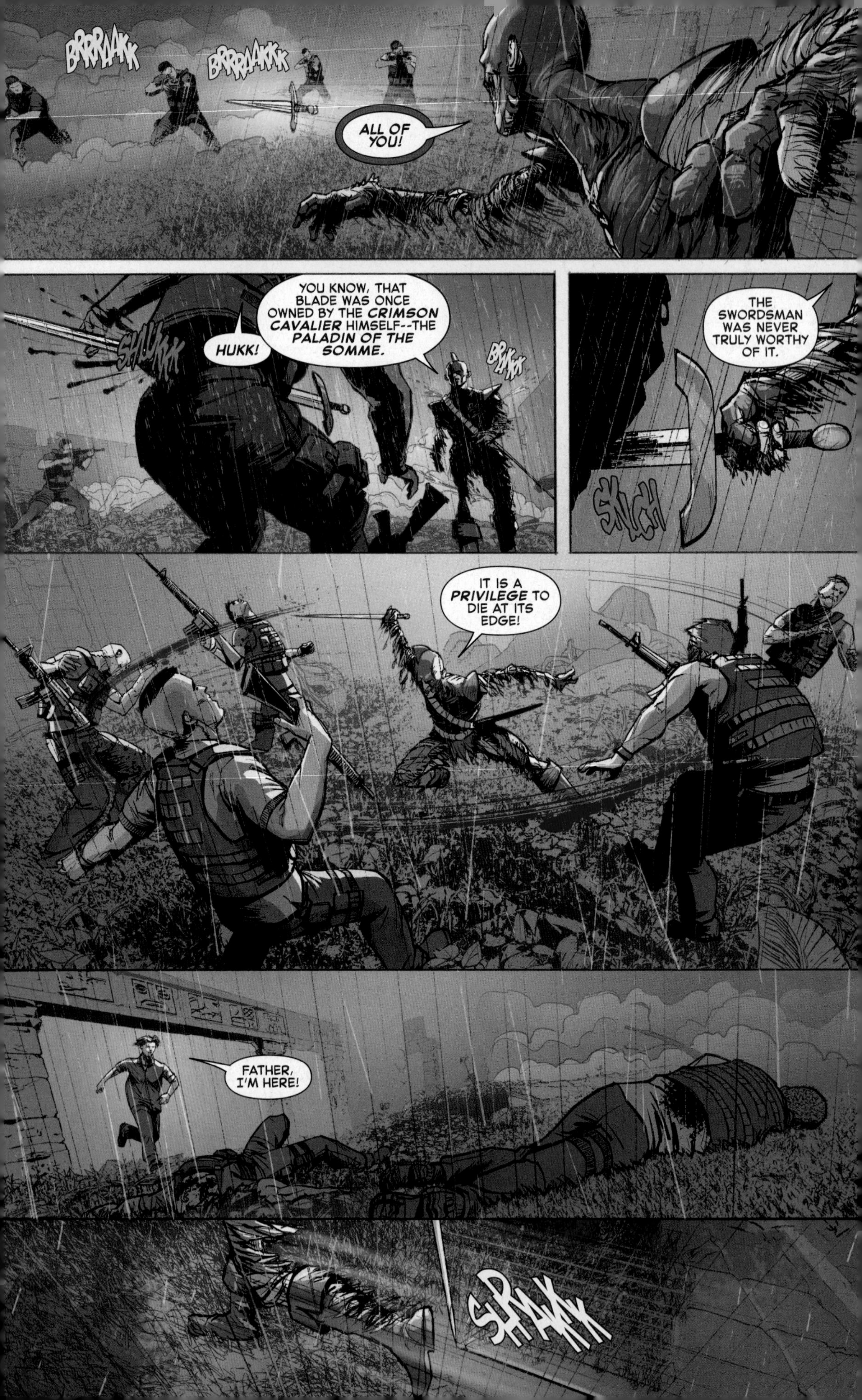
BRRRAAKK
BRRRAAKKK
ALL OF YOU!
SHUKKK
HUKK!
YOU KNOW, THAT BLADE WAS ONCE OWNED BY THE CRIMSON CAVALIER HIMSELF--THE PALADIN OF THE SOMME.
BRAKK
THE SWORDSMAN WAS NEVER TRULY WORTHY OF IT.
SKLCH
IT IS A PRIVILEGE TO DIE AT ITS EDGE!
FATHER, I'M HERE!
SHRAKK

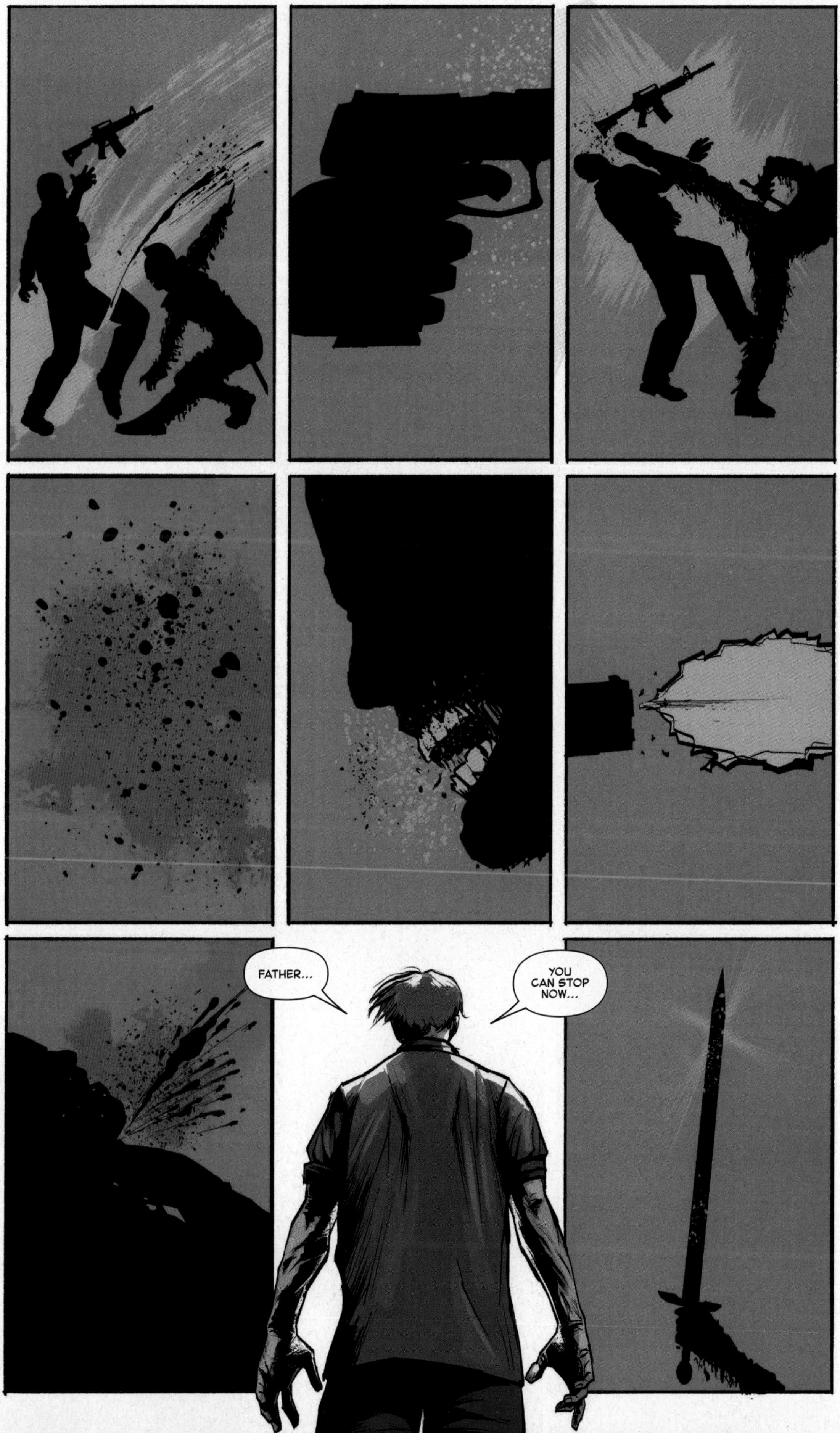
FATHER...
YOU CAN STOP NOW...

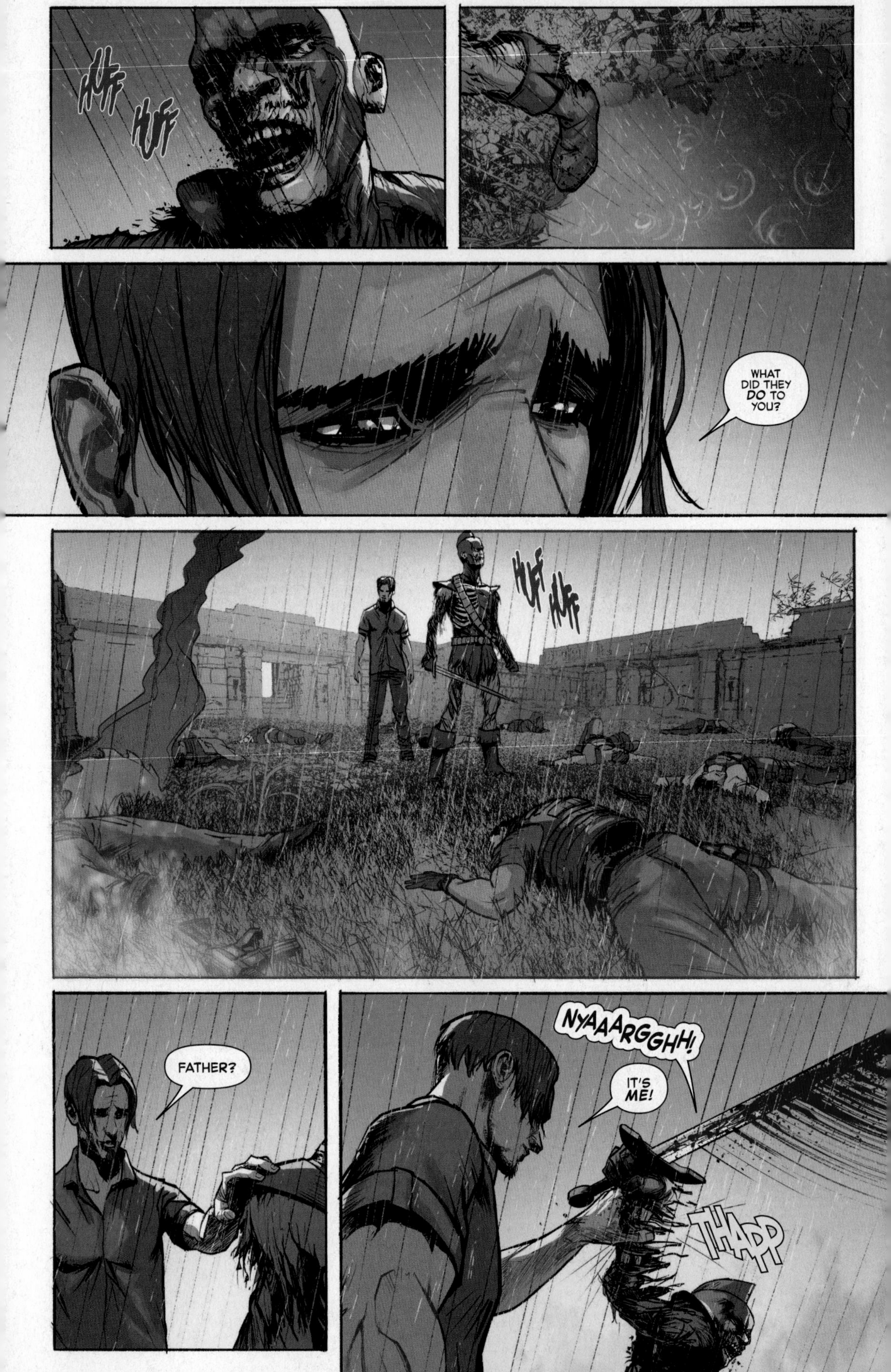
HUFF
HUFF
WHAT DID THEY DO TO YOU?
HUFF
HUFF
FATHER?
NYAAARGGHH!
IT'S ME!
THAPP

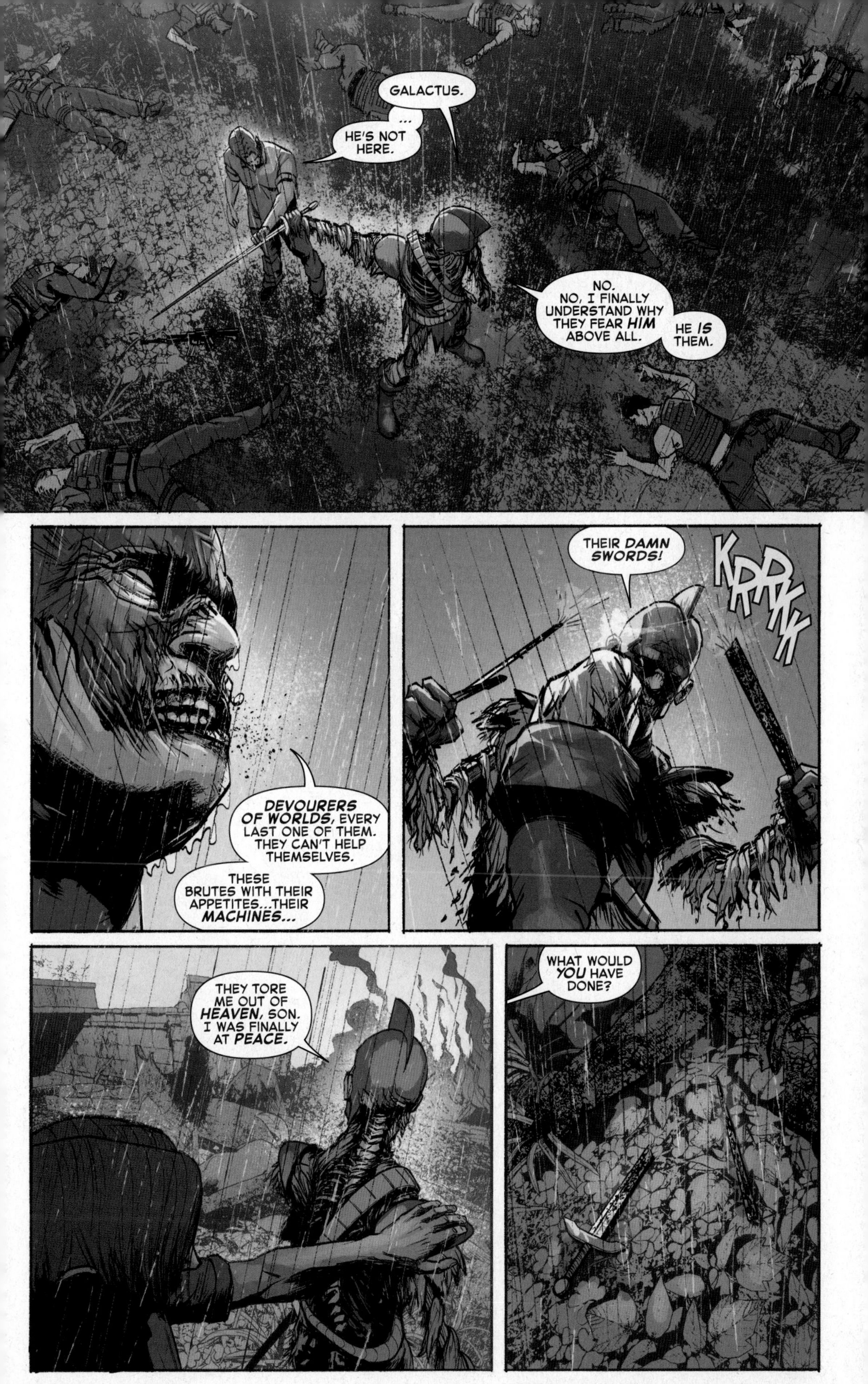
GALACTUS.
...
HE'S NOT HERE.
NO.
NO, I FINALLY UNDERSTAND WHY THEY FEAR *HIM* ABOVE ALL.
HE *IS* THEM.
DEVOURERS OF WORLDS, EVERY LAST ONE OF THEM. THEY CAN'T HELP THEMSELVES.
THESE BRUTES WITH THEIR APPETITES...THEIR *MACHINES...*
THEIR *DAMN SWORDS!*
KRRKK
THEY TORE ME OUT OF *HEAVEN*, SON. I WAS FINALLY AT *PEACE.*
WHAT WOULD *YOU* HAVE DONE?

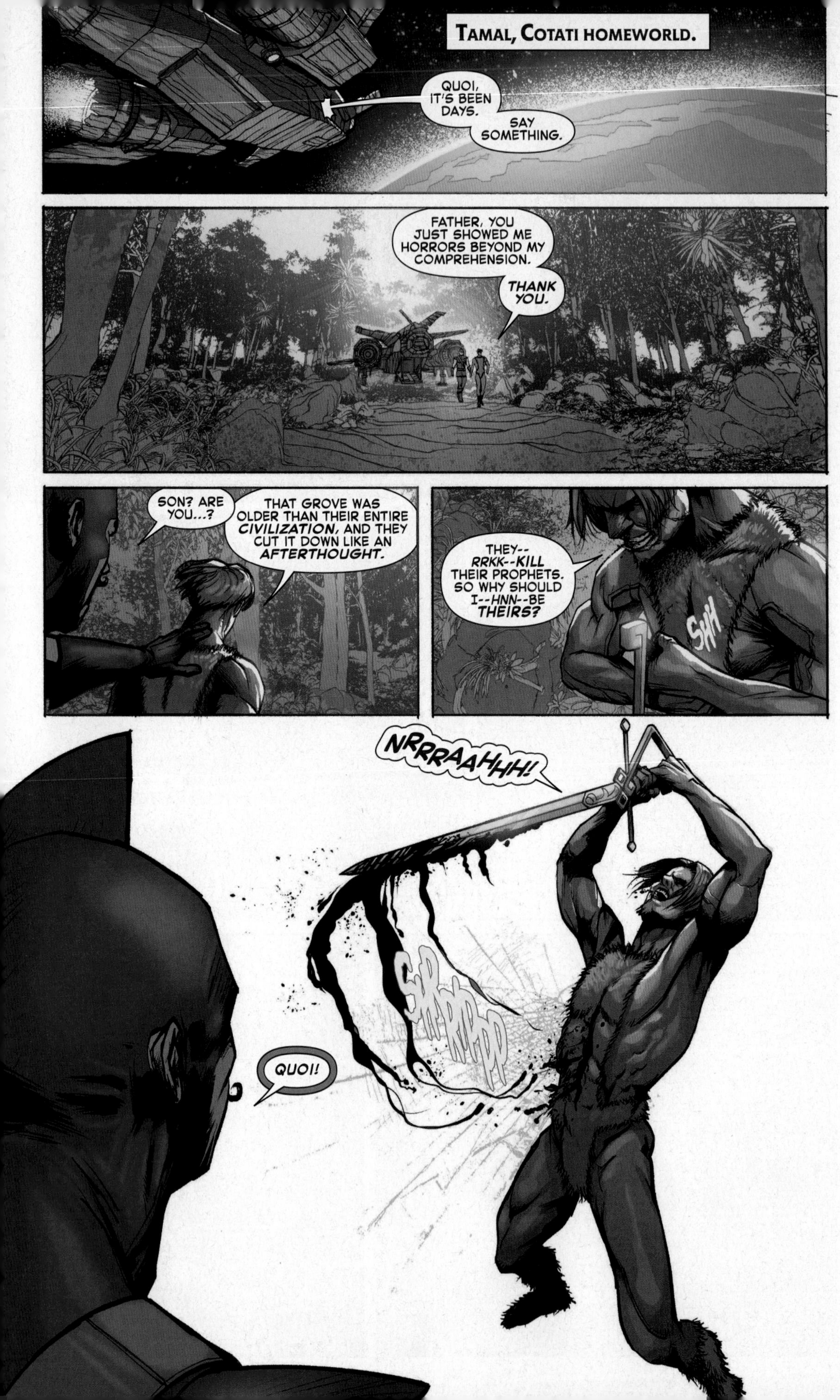
TAMAL, COTATI HOMEWORLD.
QUOI, IT'S BEEN DAYS.
SAY SOMETHING.
FATHER, YOU JUST SHOWED ME HORRORS BEYOND MY COMPREHENSION.
THANK YOU.
SON? ARE YOU...?
THAT GROVE WAS OLDER THAN THEIR ENTIRE CIVILIZATION, AND THEY CUT IT DOWN LIKE AN AFTERTHOUGHT.
THEY-- RRKK--KILL THEIR PROPHETS. SO WHY SHOULD I--HNN--BE THEIRS?
SHH
NRRRAAHHH!
SHRRIPPP
QUOI!

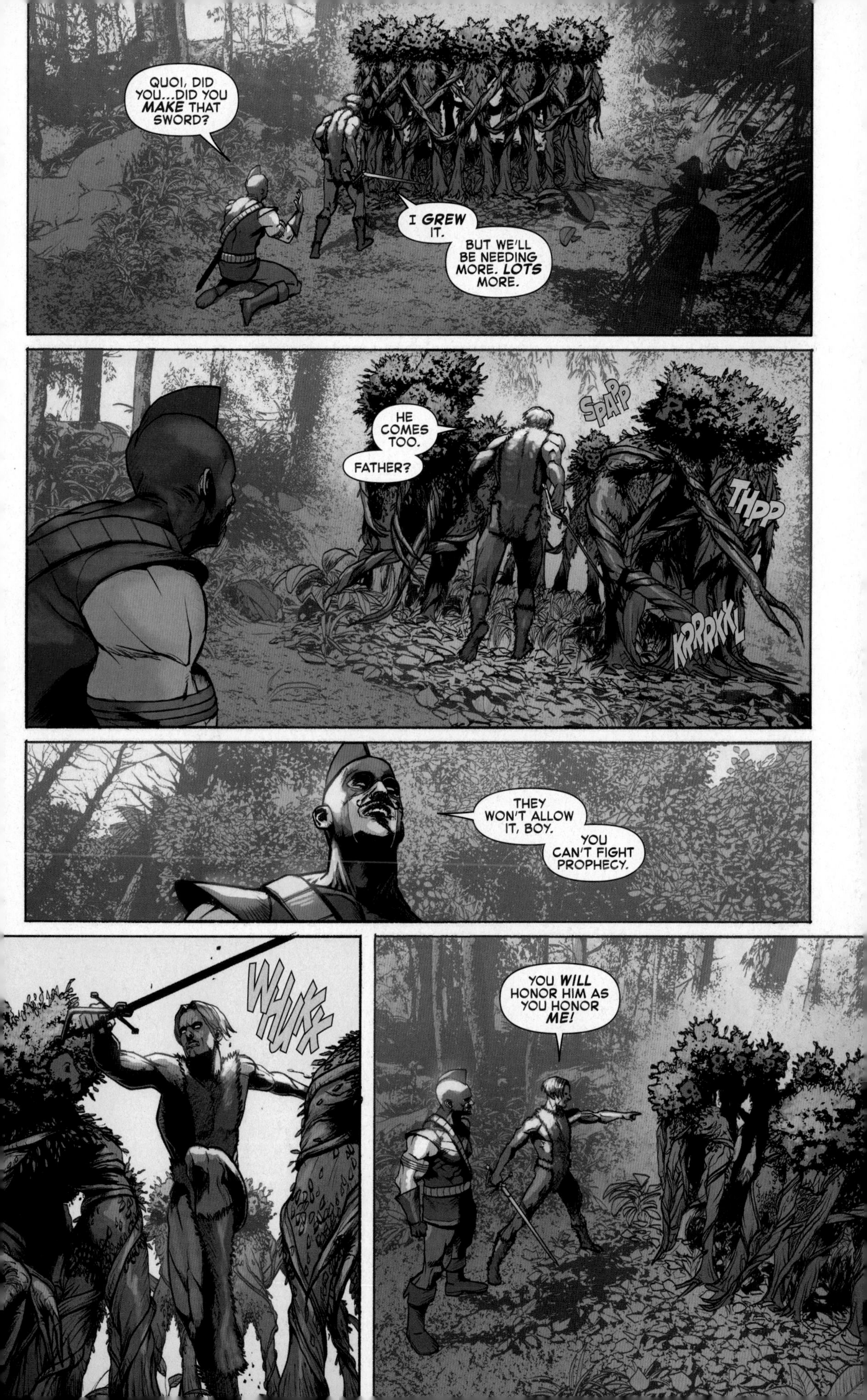
QUOI, DID YOU...DID YOU MAKE THAT SWORD?
I GREW IT.
BUT WE'LL BE NEEDING MORE. LOTS MORE.
HE COMES TOO.
FATHER?
SPAPP
THPP
KRRRKKL
THEY WON'T ALLOW IT, BOY.
YOU CAN'T FIGHT PROPHECY.
WHUKK
YOU WILL HONOR HIM AS YOU HONOR ME!

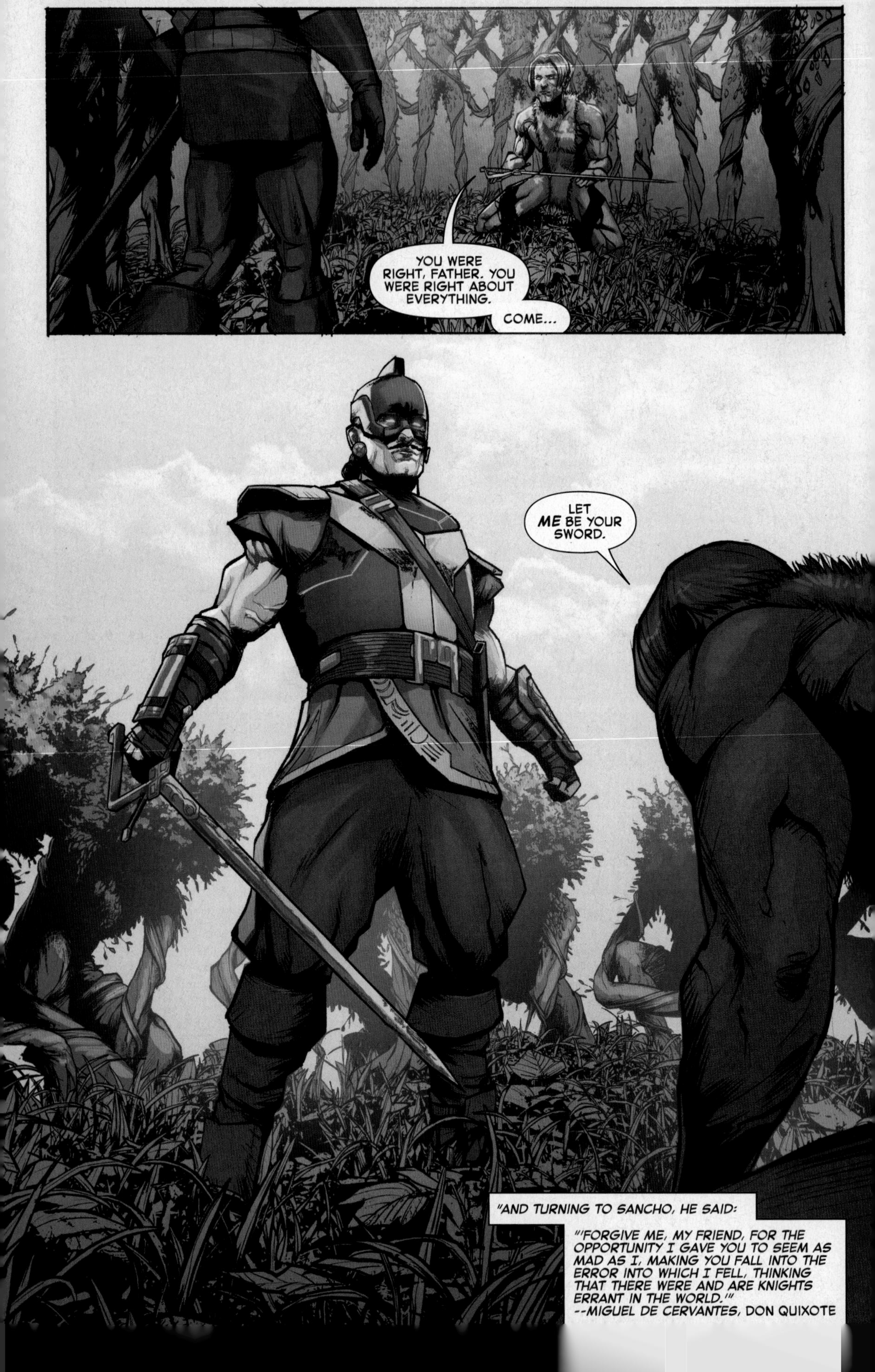
YOU WERE RIGHT, FATHER. YOU WERE RIGHT ABOUT EVERYTHING.
COME...
LET *ME* BE YOUR SWORD.
"AND TURNING TO SANCHO, HE SAID:
"'FORGIVE ME, MY FRIEND, FOR THE OPPORTUNITY I GAVE YOU TO SEEM AS MAD AS I, MAKING YOU FALL INTO THE ERROR INTO WHICH I FELL, THINKING THAT THERE WERE AND ARE KNIGHTS ERRANT IN THE WORLD.'"
--MIGUEL DE CERVANTES, DON QUIXOTE

EMPYRE: SAVAGE AVENGERS VARIANT BY
Gerardo Sandoval & **Dono Sánchez-Almara**

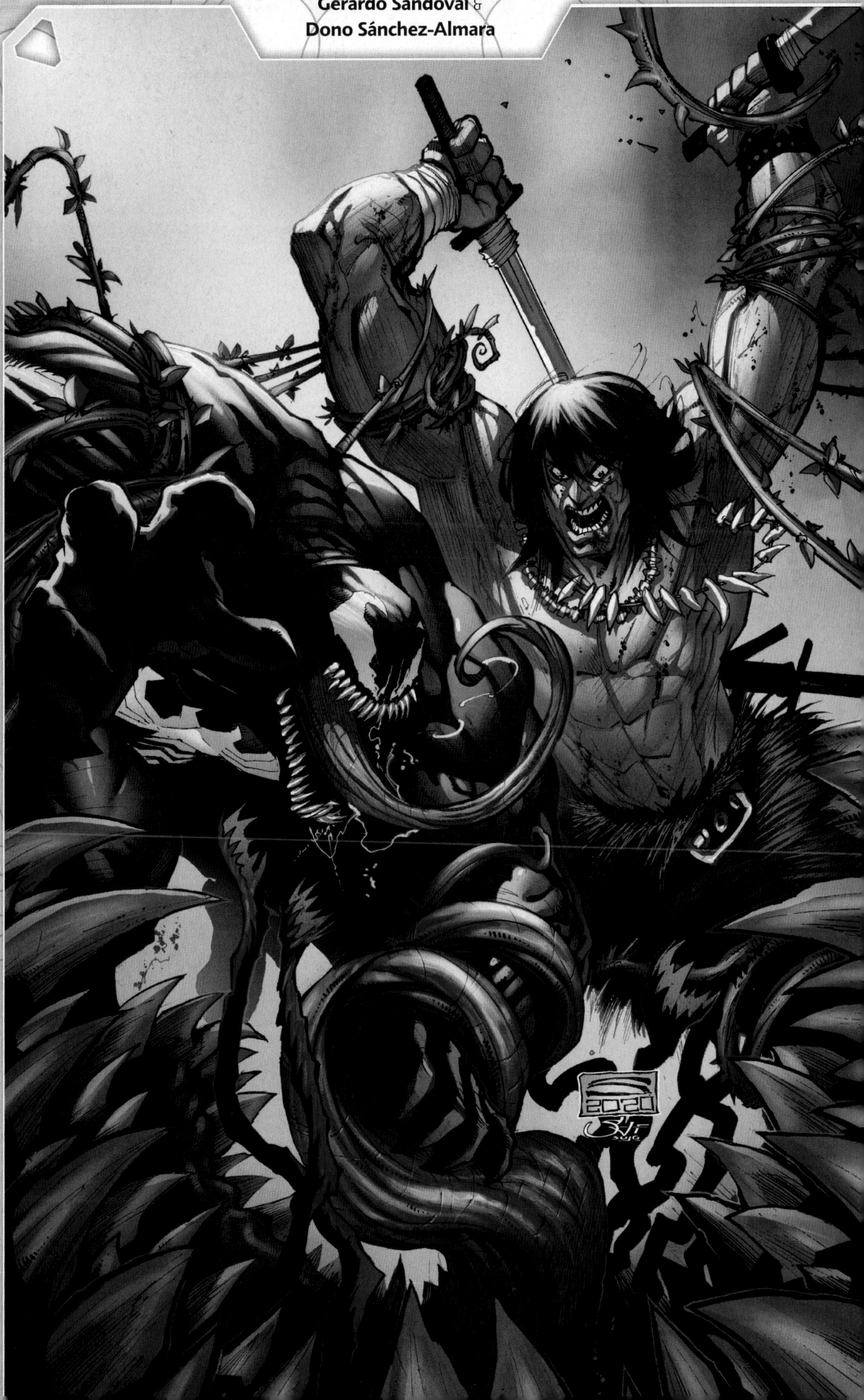

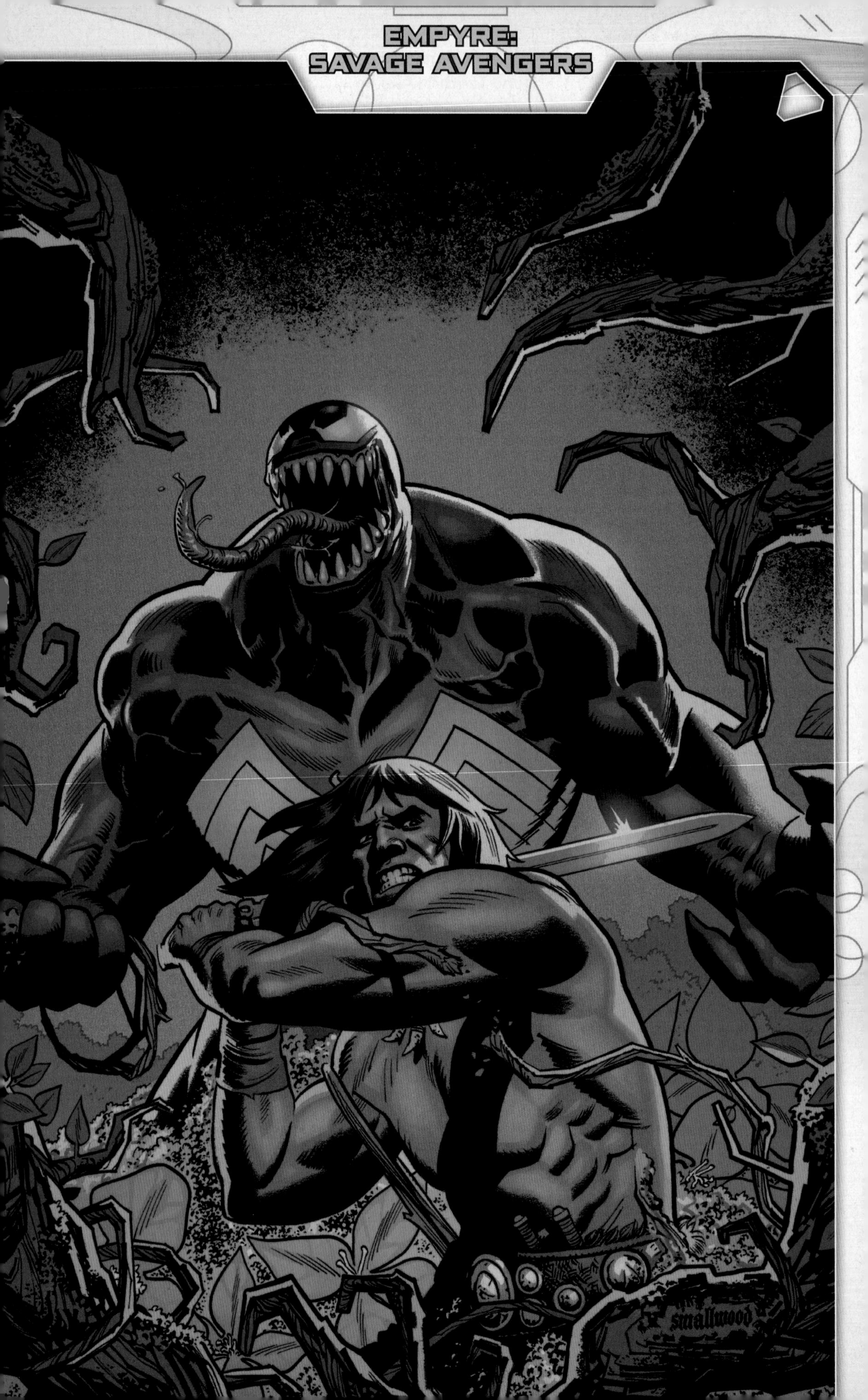
EMPYRE:
SAVAGE AVENGERS
smallwood

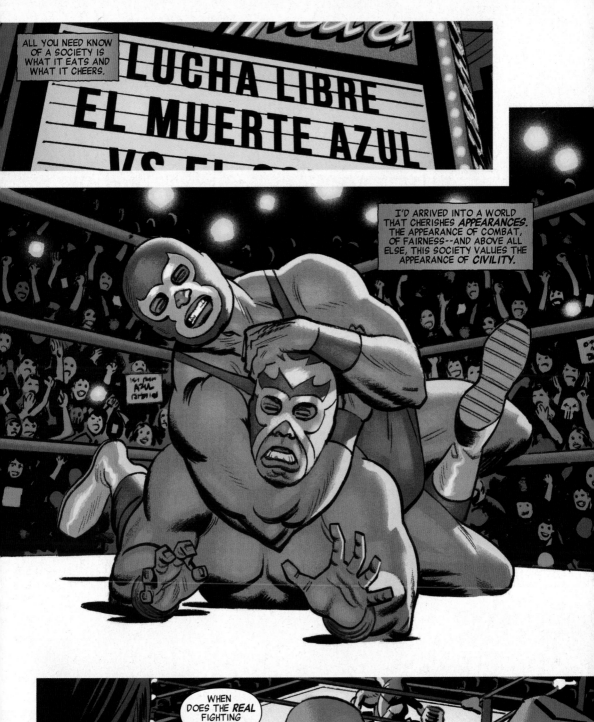

ALL YOU NEED KNOW OF A SOCIETY IS WHAT IT EATS AND WHAT IT CHEERS.

LUCHA LIBRE
EL MUERTE AZUL

I'D ARRIVED INTO A WORLD THAT CHERISHES *APPEARANCES*. THE APPEARANCE OF COMBAT, OF FAIRNESS--AND ABOVE ALL ELSE, THIS SOCIETY VALUES THE APPEARANCE OF *CIVILITY*.

WHEN DOES THE *REAL* FIGHTING BEGIN?

THOUGH THE MEN ARE WEAK, AND THEIR CODE LACKING...

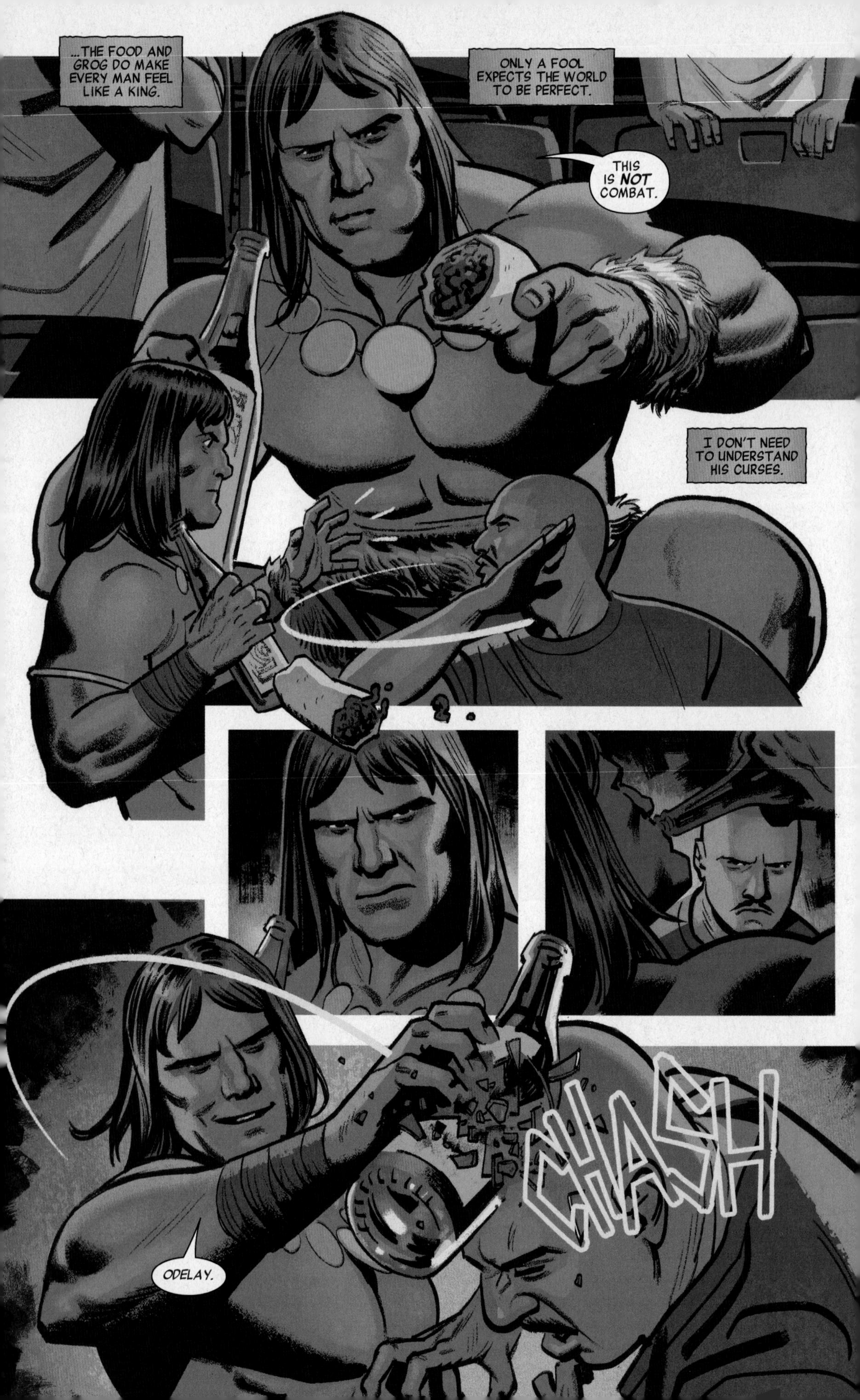
...THE FOOD AND GROG DO MAKE EVERY MAN FEEL LIKE A KING.
ONLY A FOOL EXPECTS THE WORLD TO BE PERFECT.
THIS IS NOT COMBAT.
I DON'T NEED TO UNDERSTAND HIS CURSES.
CHASH
ODELAY.

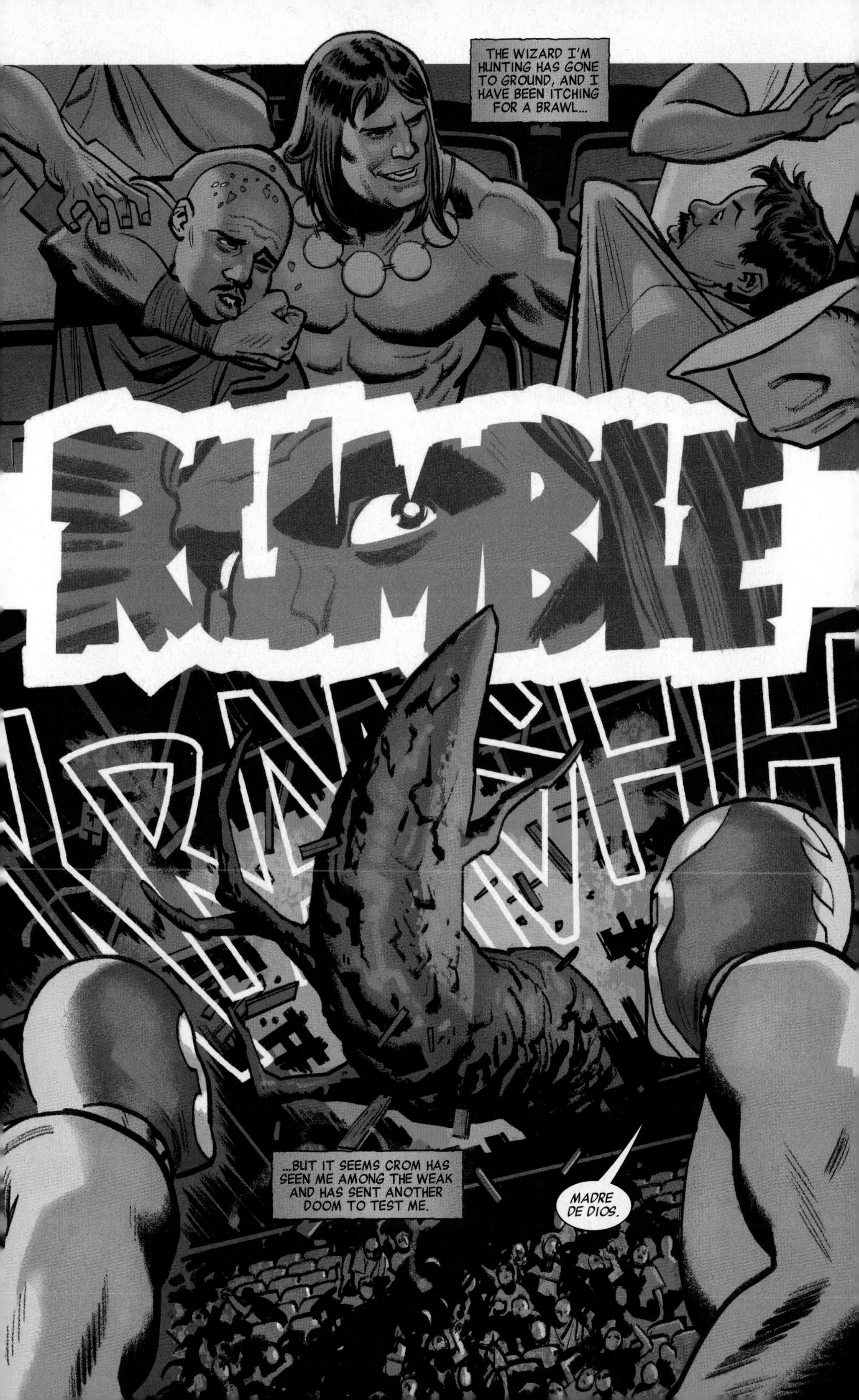
THE WIZARD I'M HUNTING HAS GONE TO GROUND, AND I HAVE BEEN ITCHING FOR A BRAWL...
RUMBLE
...BUT IT SEEMS CROM HAS SEEN ME AMONG THE WEAK AND HAS SENT ANOTHER DOOM TO TEST ME.
MADRE DE DIOS.

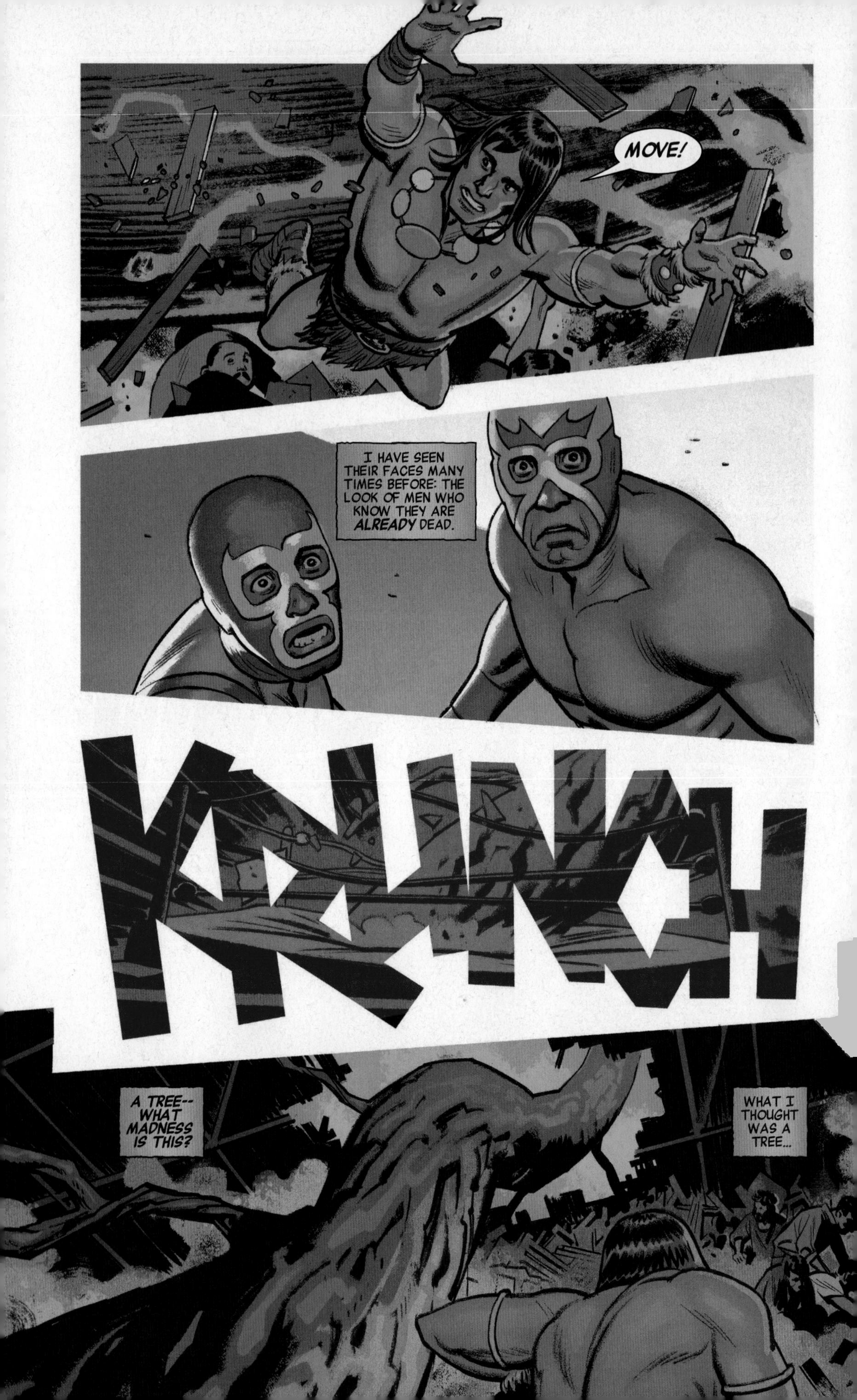
MOVE!
I HAVE SEEN THEIR FACES MANY TIMES BEFORE: THE LOOK OF MEN WHO KNOW THEY ARE ALREADY DEAD.
KRUNCH
A TREE-- WHAT MADNESS IS THIS?
WHAT I THOUGHT WAS A TREE...

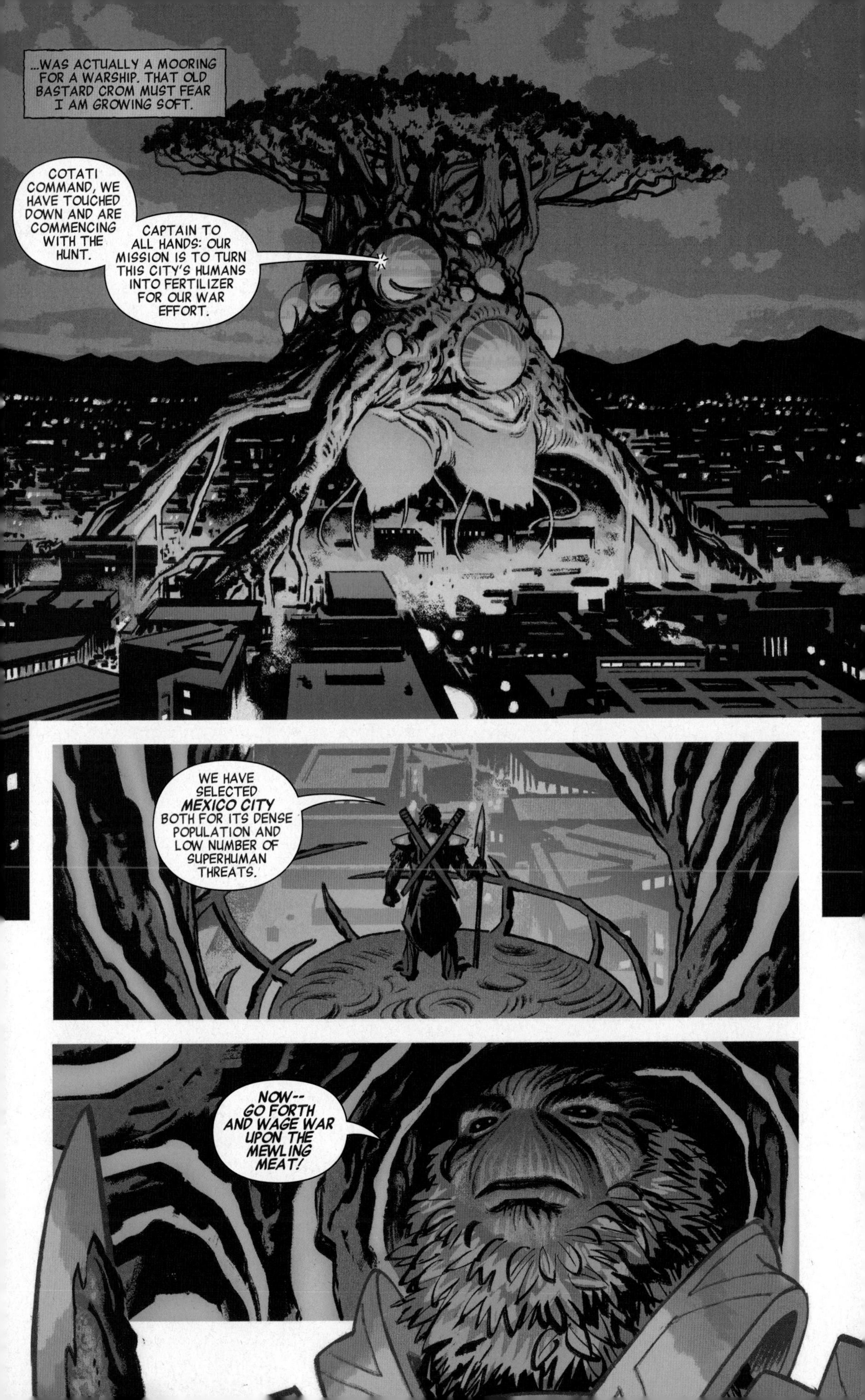

...WAS ACTUALLY A MOORING FOR A WARSHIP. THAT OLD BASTARD CROM MUST FEAR I AM GROWING SOFT.
COTATI COMMAND, WE HAVE TOUCHED DOWN AND ARE COMMENCING WITH THE HUNT.
CAPTAIN TO ALL HANDS: OUR MISSION IS TO TURN THIS CITY'S HUMANS INTO FERTILIZER FOR OUR WAR EFFORT.
WE HAVE SELECTED MEXICO CITY BOTH FOR ITS DENSE POPULATION AND LOW NUMBER OF SUPERHUMAN THREATS.
NOW-- GO FORTH AND WAGE WAR UPON THE MEWLING MEAT!

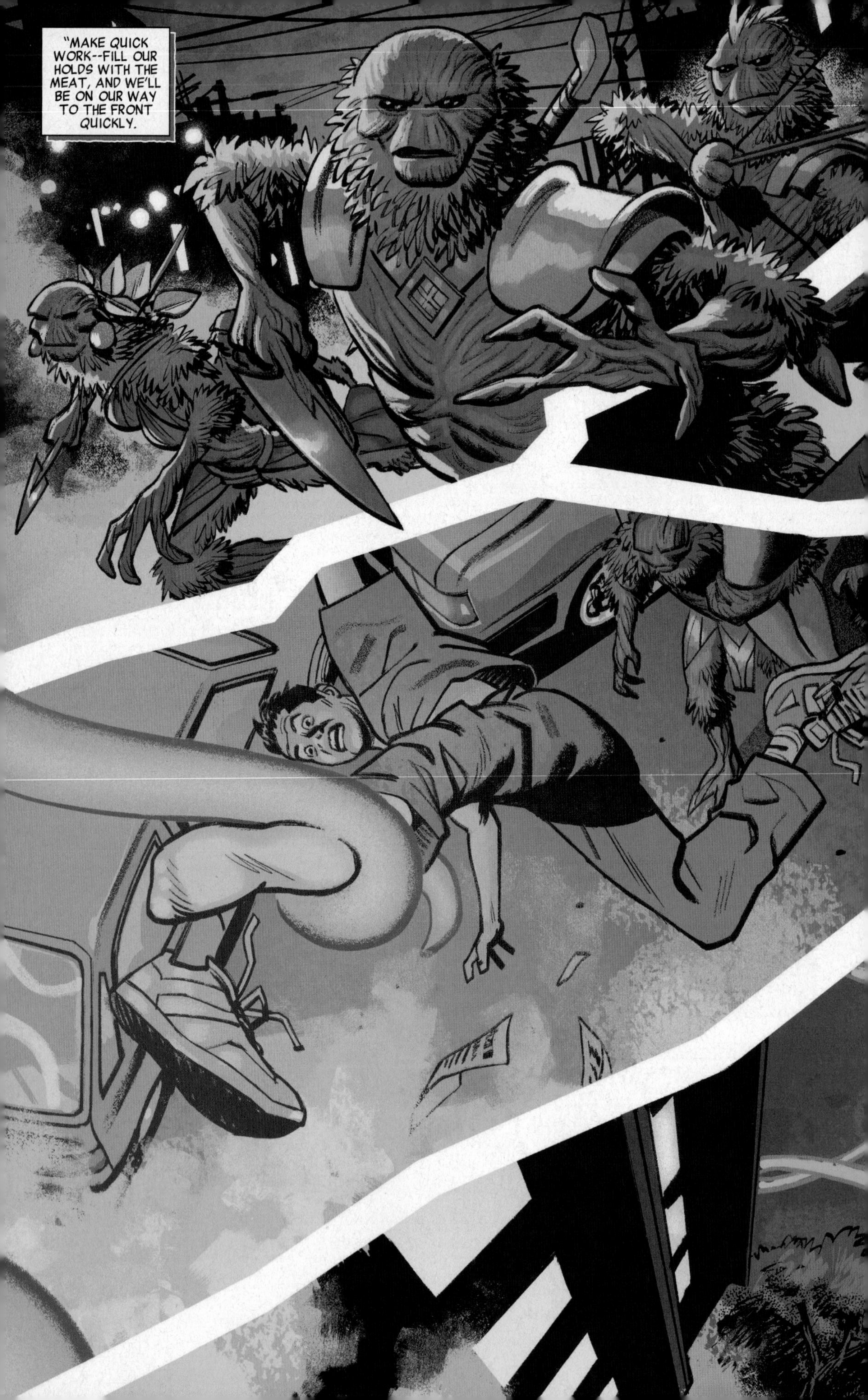
"MAKE QUICK WORK--FILL OUR HOLDS WITH THE MEAT, AND WE'LL BE ON OUR WAY TO THE FRONT QUICKLY.

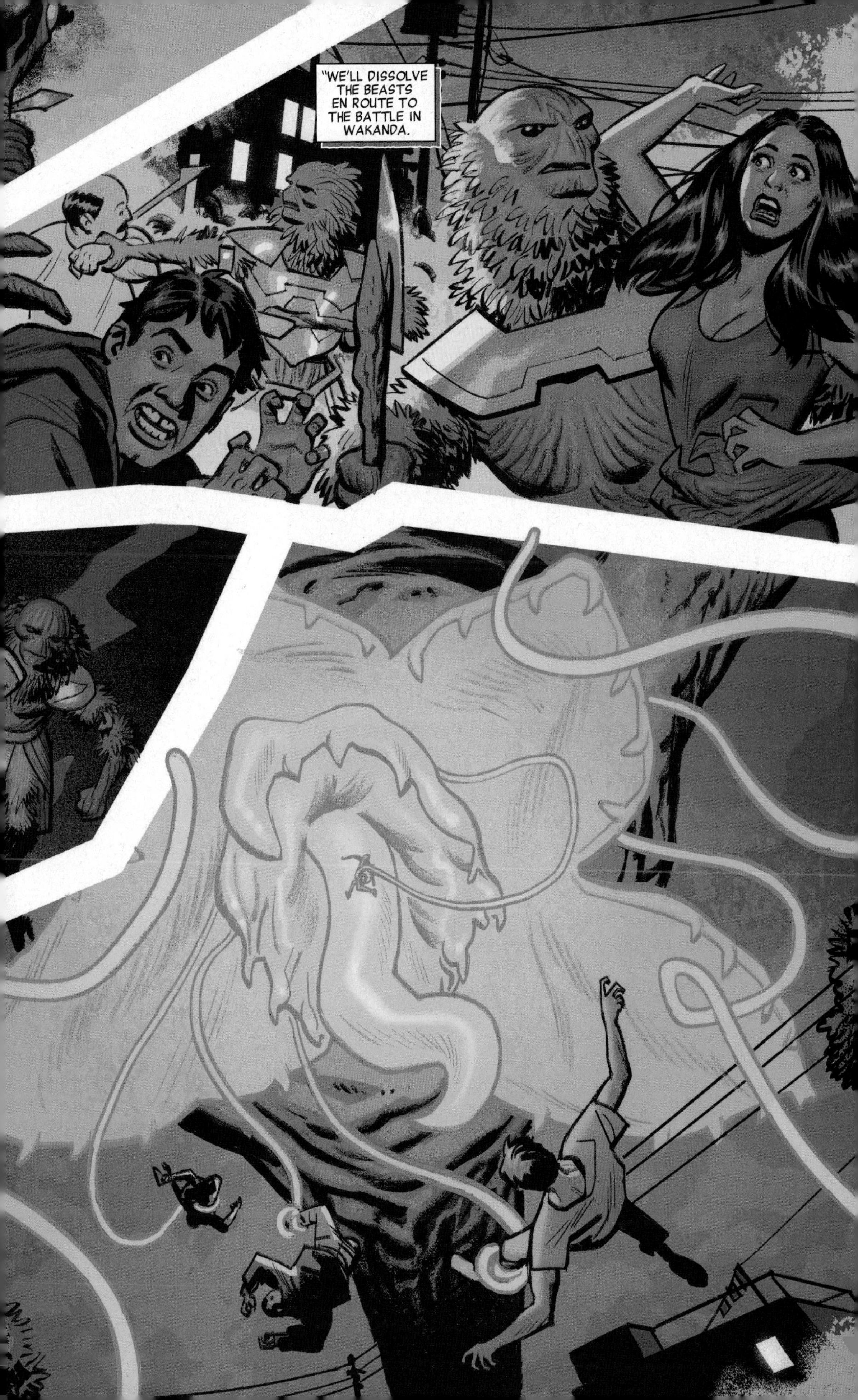
"WE'LL DISSOLVE THE BEASTS EN ROUTE TO THE BATTLE IN WAKANDA.

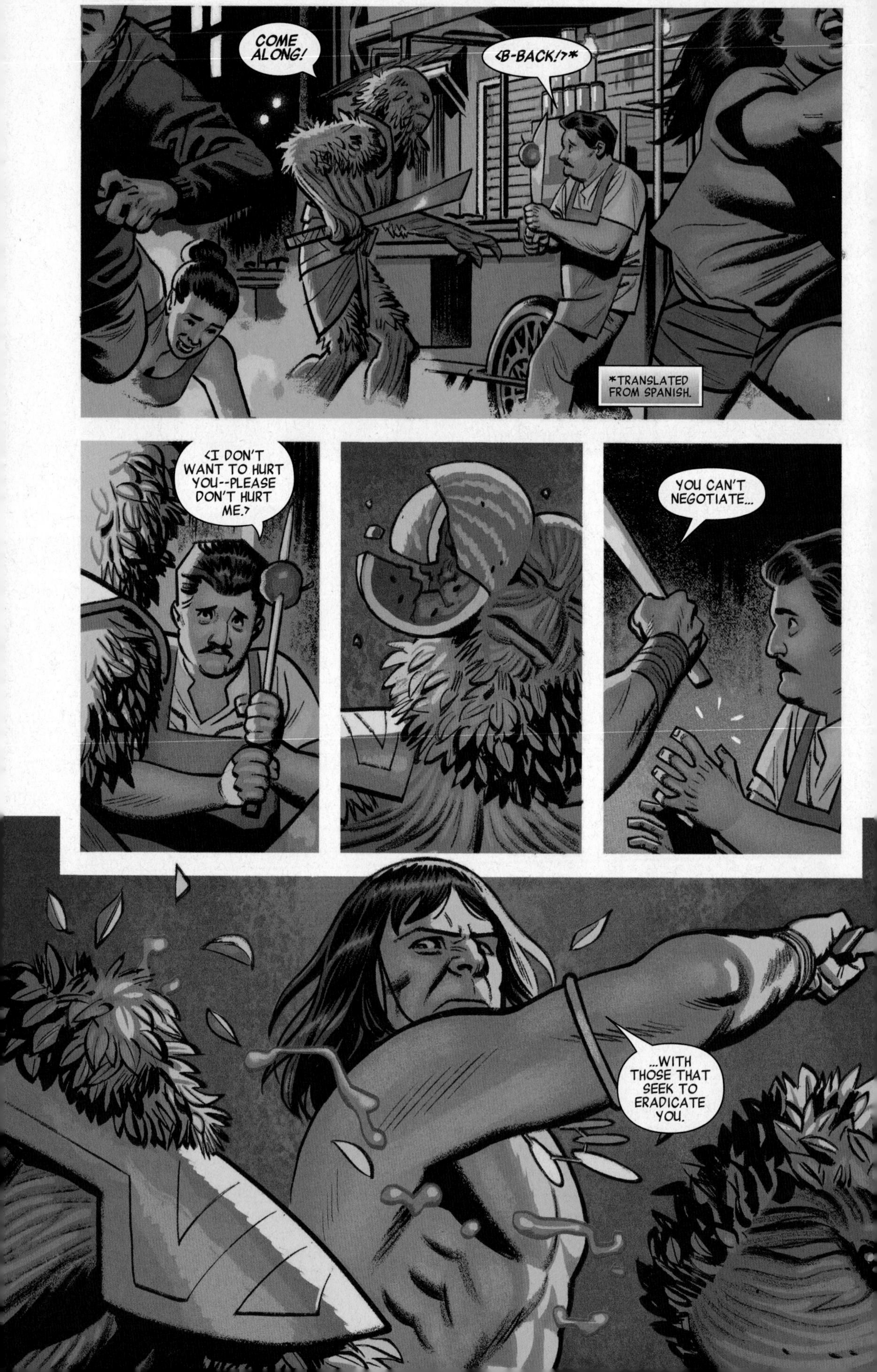
COME ALONG!
<B-BACK!?>*
*TRANSLATED FROM SPANISH.
<I DON'T WANT TO HURT YOU--PLEASE DON'T HURT ME.>
YOU CAN'T NEGOTIATE...
...WITH THOSE THAT SEEK TO ERADICATE YOU.

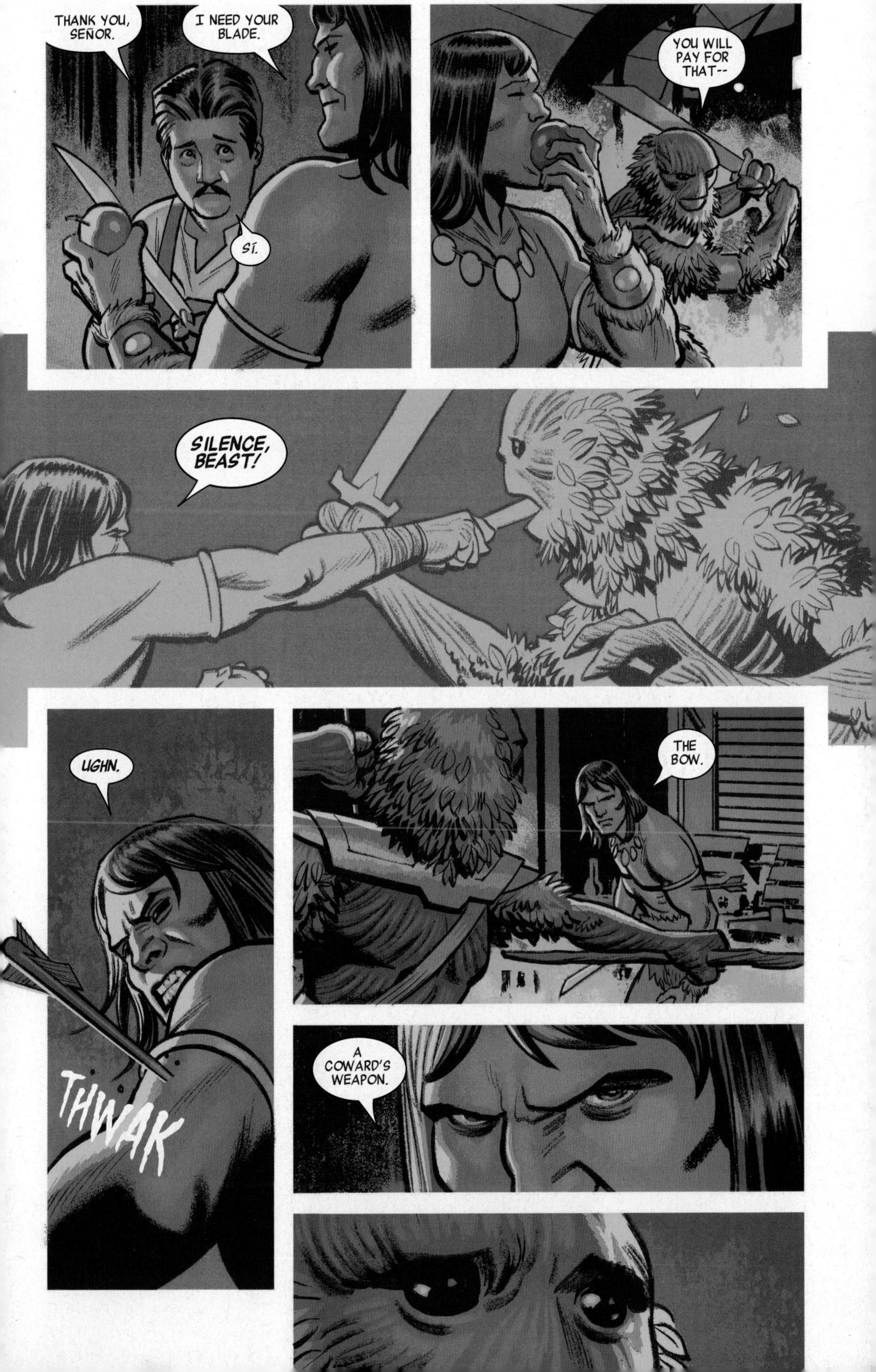
THANK YOU, SEÑOR.
I NEED YOUR BLADE.
SÍ.
YOU WILL PAY FOR THAT--
SILENCE, BEAST!
UGHN.
THWAK
THE BOW.
A COWARD'S WEAPON.

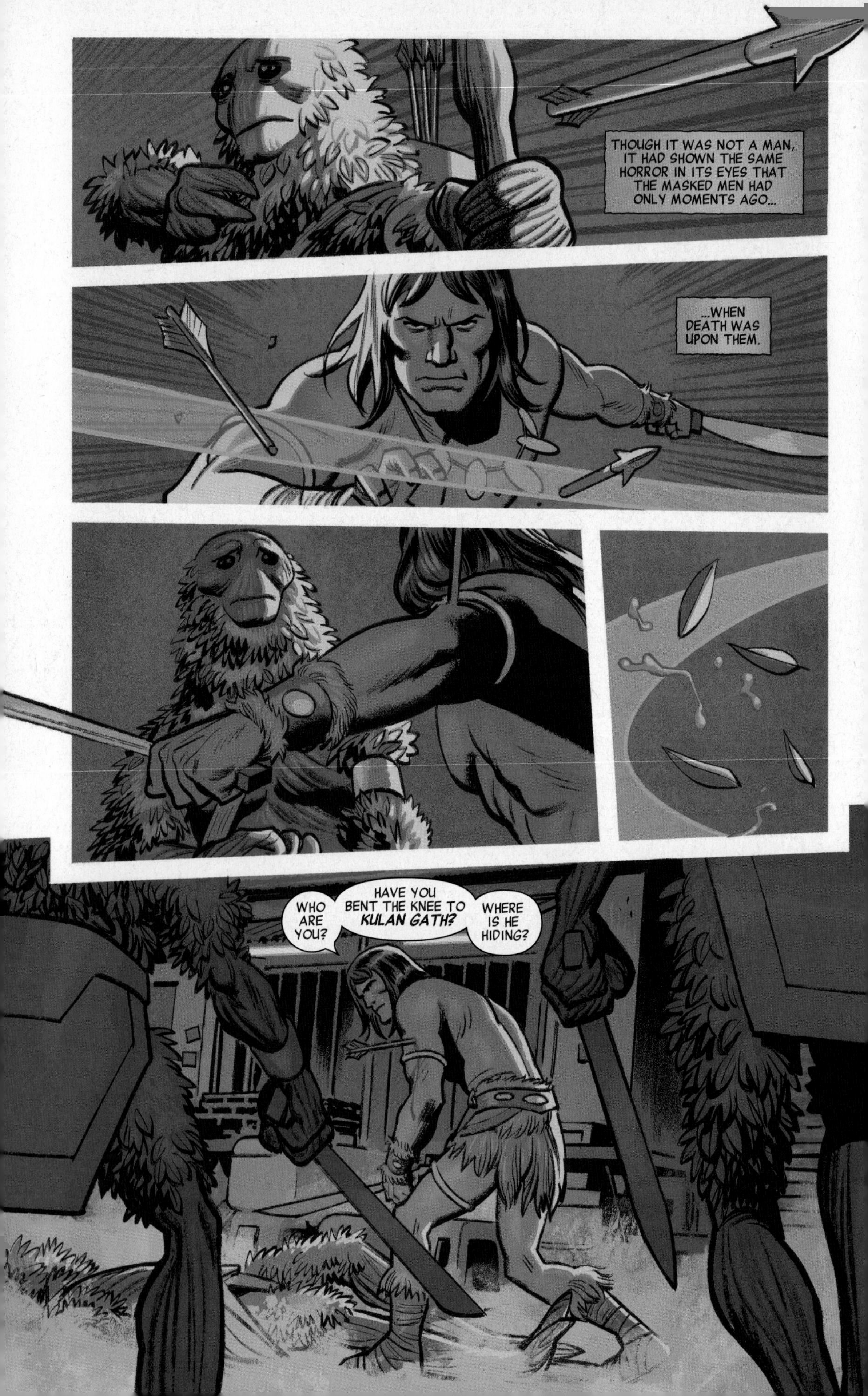
THOUGH IT WAS NOT A MAN, IT HAD SHOWN THE SAME HORROR IN ITS EYES THAT THE MASKED MEN HAD ONLY MOMENTS AGO...
...WHEN DEATH WAS UPON THEM.
WHO ARE YOU?
HAVE YOU BENT THE KNEE TO KULAN GATH?
WHERE IS HE HIDING?

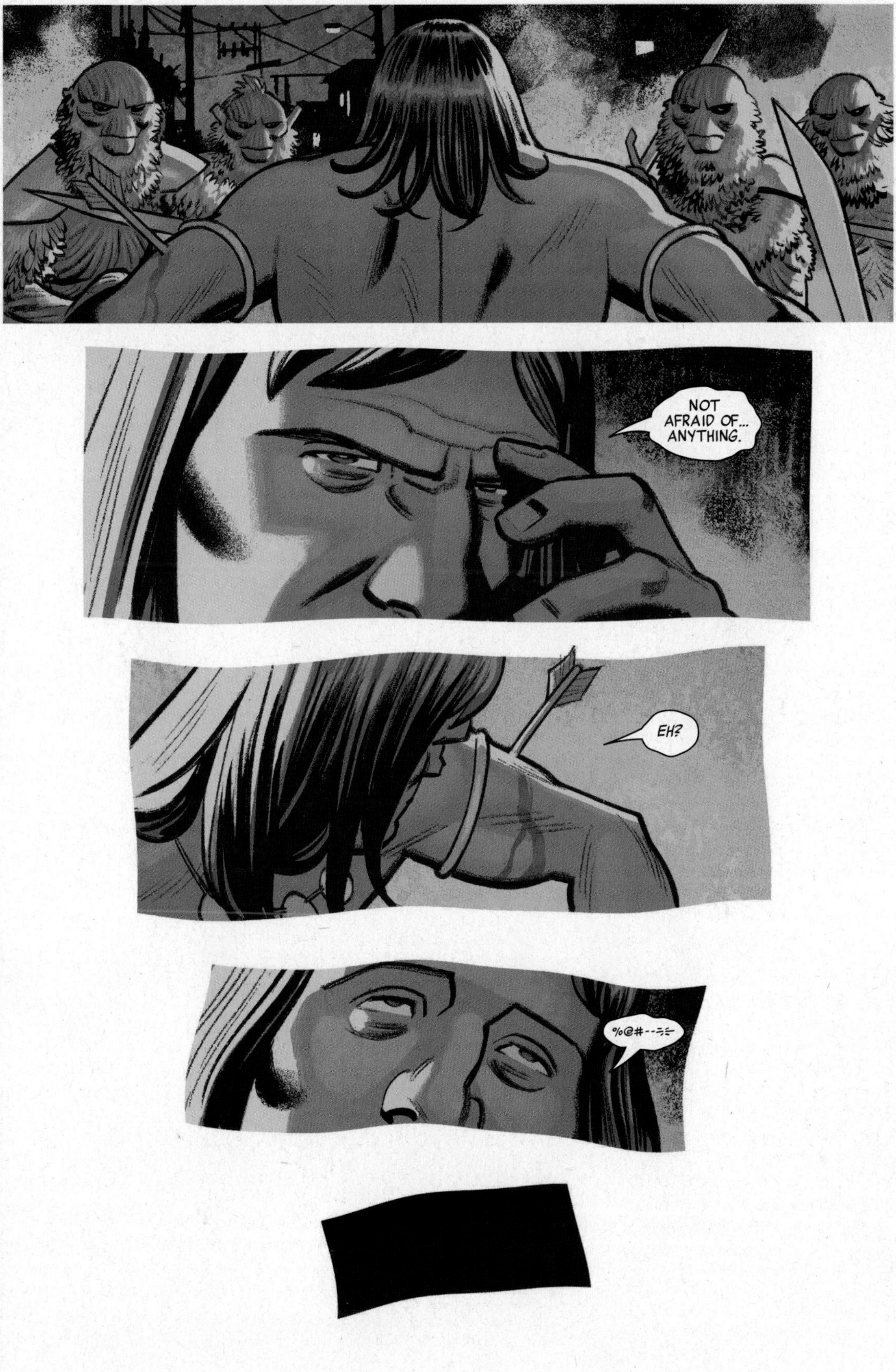
NOT AFRAID OF... ANYTHING.
EH?

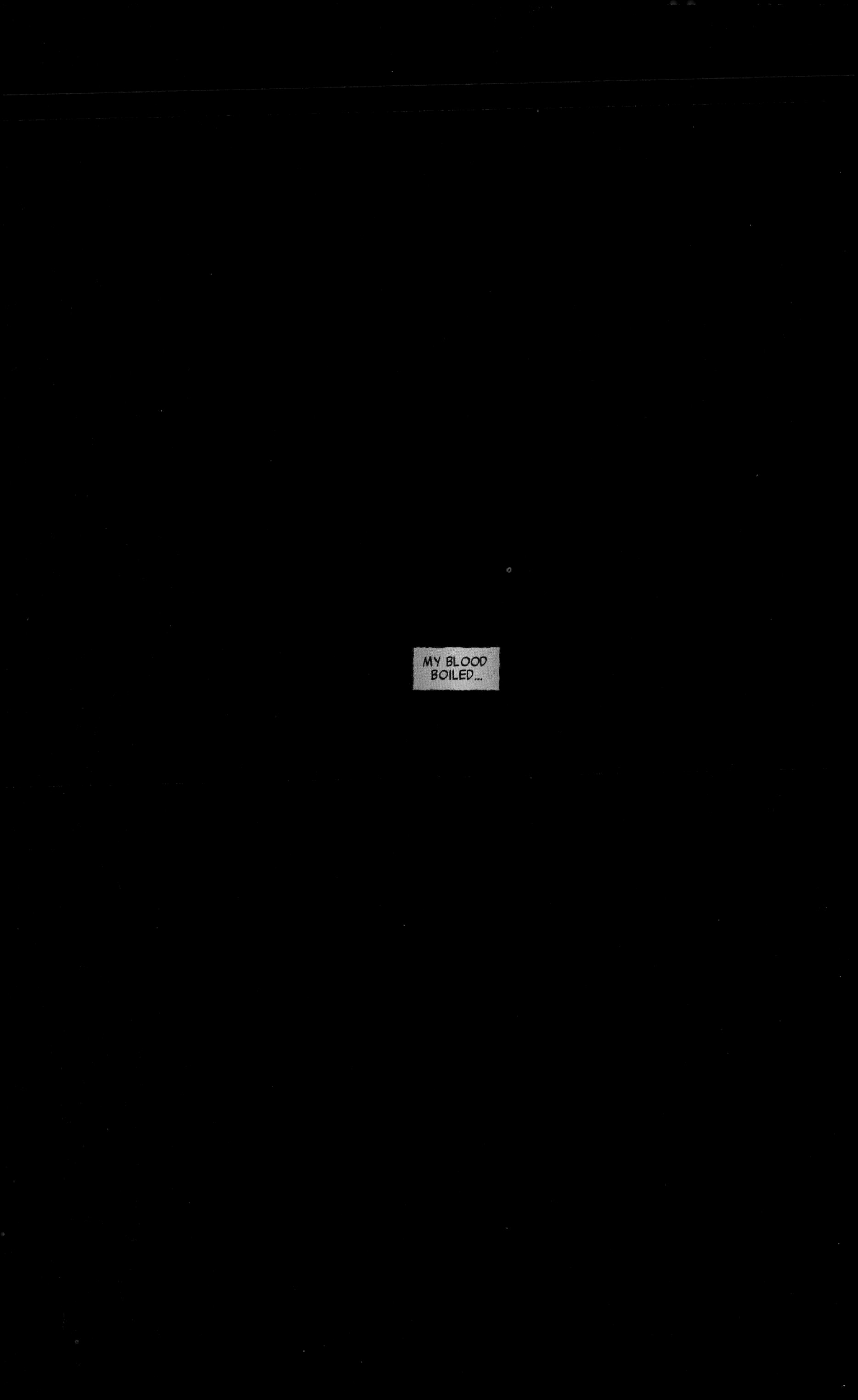
MY BLOOD BOILED...

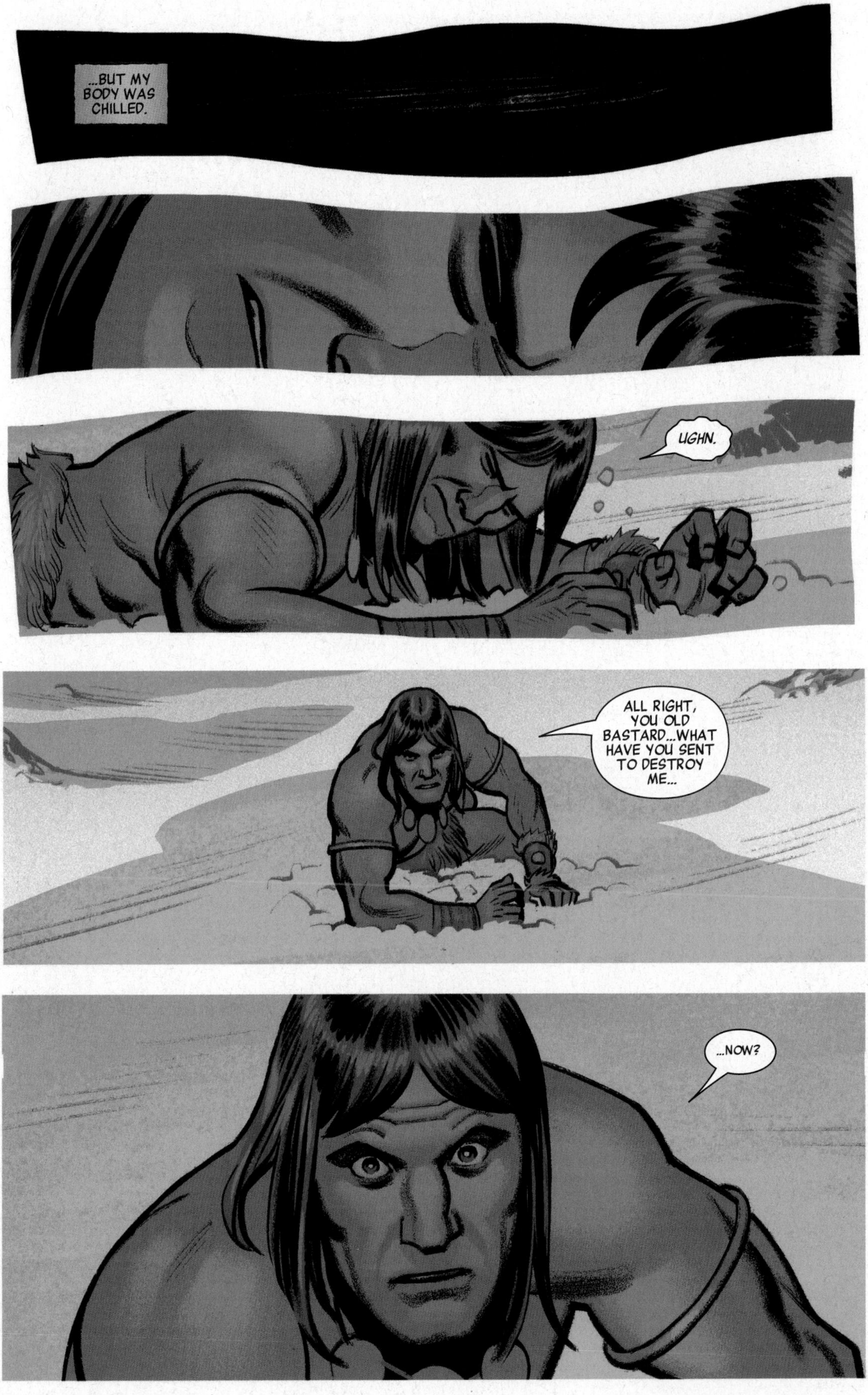
...BUT MY BODY WAS CHILLED.
UGHN.
ALL RIGHT, YOU OLD BASTARD...WHAT HAVE YOU SENT TO DESTROY ME...
...NOW?

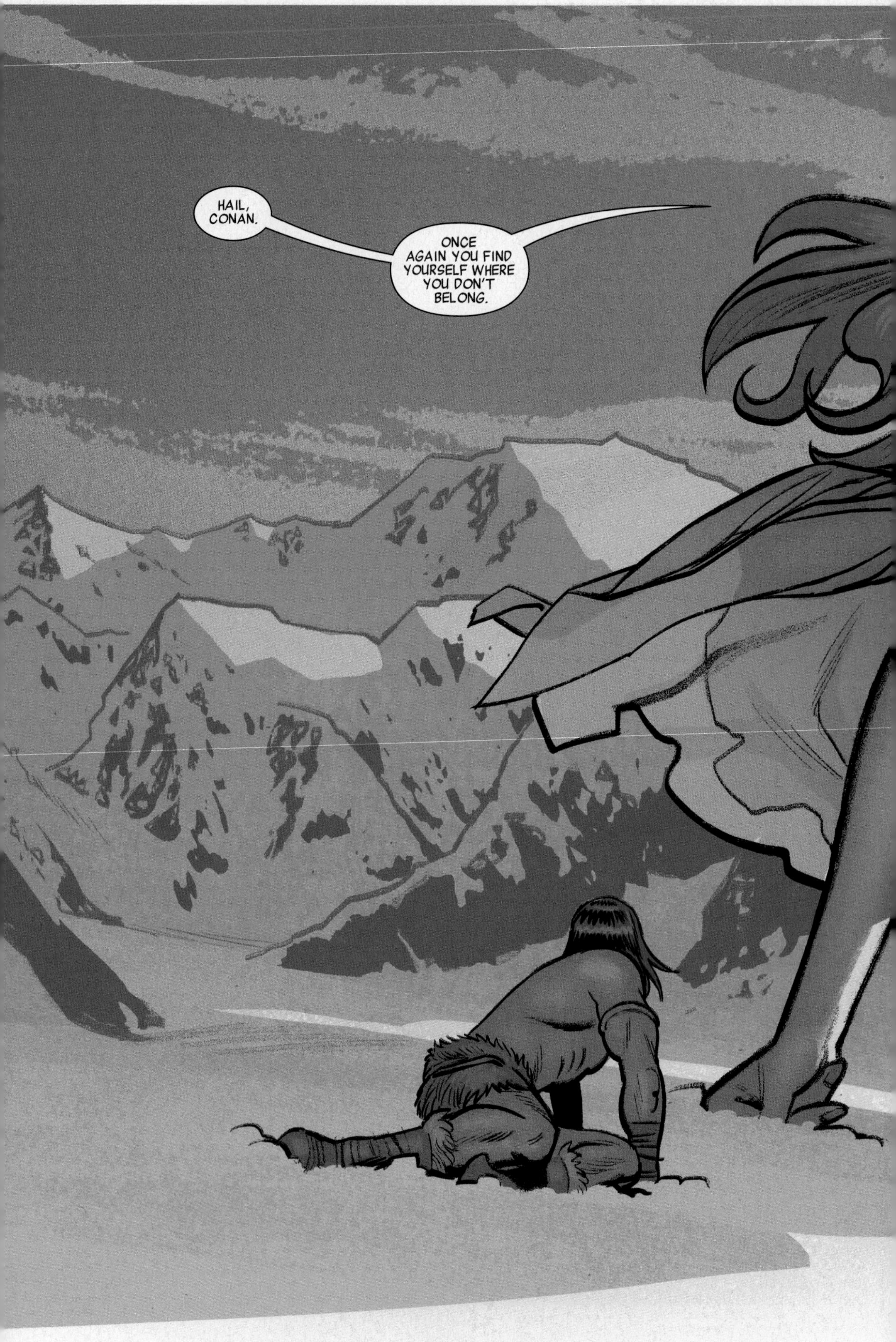
HAIL, CONAN.
ONCE AGAIN YOU FIND YOURSELF WHERE YOU DON'T BELONG.

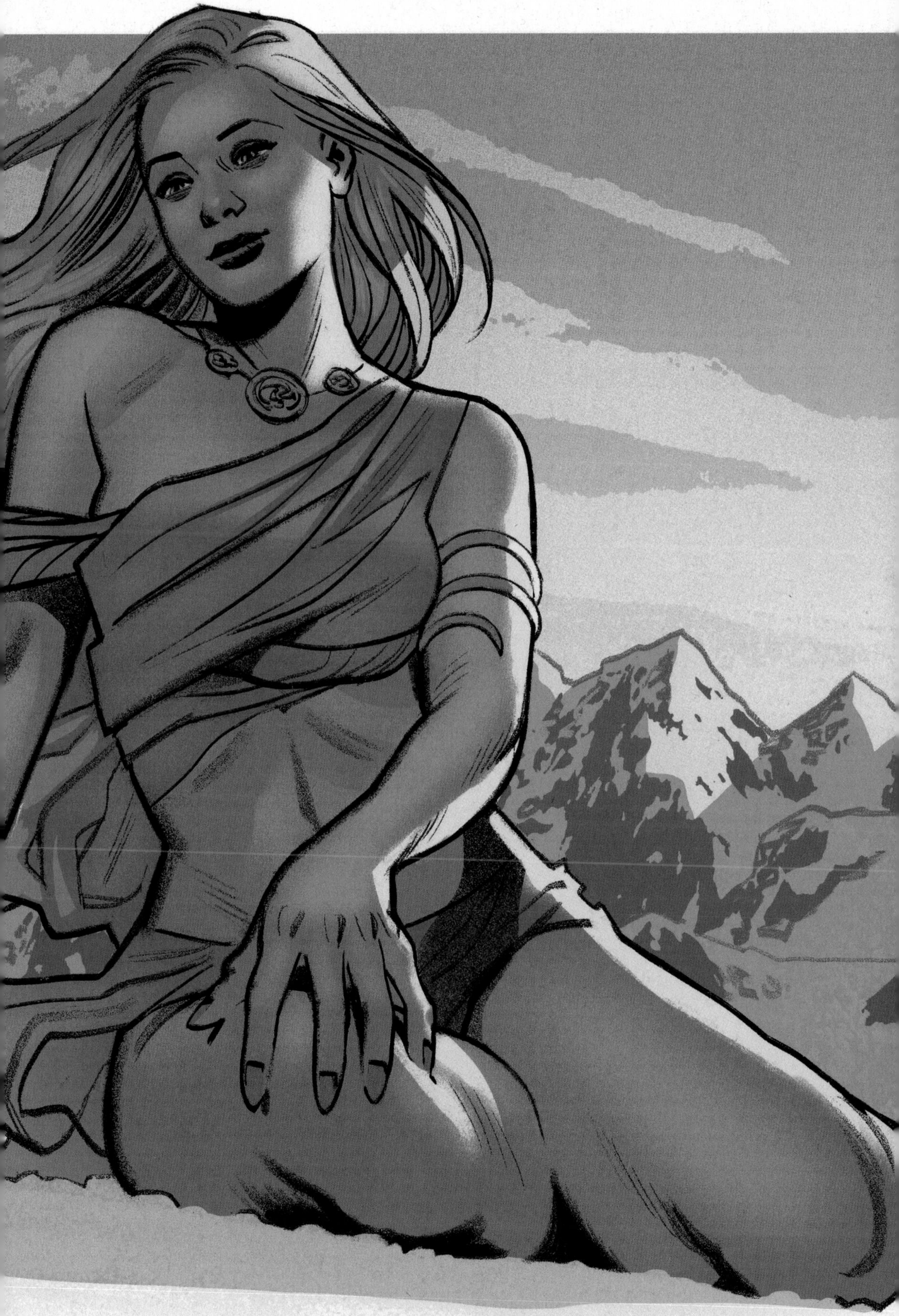

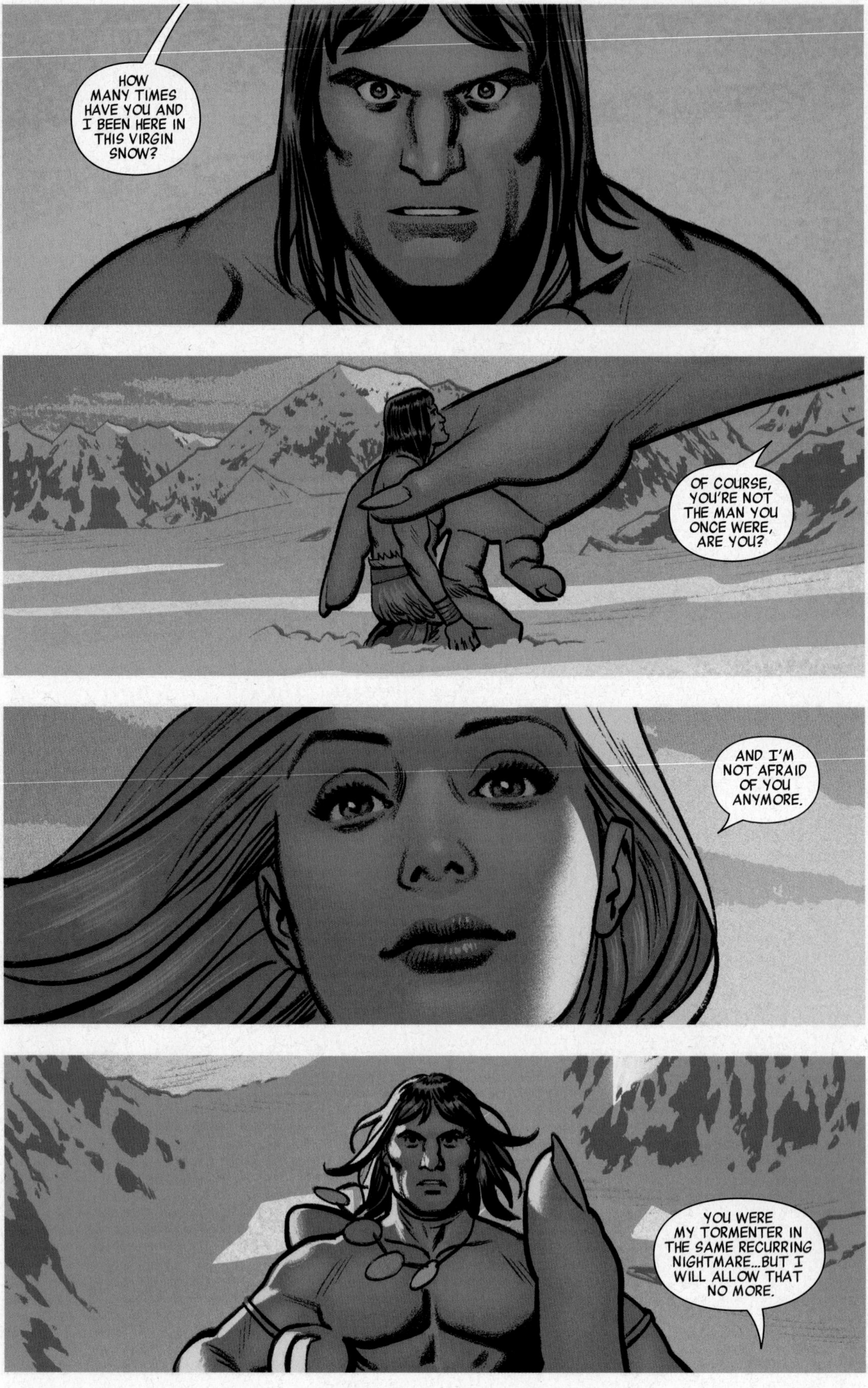
HOW MANY TIMES HAVE YOU AND I BEEN HERE IN THIS VIRGIN SNOW?
OF COURSE, YOU'RE NOT THE MAN YOU ONCE WERE, ARE YOU?
AND I'M NOT AFRAID OF YOU ANYMORE.
YOU WERE MY TORMENTER IN THE SAME RECURRING NIGHTMARE...BUT I WILL ALLOW THAT NO MORE.

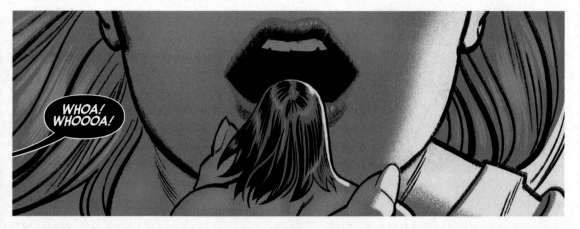

WHOA! WHOOOA!

HEY, MAN! IT'S *ME!* REMEMBER-- THE SAVAGE LAND?

IT'S ME-- EDDIE!

SHE WAS ABOUT TO EAT ME...

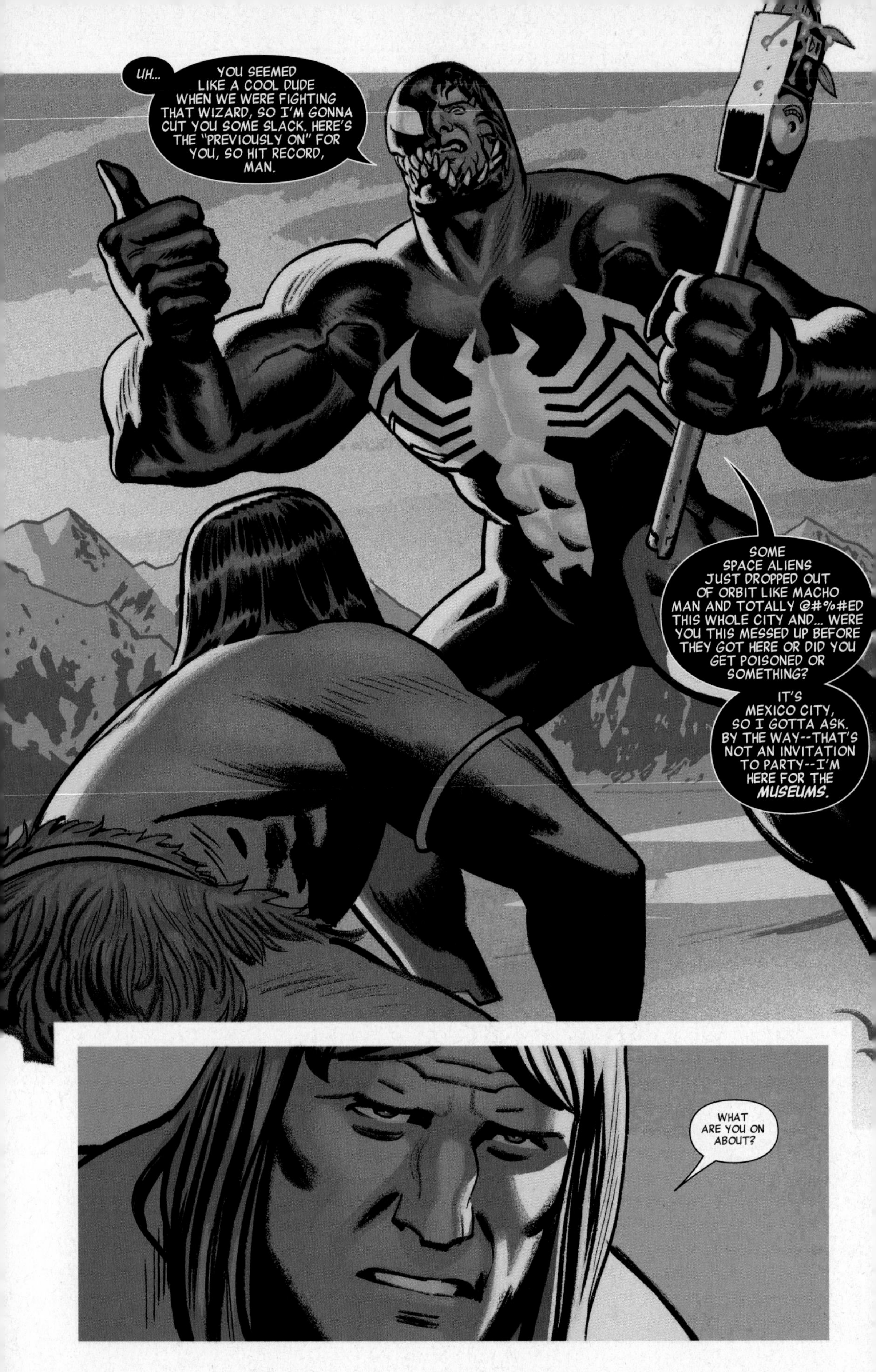
UH...
YOU SEEMED LIKE A COOL DUDE WHEN WE WERE FIGHTING THAT WIZARD, SO I'M GONNA CUT YOU SOME SLACK. HERE'S THE "PREVIOUSLY ON" FOR YOU, SO HIT RECORD, MAN.
SOME SPACE ALIENS JUST DROPPED OUT OF ORBIT LIKE MACHO MAN AND TOTALLY @#%#ED THIS WHOLE CITY AND... WERE YOU THIS MESSED UP BEFORE THEY GOT HERE OR DID YOU GET POISONED OR SOMETHING?
IT'S MEXICO CITY, SO I GOTTA ASK. BY THE WAY--THAT'S NOT AN INVITATION TO PARTY--I'M HERE FOR THE *MUSEUMS.*
WHAT ARE YOU ON ABOUT?

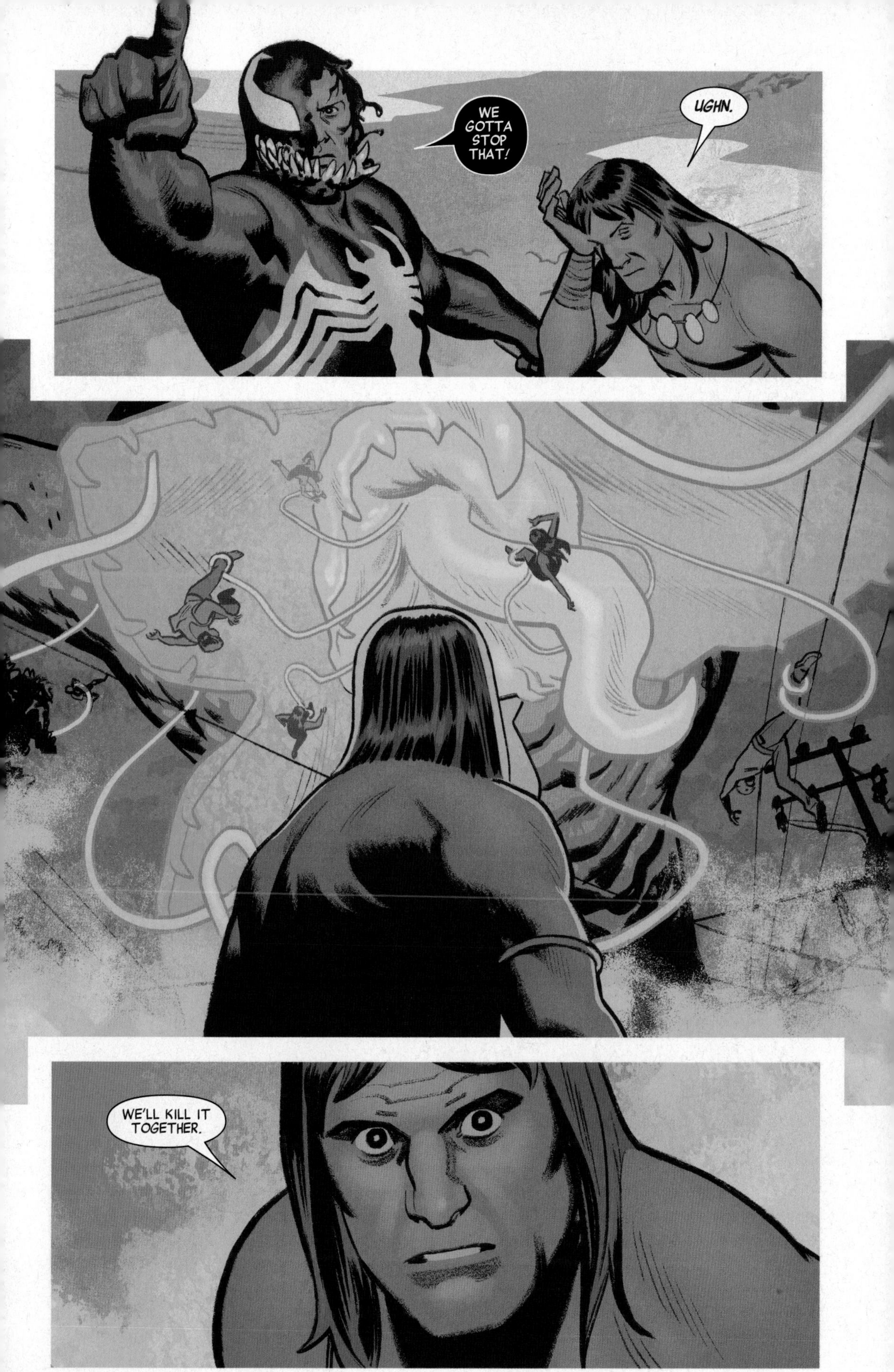
WE GOTTA STOP THAT!
UGHN.
WE'LL KILL IT TOGETHER.

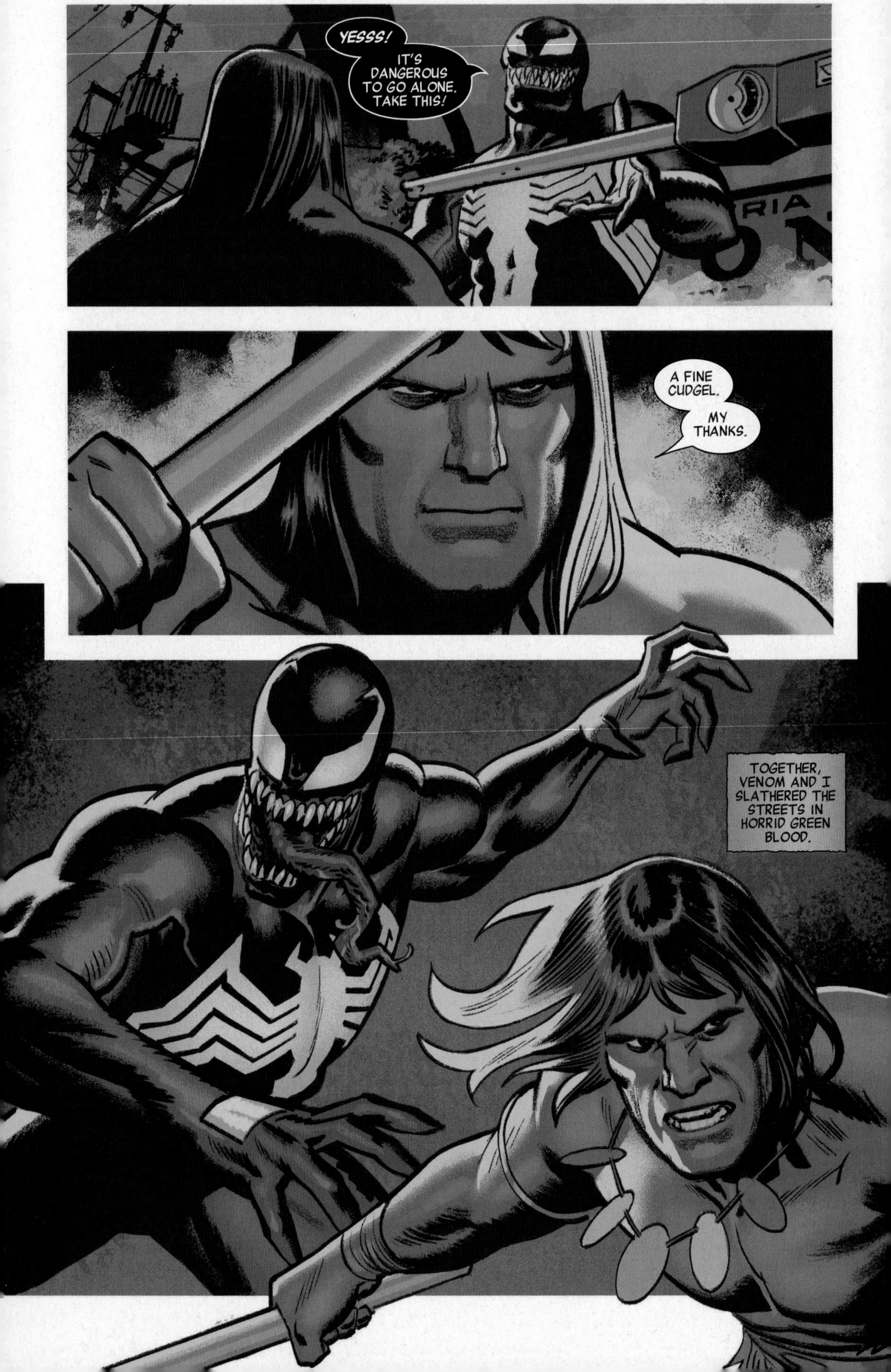
YESSS!
IT'S DANGEROUS TO GO ALONE. TAKE THIS!
A FINE CUDGEL.
MY THANKS.
TOGETHER, VENOM AND I SLATHERED THE STREETS IN HORRID GREEN BLOOD.

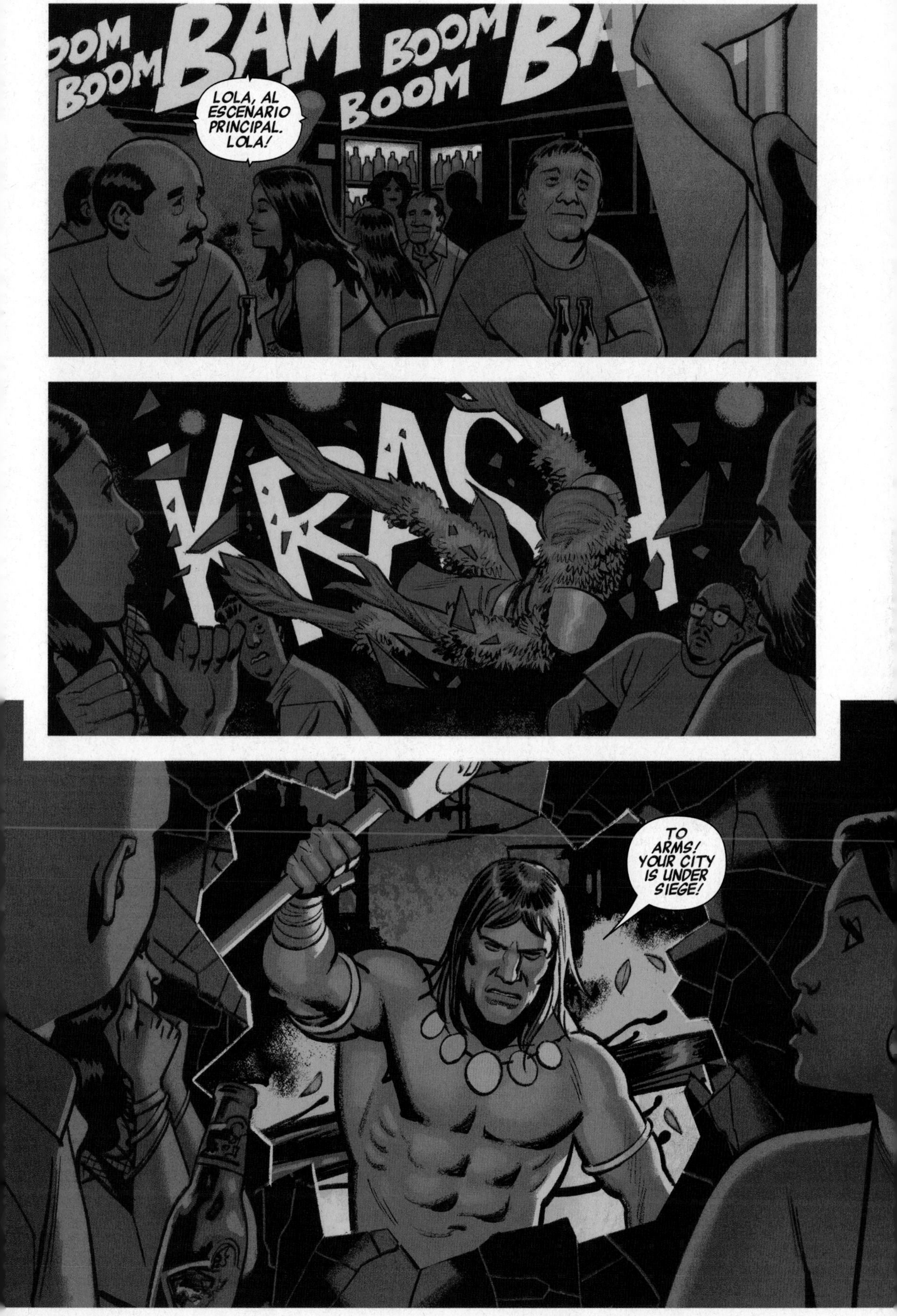
BOOM BOOM BAM BOOM BOOM BA
LOLA, AL ESCENARIO PRINCIPAL. LOLA!
KRASH
TO ARMS! YOUR CITY IS UNDER SIEGE!

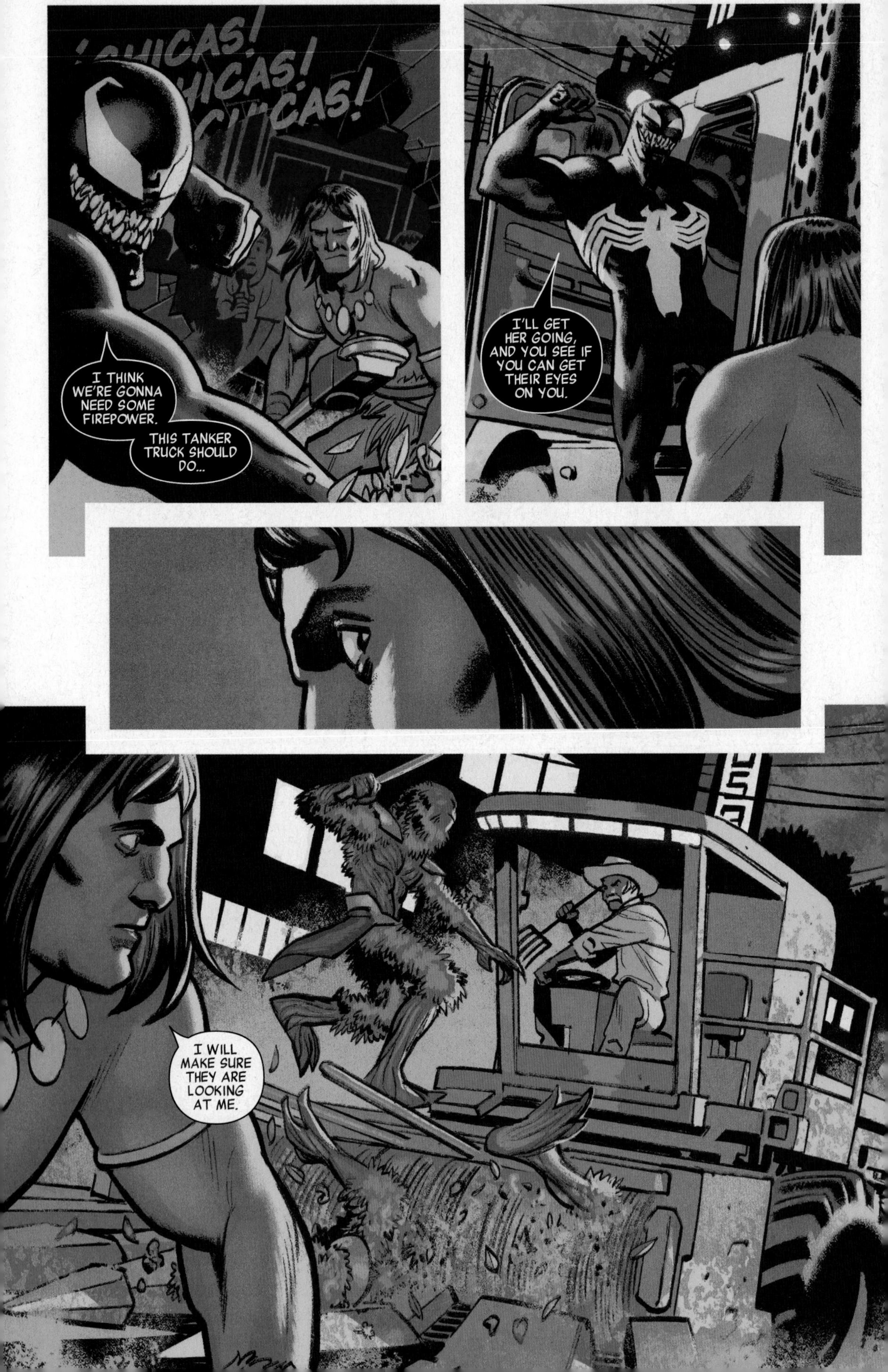
¡CHICAS! ¡CHICAS! ¡CHICAS!
I THINK WE'RE GONNA NEED SOME FIREPOWER.
THIS TANKER TRUCK SHOULD DO...
I'LL GET HER GOING, AND YOU SEE IF YOU CAN GET THEIR EYES ON YOU.
I WILL MAKE SURE THEY ARE LOOKING AT ME.

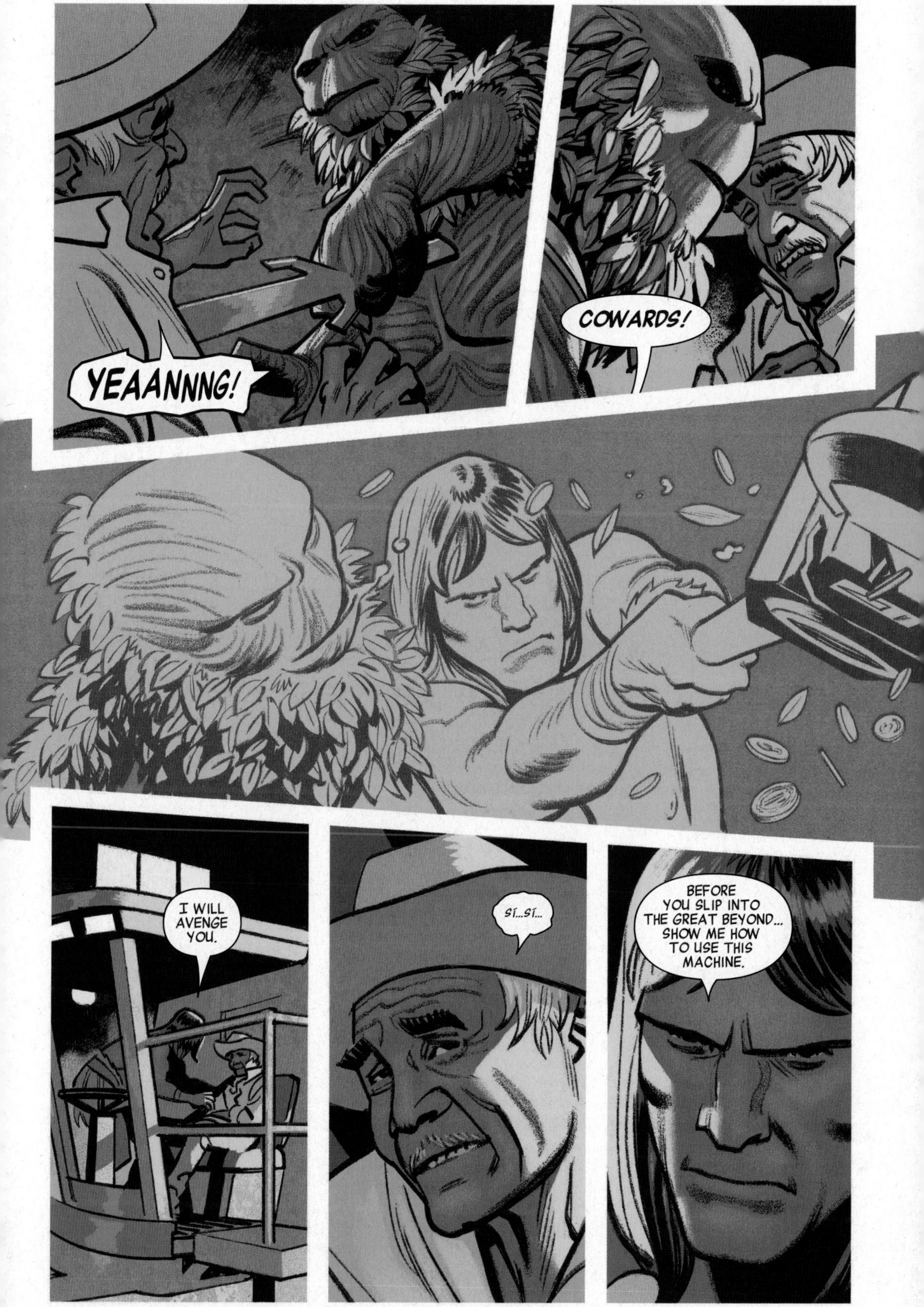
YEAANNNG!
COWARDS!
I WILL AVENGE YOU.
SÍ...SÍ...
BEFORE YOU SLIP INTO THE GREAT BEYOND... SHOW ME HOW TO USE THIS MACHINE.

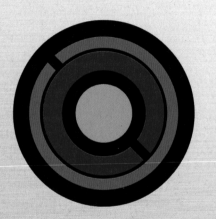

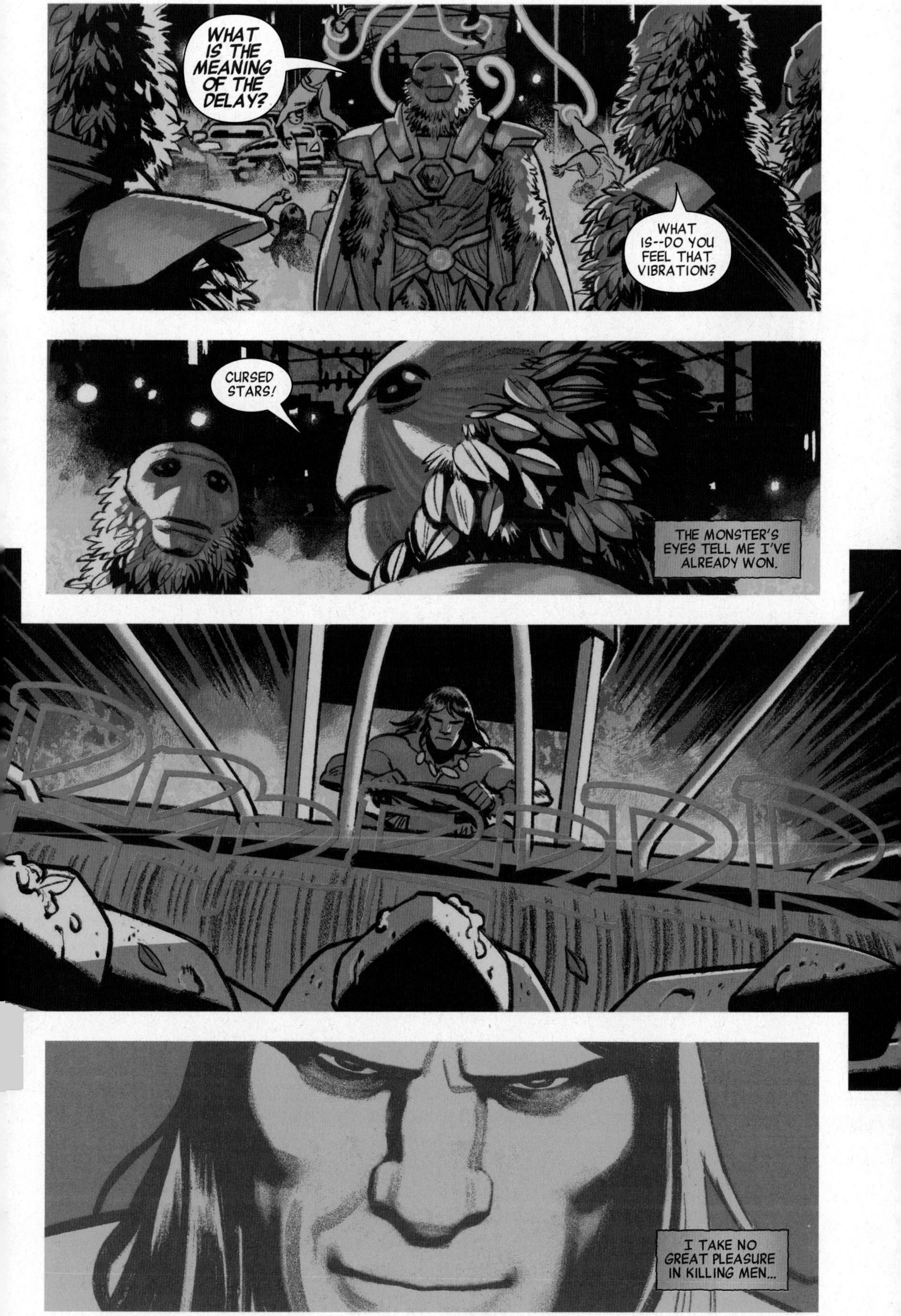
WHAT IS THE MEANING OF THE DELAY?
WHAT IS--DO YOU FEEL THAT VIBRATION?
CURSED STARS!
THE MONSTER'S EYES TELL ME I'VE ALREADY WON.
DDDDDDDDDDD
I TAKE NO GREAT PLEASURE IN KILLING MEN...

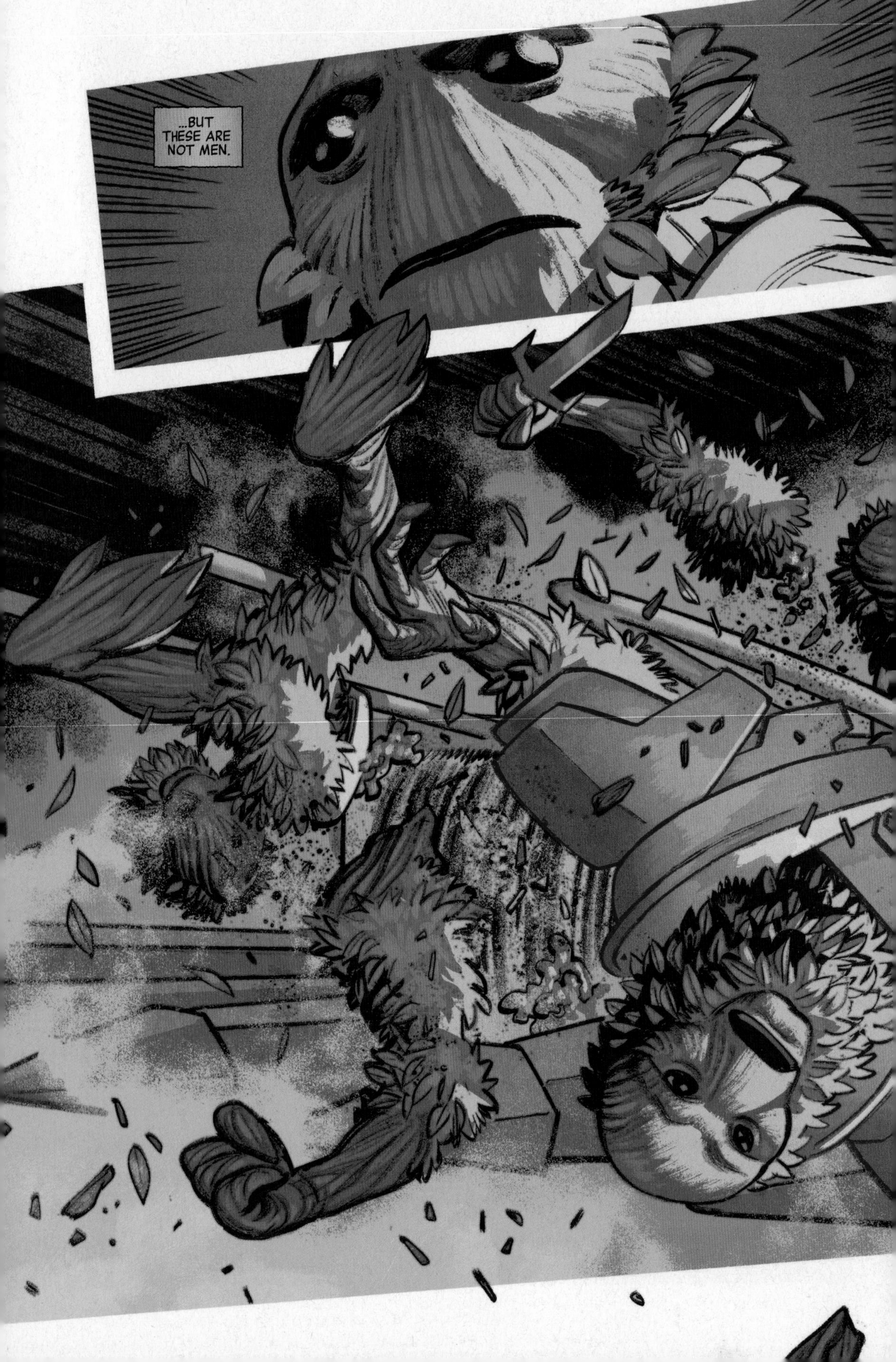
...BUT THESE ARE NOT MEN.

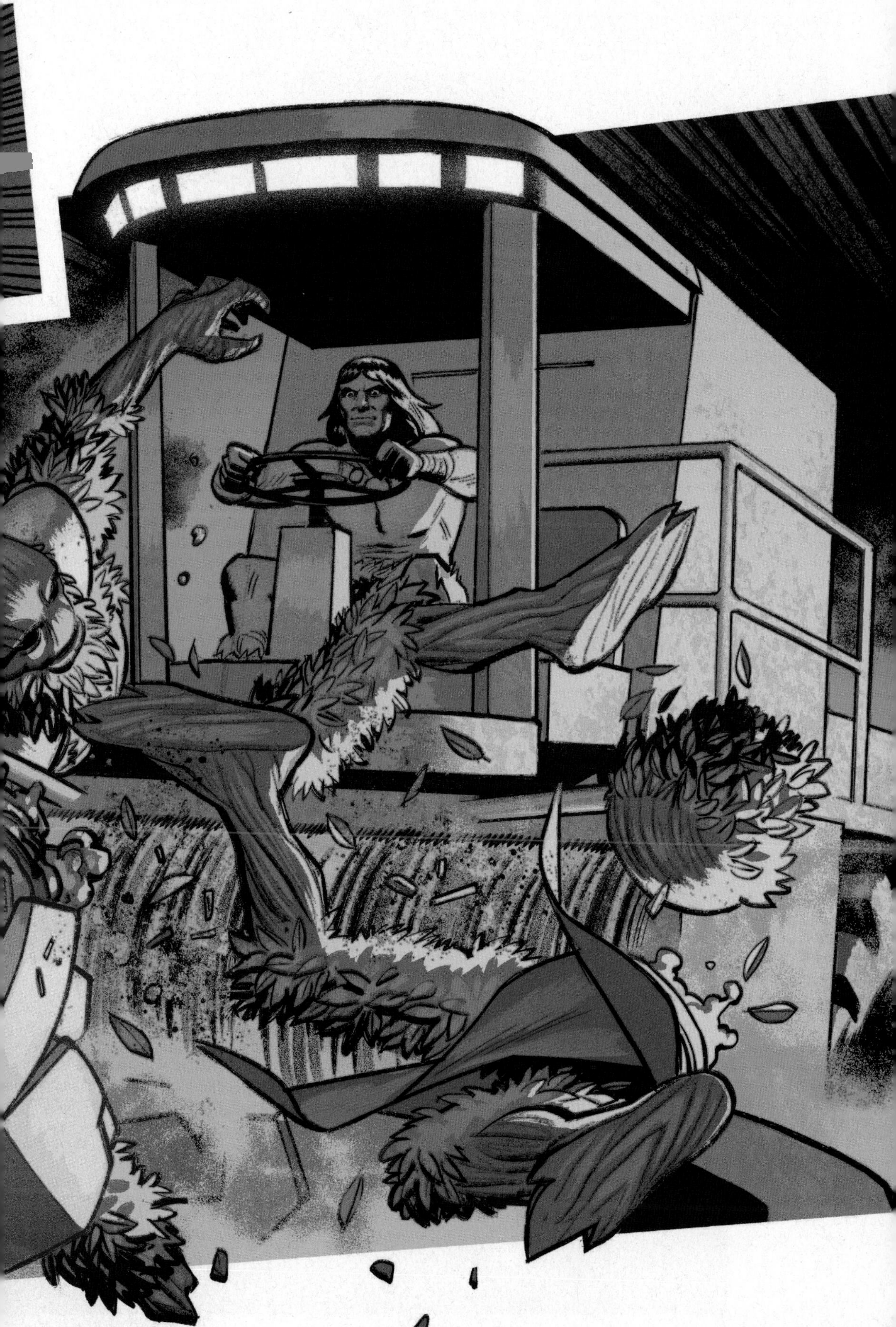

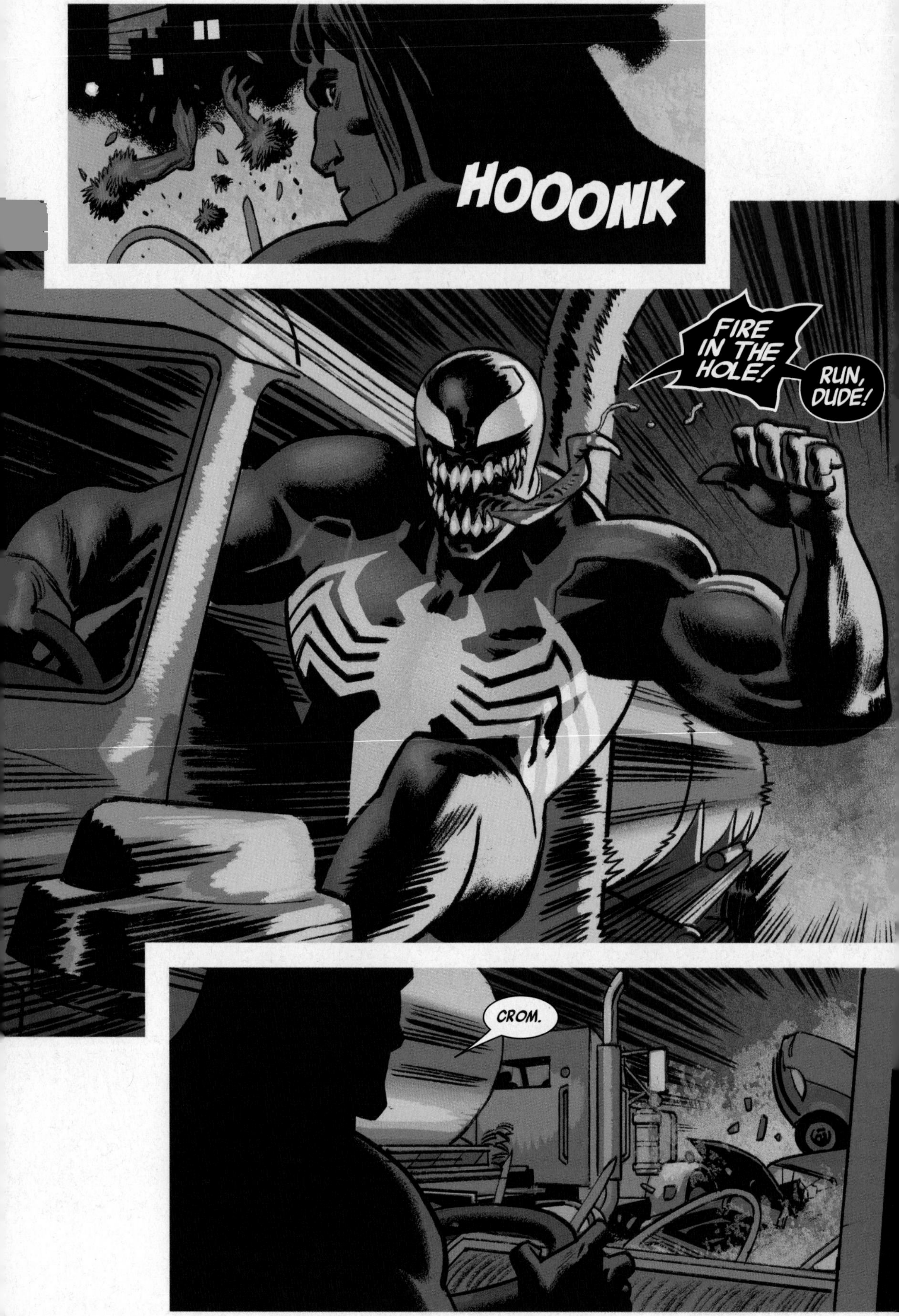
HOOONK
FIRE IN THE HOLE!
RUN, DUDE!
CROM.

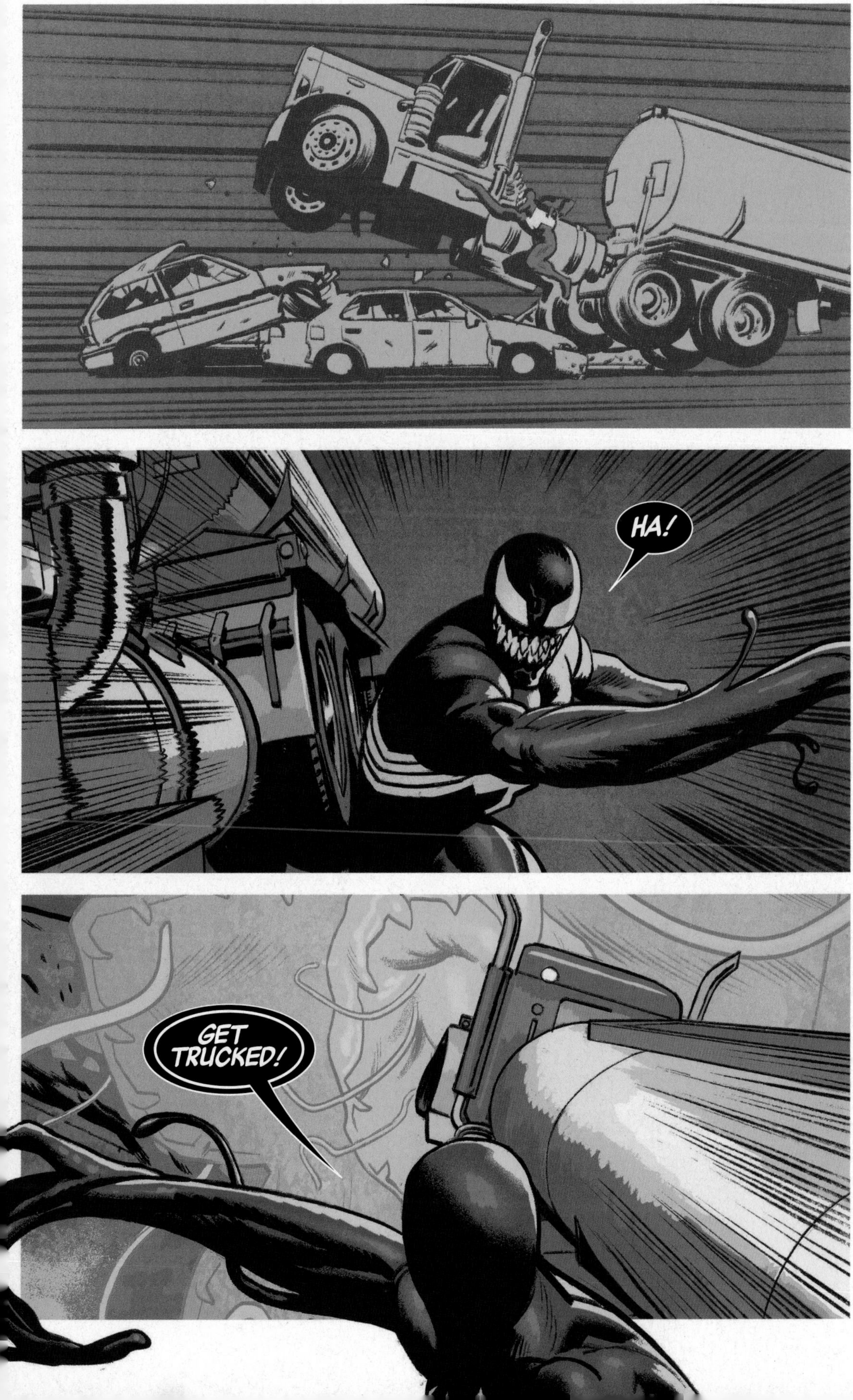
HA!
GET TRUCKED!

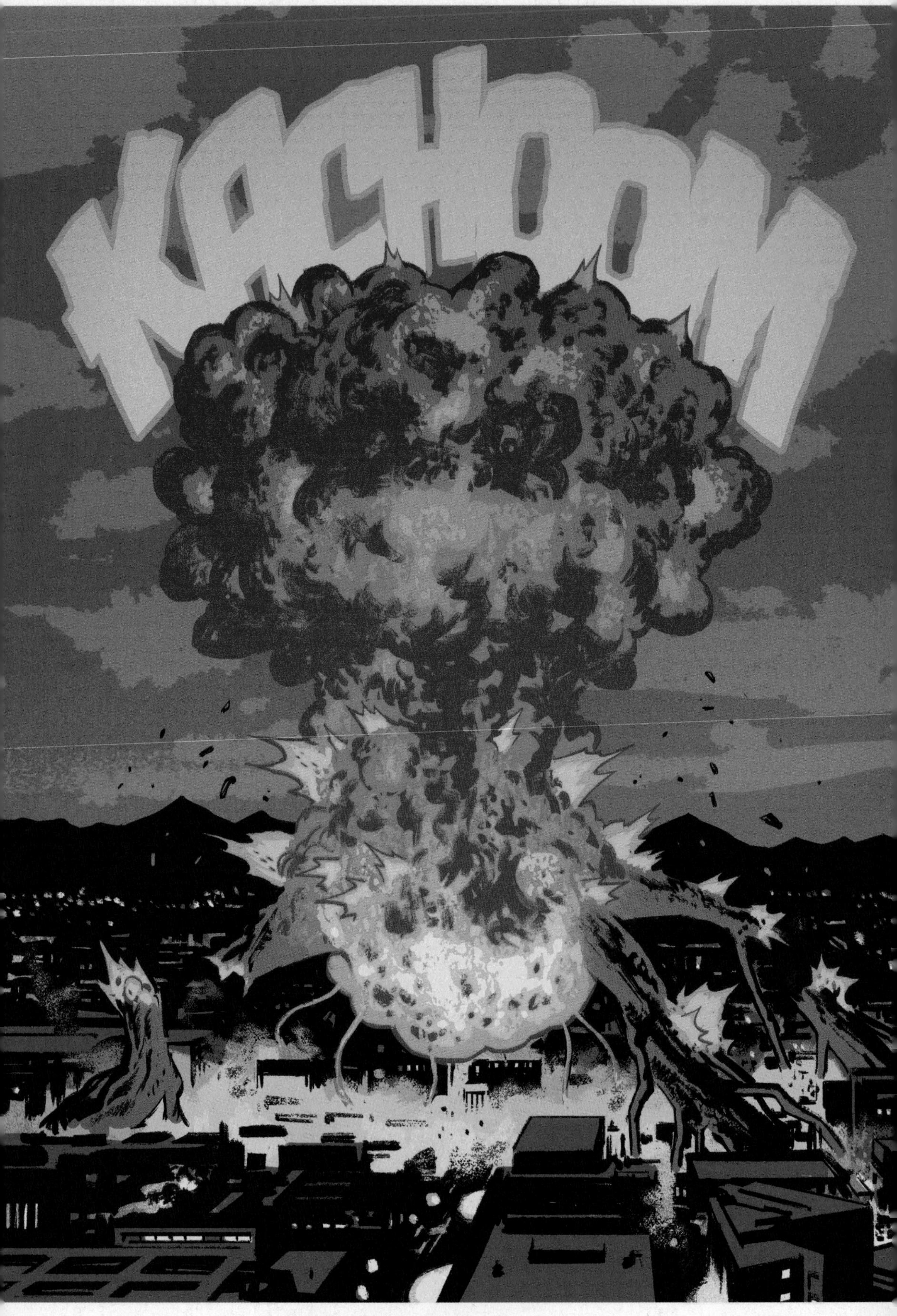
KACHOOM

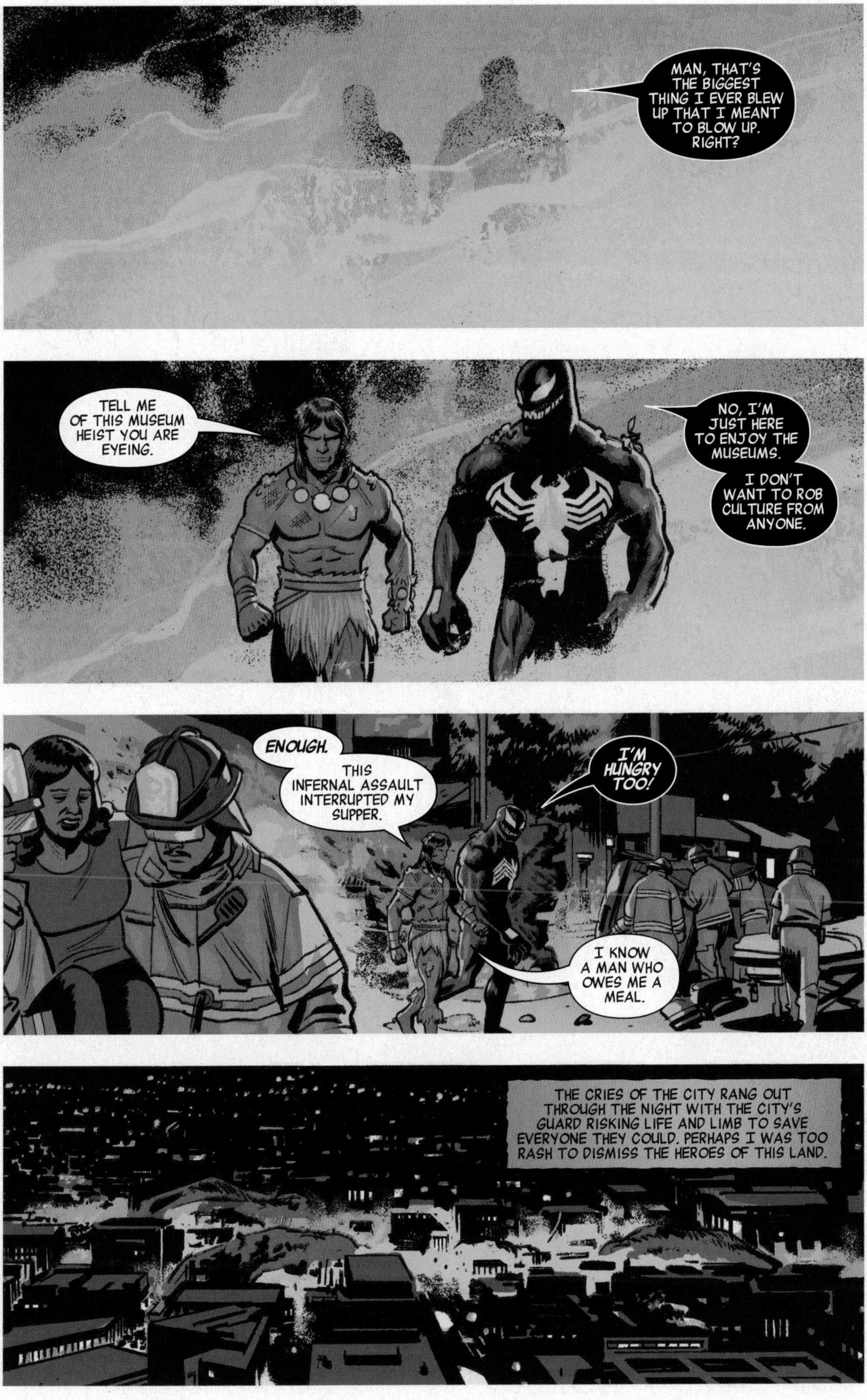
MAN, THAT'S THE BIGGEST THING I EVER BLEW UP THAT I MEANT TO BLOW UP. RIGHT?
TELL ME OF THIS MUSEUM HEIST YOU ARE EYEING.
NO, I'M JUST HERE TO ENJOY THE MUSEUMS.
I DON'T WANT TO ROB CULTURE FROM ANYONE.
ENOUGH.
THIS INFERNAL ASSAULT INTERRUPTED MY SUPPER.
I'M HUNGRY TOO!
I KNOW A MAN WHO OWES ME A MEAL.
THE CRIES OF THE CITY RANG OUT THROUGH THE NIGHT WITH THE CITY'S GUARD RISKING LIFE AND LIMB TO SAVE EVERYONE THEY COULD. PERHAPS I WAS TOO RASH TO DISMISS THE HEROES OF THIS LAND.

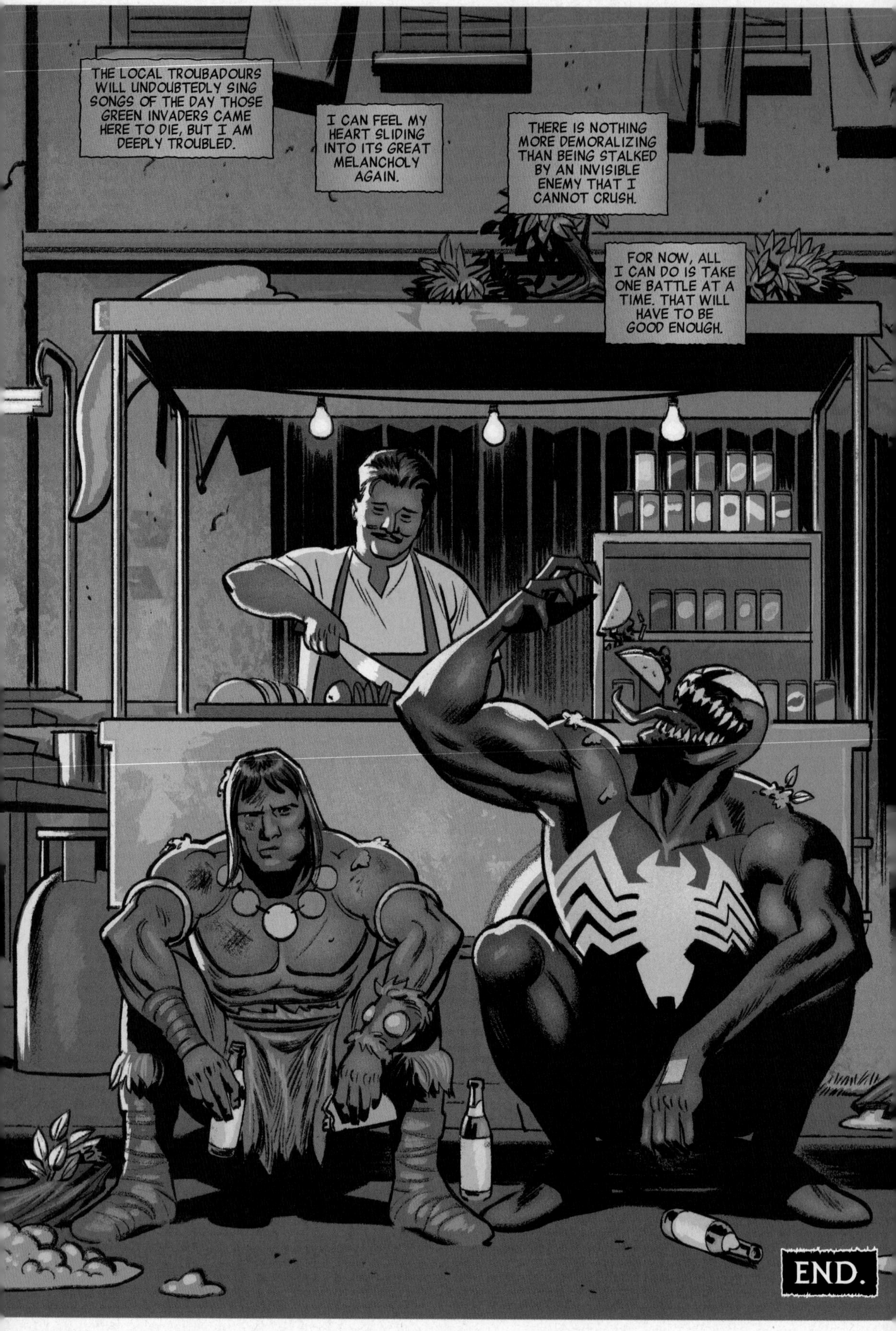
THE LOCAL TROUBADOURS WILL UNDOUBTEDLY SING SONGS OF THE DAY THOSE GREEN INVADERS CAME HERE TO DIE, BUT I AM DEEPLY TROUBLED.
I CAN FEEL MY HEART SLIDING INTO ITS GREAT MELANCHOLY AGAIN.
THERE IS NOTHING MORE DEMORALIZING THAN BEING STALKED BY AN INVISIBLE ENEMY THAT I CANNOT CRUSH.
FOR NOW, ALL I CAN DO IS TAKE ONE BATTLE AT A TIME. THAT WILL HAVE TO BE GOOD ENOUGH.
END.

LORDS OF EMPYRE: EMPEROR HULKLING
VARIANT BY
Jen Bartel

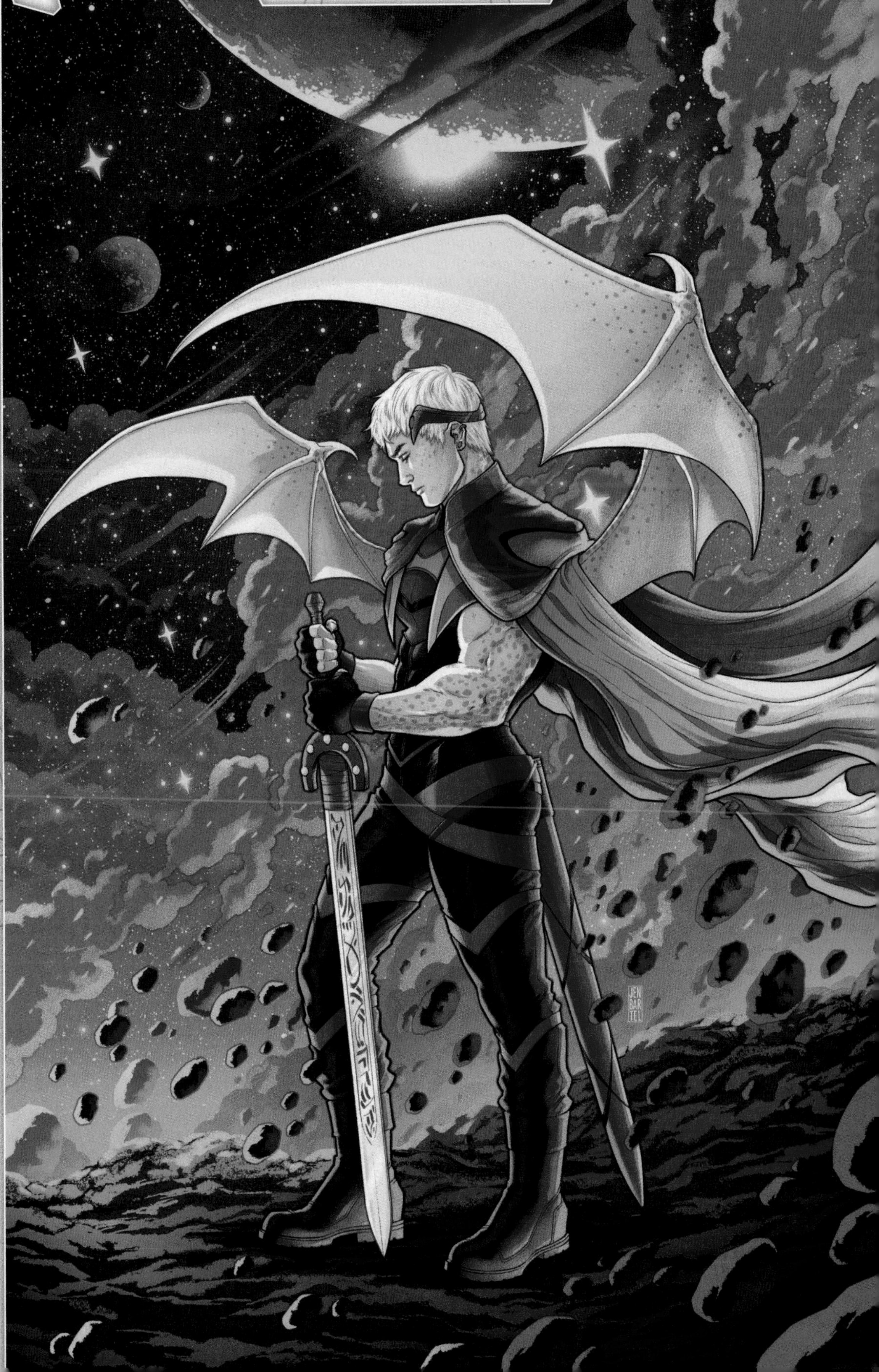
JEN BARTEL

LORDS OF EMPYRE: EMPEROR HULKLING
VARIANT BY
Luciano Vecchio

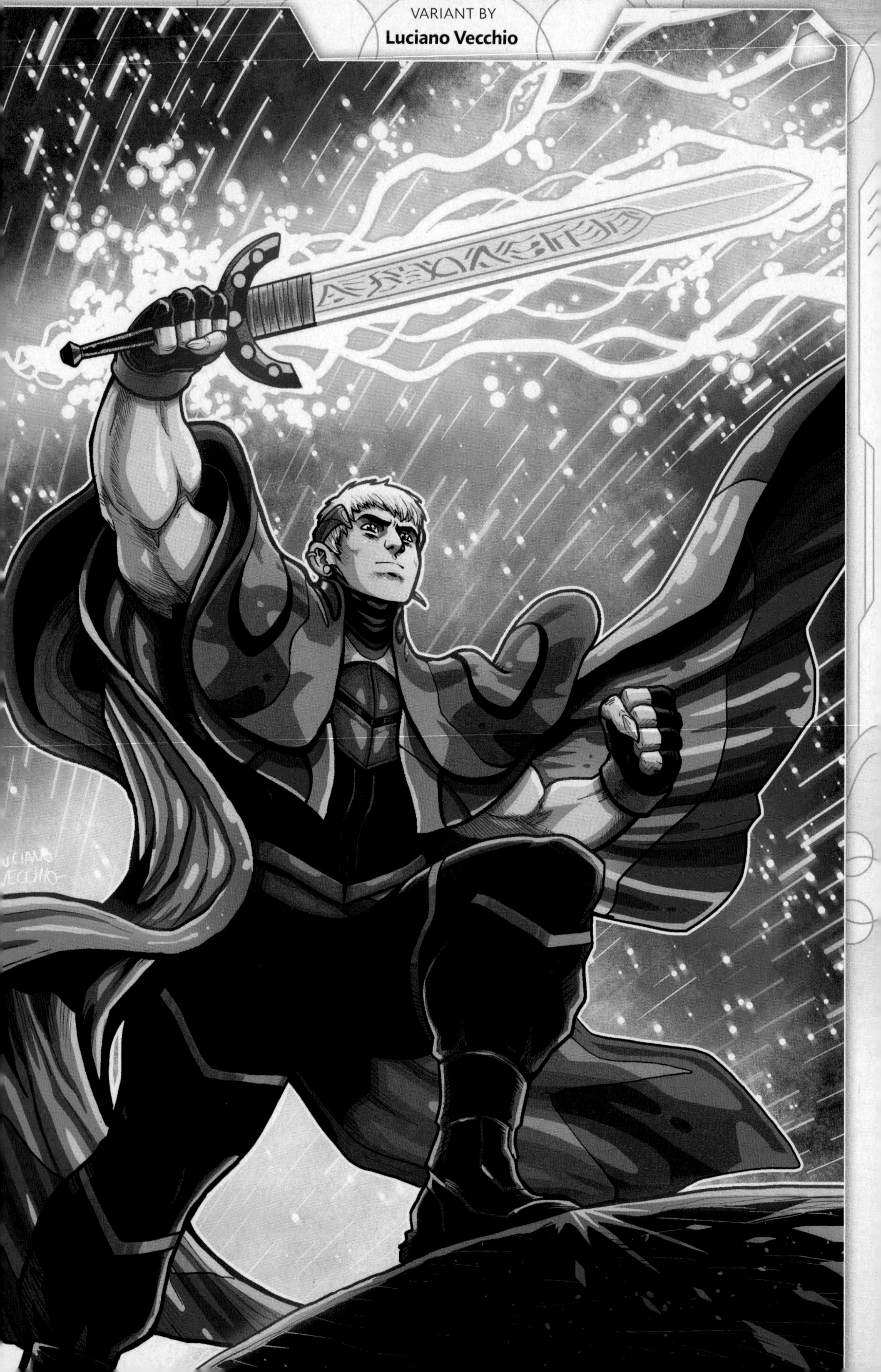

LORDS OF EMPYRE: EMPEROR HULKLING
VARIANT BY
Jeff Dekal

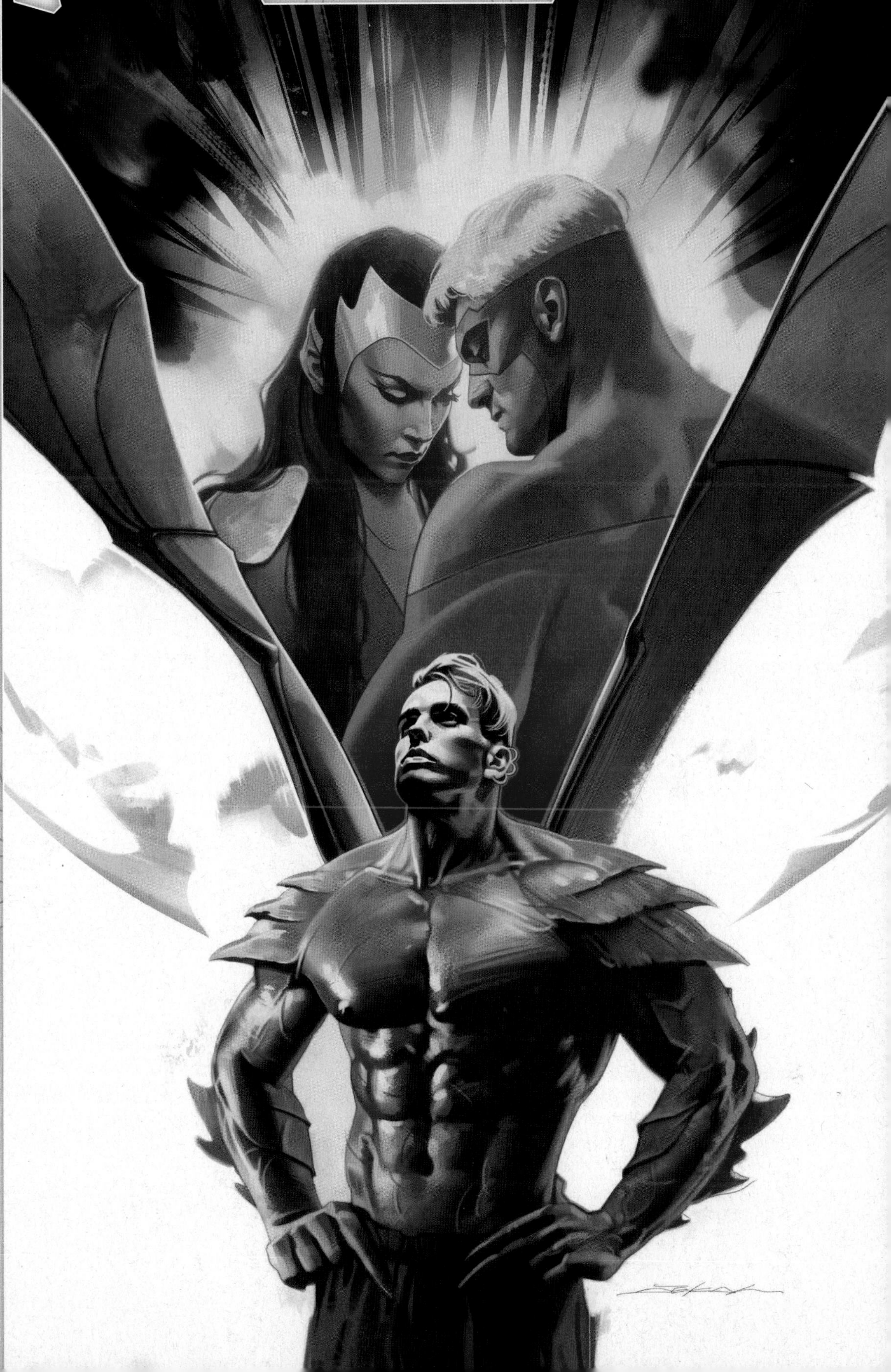

LORDS OF EMPYRE: CELESTIAL MESSIAH
VARIANT BY
Joshua Cassara & **Dean White**

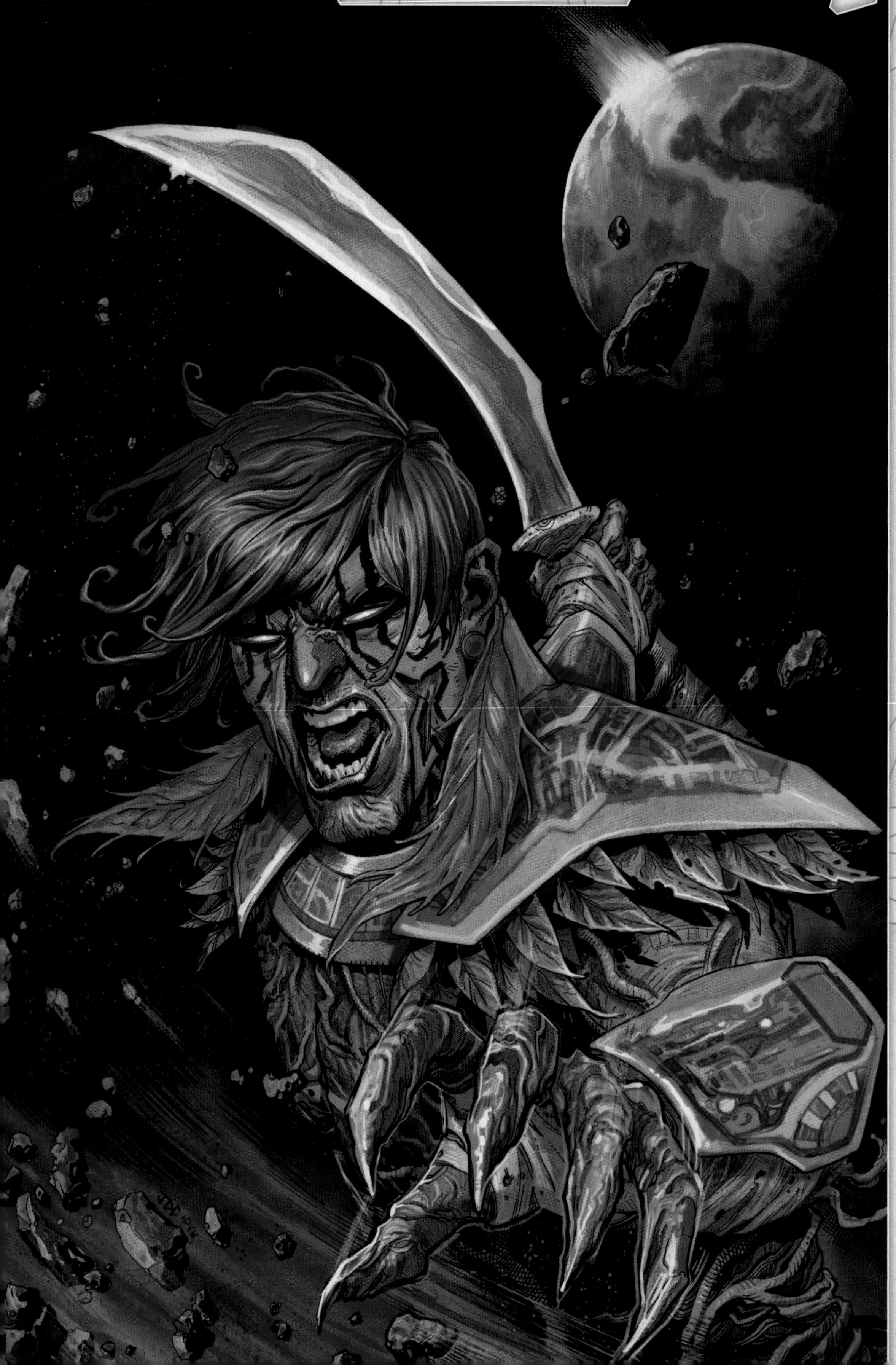

LORDS OF EMPYRE: SWORDSMAN
VARIANT BY
Salvador Larroca & **Guru-eFX**

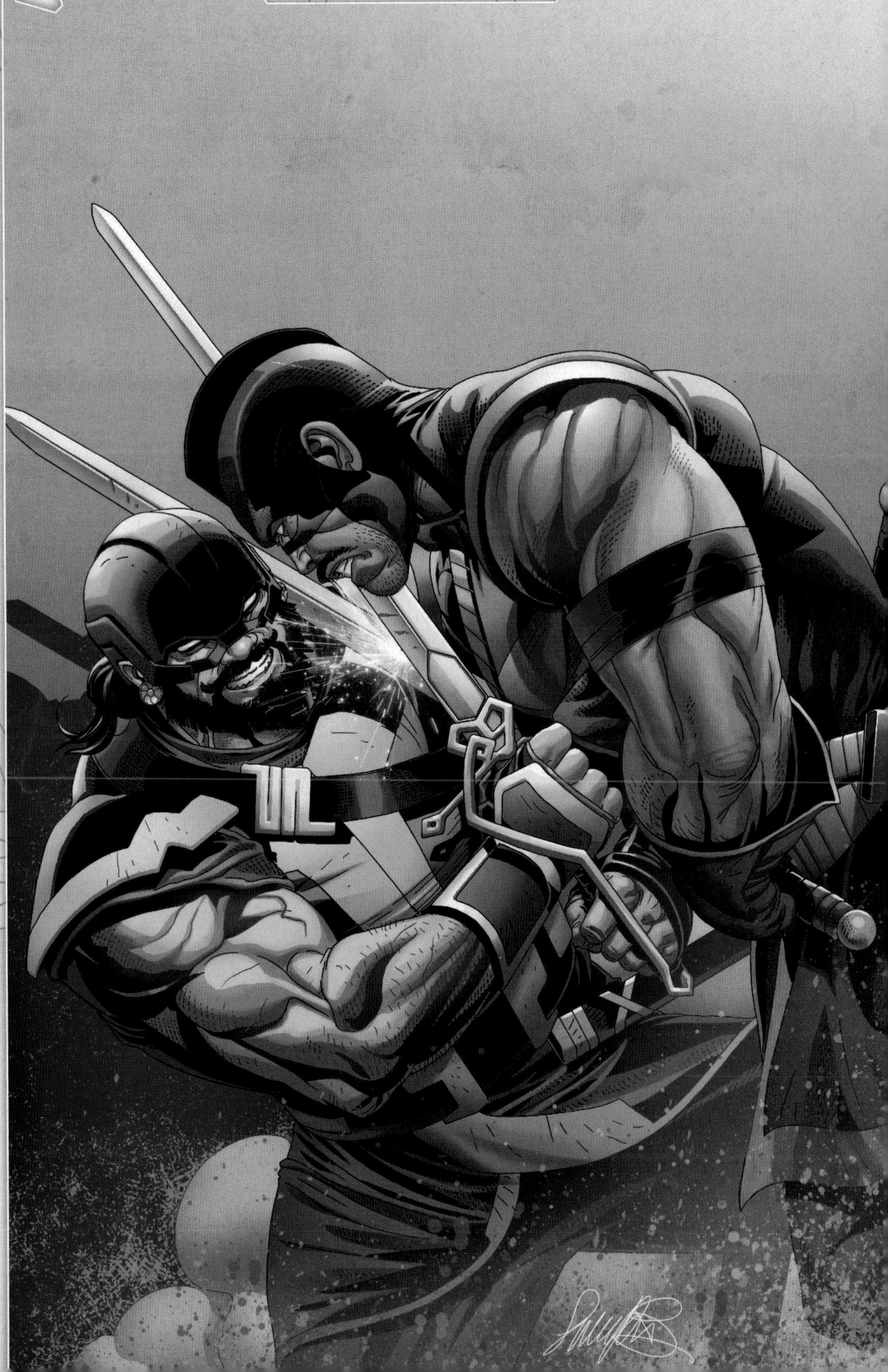

LORDS OF EMPYRE: EMPEROR HULKLING
PAGE 30 PENCILS, INKS AND COLORS BY
Manuel Garcia, **Cam Smith**
& **Tríona Farrell**

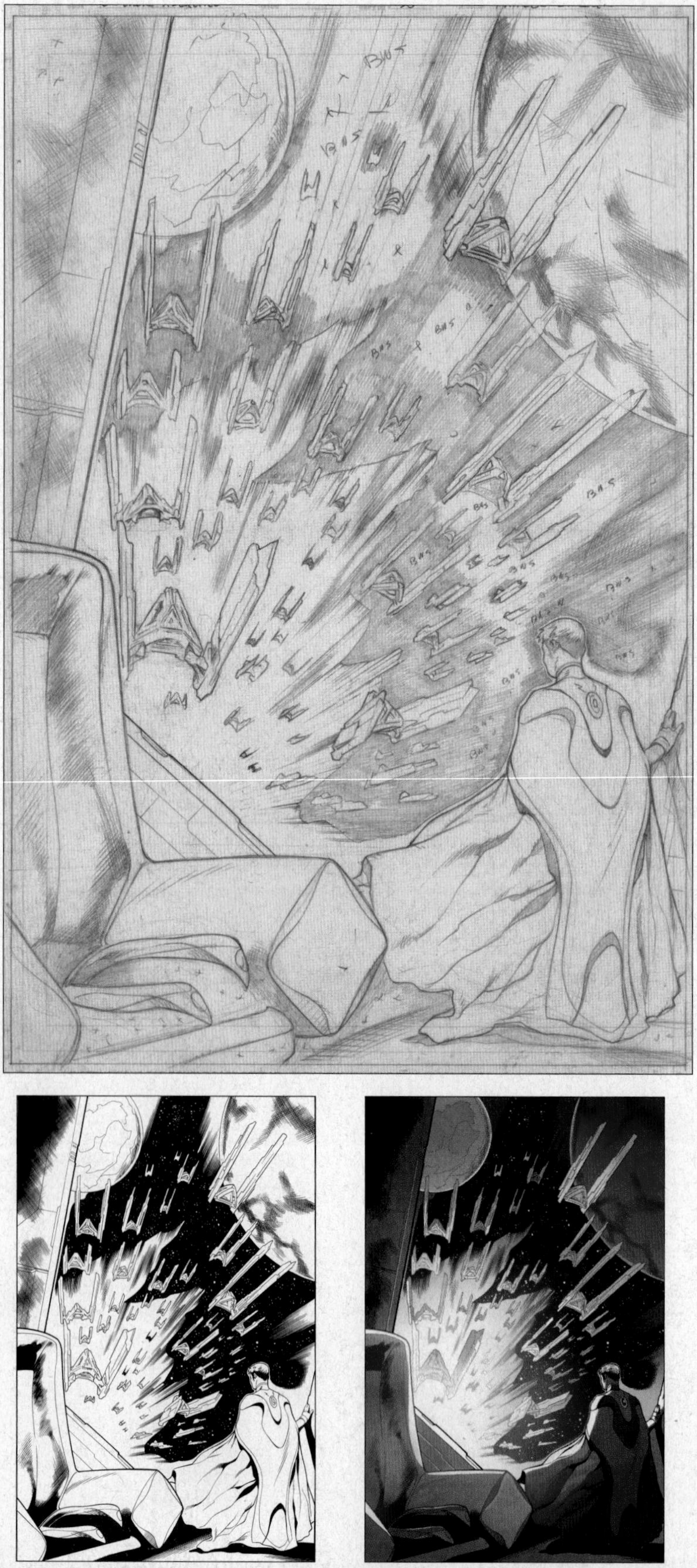